THE

RULES
OF LIFE

CW00671607

THE

RULES

OF LIFE

A personal code for living
a better, happier, more
successful kind of life

RICHARD TEMPLAR

PEARSON
Prentice
Hall

Harlow, England • London • New York • Boston • San Francisco • Toronto
Sydney • Tokyo • Singapore • Hong Kong • Seoul • Taipei • New Delhi
Cape Town • Madrid • Mexico City • Amsterdam • Munich • Paris • Milan

PEARSON EDUCATION LIMITED

Edinburgh Gate
Harlow CM20 2JE
Tel: +44 (0)1279 623623
Fax: +44 (0)1279 431059
Website: www.pearsoned.co.uk

First published in Great Britain in 2006

UK edition:
ISBN-13: 978-0-273-70625-0

Asian edition:
ISBN-13: 978-0-273-70762-2

British Library Cataloguing-in-Publication Data
A catalogue record for this book can be obtained from the British Library

Library of Congress Cataloging-in-Publication Data
A catalog record for this book is available from the Library of Congress

10 9 8
09 08 07

Typeset in 11pt Iowan Old Style by 70
Printed and bound in Great Britain by Clays Ltd, Bungay, Suffolk

The Publisher's policy is to use paper manufactured from sustainable forests.

This book is dedicated to Miyamoto Musashi, who taught me the strategy of simplicity, and Jamie Greenwood, who taught me economy of movement. I am indeed deeply indebted to both of them.

No Fear

No Surprise

No Hesitation

No Doubt

Contents

Introduction

For reasons that are too long and complicated to go into here, I had to live with my grandparents for a couple of years when I was very young. They, like many of their generation, were hard-working, contented sort of people. My grandfather had taken early retirement owing to an industrial accident (a lorry-load of bricks fell on his foot) and my grandmother worked in a large department store in London. Having me dumped unexpectedly on her for a while obviously caused logistical problems. I was too young for school and my grandfather wasn't to be trusted to look after me at home (men didn't look after children in those days . . . my, how things have changed). Her solution was to tuck me under her wing – on some days physically as well as metaphorically, as she smuggled me past managers and supervisors – and we went to work together.

Now going to work with 'Nan' was fun. I was expected to keep quiet and still for long periods and, as I didn't know any different, assumed this was normal. I found that by watching customers – often from my safe refuge under a huge desk – I could pass the time quite happily. Thus was born an immense appetite for people-watching.

My mother – later I went back to live with her – said it wouldn't ever get me anywhere. I'm not so sure. You see, early in my career, observation of those around showed that there were a distinct set of behaviours that got people promoted. If there were two people of equal ability for example, and one dressed, thought and behaved as if they had already been promoted, they would be the one who got the next available job at that next level. Putting these behaviours into practice gave me a fast track up the career ladder. These 'rules' formed the basis of my book *Rules of Work*, now a bestseller in its field.

Just as you can identify behaviours that make some people glide effortlessly onwards and upwards at work, so you can in life. Observing life in general, people very broadly seem to fall into two main camps: those who seem to have mastered the knack of successful living and those who still find it all a bit of a struggle. And when I say successfully mastered it, I don't mean by amassing wealth or being at the top in some stressful career. No, I mean mastered it in the old-fashioned sense that my hard-working grandparents would have understood. People who are content, mostly happy on a day-to-day basis and in general healthy and getting more out of life. Those who are still struggling tend to be not so happy on the whole, and the enjoyment of life just isn't what it should be.

So what's the secret? The answer is all down to a simple choice. We can all choose to do certain things every day of our lives. Some things we do will make us unhappy and some things we choose to do will make us happier. By observing people, I have reasoned that if we follow a few basic 'Rules of Life' we tend to get more done, shrug off adversity more easily, get more out of life and spread a little happiness around us as we go. People who play by the Rules seem to bring their luck with them, light up a room when they enter, have more enthusiasm for life and cope better.

So what follows are my Rules of Life. They aren't set in stone, aren't secret or difficult. And they are based entirely on my observations of happy and successful people. I have noticed that those who are happy are those who follow most of them. Those who seem miserable are the ones who don't follow them. And the successful ones often don't even realize this is what they are doing – they are natural Rules Players. Whereas the less instinctive ones often feel something is missing and spend their entire life looking for something – often themselves – that will miraculously give their life meaning or fill some empty void within them. But the answer lies much closer to home – simple changes in behaviour are all that is required.

Can it really be that easy? No, of course not. To live by the Rules is never easy. If it was, we would all have stumbled on this a long time ago. It has to be hard to make it worthwhile. But, and this is the beauty of the Rules, they are all individually simple and attainable. You can aim high and go for them all or take one or two and start there. Me? No, I never get it all right, ever. I fall by the wayside as often as any one else but I do know what to do to get back up again. I know what I have to do to make my life make sense again.

By watching people I came to realize that all of these Rules of Life are sensible. Personally I love the sort of advice that begins 'Go quietly . . .' but I'm not sure how I'm supposed to do that. However, a bit of advice such as 'Clean your shoes before you go out' makes more sense to me because that is something I can do and, more importantly, in which I can immediately see the logic. Incidentally, I still feel polished shoes make a better impression than scruffy ones.

You won't actually find shoe polishing here, nor will you find anything inspirational and New Age, which doesn't mean those things don't count. It's just that I feel it is better to have realistic things we can do rather than uplifting clichés that may well be true – time is a great healer, for example, and love does conquer all – but when you want things to do, they don't hit the button as far as I'm concerned.

What you will find is good old-fashioned common sense. There is nothing here you don't already know. This book isn't a revelation, it's a reminder. It reminds you that the Rules of Life are universal, obvious, simple. Do them, they work.

But what about those who don't do them and still seem successful? Well, I'm sure we all know people who have acquired great wealth and who are ruthless, unpleasant, dictatorial and sail morally pretty close to the wind. And if that is what you want, it is attainable. But I'm assuming you want to be able to sleep nights, live with yourself and be a thoroughly nice person. And the beauty of all this is it is entirely down to personal choice. We all choose every day whether we are on the side of the angels or the beasts. The Rules of Life help you choose to be on the side of the angels but it's not compulsory. Personally, when I go to sleep at night, I like to do a quick recap of my day and then, hopefully, I can say to myself 'Yep, good day, did OK', and feel proud of what I've achieved, rather than feeling regretful and dissatisfied with my actions and life. I like to go to sleep feeling I've made a difference, been kind to people rather than hurting them, spread a little happiness, had some fun and generally got nearer to 10 than 1 out of 10 for good behaviour.

The Rules of Life aren't about making lots of money and being incredibly successful (you might need to read *The Rules of Work* for that). It is quite simply about how you feel inside, how you affect people around you, what sort of a friend, partner and parent you are, what sort of impact you make on the world, and what sort of impression you leave in your wake.

I regard my books, sometimes, a little like children. I pat them on the head, wipe their nose and send them out into the world. I like to know how they've got on. So if *The Rules of Life* makes a difference to you, or you have a Rule or two of your own that I've missed, I'm always interested in hearing from you. You can email me at *Richard.Templar@RichardTemplar.co.uk*.

Richard Templar

RULES
FOR YOU

I've divided the Rules of Life into five areas – you, your partner, your family, your social circle (including work and friends) and lastly the world – to represent the five unconscious circles we all draw around ourselves.

Let's begin with the most important of these, the Rules for ourselves – personal rules, rules for us. These are the Rules that will help get us out of bed in the mornings, face the world with a positive air and navigate our way safely and successfully through our day, no matter what may arise. These are the Rules that will help reduce stress levels, give us the right kind of outlook, encourage us to set our own standards and have goals to aim for.

I guess that for each and every one of us, these Rules will have to be adapted to take into account our upbringing, our age and our situation. We all need to have personal standards to live up to. They will vary from person to person, but it is vitally important to have them. Without them we are adrift and unable to monitor how we are doing. With them we have a firm centre, somewhere we can get back to, somewhere to touch base and recharge. They are our benchmark for personal progress.

But it's not all about standards; it's also about lightening up, having fun, enjoying life.

Keep it under your hat

You are about to become a Rules Player. You are about to embark on a life-changing adventure, possibly, if you choose to accept your mission. You are about to discover ways to become positive, happier, more successful in everything you do. So there's no need to say anything to anybody about it. Keep quiet. No one likes a smart arse. That's it. First Rule: *Keep it under your hat*.

There may well be times when you do want to talk to other people about what you're doing because, quite naturally, you want to share it with somebody. Well, you can't and you don't. Let them find out for themselves with no clues from you. You may think this unfair but it is actually fairer than you believe. If you tell them, they'll shy away. And quite rightly so – we all hate being preached at. It's a bit like when you give up smoking and suddenly find this new healthier way of living and you simply have to convert all your old smoking friends. Trouble is, they aren't ready to quit yet and you find they label you as smug or a prig or, even worse, an ex-smoker. And how we all hate those.

> DON'T PREACH,
> PROPAGATE, EVEN
> MENTION THIS

RULE 1

So the first Rule is, quite simply, don't preach, propagate, try to convert, shout from the rooftops or even mention this.

You will get a warm glow from changing your attitude to life and having people ask what it is you have done, are doing and you can say that it's nothing, merely a sunny day and you feel better/happier/livelier/jollier/whatever. There is no need to go into any detail because that's not really what people want to know. In fact it's exactly the opposite of what they want to know. It's a bit like when someone asks how you are. What they want to really hear is just the one word, 'Fine'. Even if you are in the very pits of despair, that's all they want to hear because anything more requires commitment on their part. And for a casual 'How are you?' that's most certainly not what they want. What they want is just 'Fine'. And then they can be about their business without any further involvement. If you don't say 'Fine', but instead unburden yourself, they will back off pretty quickly.

And it's the same with being a Rules Player. No one really wants to know, so keep quiet. How do I know? Because when I wrote *The Rules of Work*, which turned a lot of people onto the ability to be successful in the workplace without having to resort to underhand means, I suggested the same thing and found it worked. Just get on with it, do it quietly and go about your daily life happily and smugly without having to tell anyone anything.

You'll get older but not necessarily wiser

There is an assumption that as we get older we will get wiser; not true I'm afraid. The rule is we carry on being just as daft, still making plenty of mistakes. It's just that we make new ones, different ones. We do learn from experience and may not make the same mistakes again, but there is a whole new pickle jar of fresh ones just lying in wait for us to trip up and fall into. The secret is to accept this and not to beat yourself up when you do make new ones. The Rule really is: be kind to yourself when you do muck things up. Be forgiving and accept that it's all part of that growing older but no wiser routine.

Looking back, we can always see the mistakes we made but we fail to see the ones looming up. Wisdom isn't about not making mistakes, but about learning to escape afterwards with our dignity and sanity intact.

When we are young, ageing seems to be something that happens to, well, old people. But it does happen to us all and we have no choice but to embrace it and roll with it. Whatever we do and however we are, the fact is we are going to get older. And this ageing process does seem to speed up as we get older.

You can look at it this way – the older you get, the more areas you've covered to make mistakes in. There will always be new areas of experience where we have no guidelines and where we'll handle things badly, overreact, get it wrong. And the more flexible we are, the more adventurous, the more life-embracing, then the more new avenues there will be to explore – and make mistakes in of course.

RULE 2

> WISDOM ISN'T ABOUT NOT MAKING MISTAKES BUT ABOUT LEARNING TO ESCAPE AFTERWARDS WITH OUR DIGNITY AND SANITY INTACT

As long as we look back and see where we went wrong and resolve not to repeat such mistakes, there is little else we need to do. Remember that any Rules that apply to you also apply to everyone else around you. They are all getting older too. And not any wiser particularly. Once you accept this, you'll be more forgiving and kinder towards yourself and others.

Finally, yes, time does heal and things do get better as you get older. After all, the more mistakes you've made, the less likely that you'll come up with new ones. The best thing is that if you get a lot of your mistakes over and done with early on in life, there will be less to learn the hard way later on. And that's what youth is all about, a chance to make all the mistakes you can and get them out of the way.

RULE 3

Accept what is done is done

People make mistakes. Sometimes very serious ones. As often as not, the mistakes aren't deliberate or personal. Sometimes people just don't know what they are doing. This means that if, in the past, people have behaved badly towards you, it wasn't necessarily because they meant to be horrid, but because they were as naïve, as foolish, as human as the rest of us. They made mistakes in the way they brought you up or finished a relationship with you or whatever, not because they wanted to do it that way, but because they didn't know any different.

If you want to, you can let go of any feelings of resentment, of regret, of anger. You can accept that you are a fabulous human being *because* of all the bad things that have happened to you, not in spite of them. What is done is done and you need to just get on with things. Don't use the labels 'good' and 'bad'. Yes, I know some of it is indeed bad, but it is how we let it affect us that is the real 'bad'. You could let all these things get you down, fizzle away internally like some emotional acid making you ill and resentful and stuck. But you will let them go, embrace them as character forming and in general as positive rather then negative.

On paper I had a seriously dysfunctional childhood and for a while was resentful. I blamed my bizarre upbringing for all that was weak or dispirited or badly formed in me. It's so easy to do. But once I accepted that what was done was done, and that I could choose to forgive and get on with my life, things improved enormously. For at least one of my siblings this was not the route they chose, and they carried on building up the resentment until it overwhelmed them.

> ## WHAT IS DONE IS DONE AND YOU NEED TO JUST GET ON WITH THINGS

For me it was essential, if I wanted more out of my life, to embrace all the bad things as being an important part of me and to move on. In fact I wanted them to fuel me into my future, to become positive to such an extent that I couldn't imagine being me without them. Now, if given the choice, I wouldn't change a thing. Yes, looking back, it was tough being the kid I was, living the life I did, but it has certainly helped make me, me.

I think the change occurred once I realized that even if I could get in front of me all the people who had 'done me wrong', there would still be nothing they could do. I could shout at them, berate them, rant at them, but there would be nothing they could do to make amends or put things right. They too would have to accept that what's done is done. There is no going back, only forwards. Make it a motto for life – keep moving forwards.

Accept yourself

If you accept that what's done is done, you are left with yourself exactly as you are. You can't go back and change anything, so you've got to work with what you've got. I'm not suggesting anything New Age here such as love yourself – that's far too ambitious. No, let's begin with simple accepting. Accepting is easy because it is exactly what it says – accepting. You don't have to improve or change or strive for perfection. Quite the opposite. Just accept.

> ## YOU DON'T HAVE TO IMPROVE OR CHANGE OR STRIVE FOR PERFECTION. QUITE THE OPPOSITE. JUST ACCEPT

That means accepting all the warts and emotional lumps and bumps, the bad bits, the weaknesses and the rest of it. This doesn't mean we are happy with everything about ourselves, or that we are going to be lazy and lead a bad life. We are going to accept the way we are, initially, and then build on that. What we are *not* going to do is beat ourselves up because we don't like some bits. Yes, we can change lots but that will come later. We're only up to Rule 4 here.

This has to be a Rule because there can be no choice here. We have to accept that we are the way we are – the result of everything that has happened. It all just is. You, like me, like all of us, are human. That means you're pretty complex. You come fully loaded with desires, anguish, sins, pettiness at times, mistakes, ill temper, rudeness, deviation, hesitation and repetition. That's what makes a human being so wonderful, the complexity. None of us can ever be perfect. We start with what we've got and who we are and then we can only make a choice, each day, to strive for some kind of better. And that's all they can ask of us – to make that choice. To be awake and aware, to be ready to do the right thing. And accept that some days you aren't going to make it. Some days you will, like all of us, fall far short. That's OK, don't beat yourself up. Pick yourself up and start again. Accept that you will fail from time to time and that you are human.

I know it can be hard at times, but once you have picked up the gauntlet of becoming a Rules Player, you're well on the path to improvement. Stop picking faults with yourself, or giving yourself a hard time. Instead, accept that you are what you are. You're doing the best you can at this point in time, so give yourself a pat on the back and press on.

RULE 5

Know what counts and what doesn't

Being here counts. Being kind and considerate counts. Getting through each day without seriously offending anyone or hurting anyone counts. Having the latest technology doesn't.

Sorry, I don't have a downer on technology. In fact, I probably have pretty much all the latest gizmos. I just (a) don't overly rely too much on any of it and (b) see them all as useful tools rather than having any intrinsic meaning in themselves, in a status symbol or one-up-personship kind of way.

Doing something useful with your life counts. Going shopping because you're bored doesn't. Yes, by all means go shopping, but see what you do as counting or not counting, being real or not being real, having real value or not, being of some benefit or not. This does not mean chucking it all up and going off to some fly-infested swamp to work with the locals and catch malaria – although that in itself *would* count, but you don't have to go to quite those extremes to make your life meaningful.

I guess the Rule means focusing on what is important, to you in your life, and making positive changes to ensure you feel happy with what you are dedicating your life to (*see Rule 6*). This doesn't mean long-term plans mapped out to the smallest detail. It means knowing, roughly, where you are going and what you are doing. Awake rather than asleep. A fellow author, Tim Freke, calls it 'lucid living'* – a perfect term for what we are talking about.

---

* *Lucid Living* by Tim Freke (Books for Burning, 2005).

There are some things in this life that are important and a whole lot of things that aren't. It doesn't take too much discrimination to work out which are which. And there are a whole lot more things that don't count, aren't really important, to choose from. I'm not saying we can't have trivia in our lives – we can and it's fine. Just don't go mistaking the trivia for what is really important. Having time for loved ones and friends is important, watching the latest soap isn't. Repaying a debt is important, what brand of washing powder you use isn't. Nurturing our children and teaching them real values is important, dressing them in designer fashion isn't. You get the idea. Think about what you do that counts – and do more of it.

> ## THERE ARE SOME THINGS IN THIS LIFE THAT ARE IMPORTANT AND A WHOLE LOT OF THINGS THAT AREN'T

RULE 6

Dedicate your life to something

To know what counts and what doesn't, you have to know what you are dedicating your life to. There are, of course, no right or wrong answers to this one as it's a very personal choice – but it's really useful to have an answer, rather than not really knowing.

As an example, my own life has been driven by two things: (a) someone once told me that if my soul or spirit was the only thing I was likely to be taking with me when I went, then it ought to be the best thing I had; (b) my curious upbringing.

The first one isn't, for me at least, in any way religious. It just struck a chord with me, triggered something. Whatever it was I was taking with me, then perhaps I ought to do a bit of work on it. Make sure it really is the very best thing about me. That got me thinking. How on earth do you go about that? The answer still is that I haven't got a clue. I have explored and experimented, learned and made mistakes, been a seeker and a follower, read and observed and wrestled with this great problem all my life. How do you go about improving your life on that level? I think the only conclusion I have come to is to live as decent a life as possible, to go through causing as little damage as possible, to treat everyone with whom you come into contact with respect and dignity. It's something to dedicate my life to and it works for me.

And how can my curious upbringing cause me to focus on what I am dedicating my life to? Well, having had a 'dysfunctional' upbringing and having chosen to let it motivate me rather than affect me, I am acutely aware that many people also need to throw off that feeling of being badly affected by what has gone before. This is what I dedicate my life to. Yes, it might be crazy; I might be crazy. But at least I have something I can focus on, something (for me) that counts.

Now none of this is big stuff and by that I mean I don't go around with this emblazoned on my forehead – 'Templar dedicates his life to . . .' sort of thing. It's more that quietly, in my heart, I have something that I can devote my attention to. It's a yardstick by which I can measure (a) how I'm doing, (b) what I'm doing and (c) where I'm going. You don't need to trumpet it. You don't need to tell anyone (*see Rule 1*). You don't even need to think it out in too much detail. A simple internal mission statement will do. Disney's mission for example is: 'To make people happy'. Decide what it is you are dedicating your life to. It makes the rest much easier.

> ## IT'S A YARDSTICK TO MEASURE (A) HOW I'M DOING, (B) WHAT I'M DOING AND (C) WHERE I'M GOING

Be flexible in your thinking

Once your thinking gets crystallized, rigid, formed, you've lost the battle. Once you think you have all the answers, you might as well hang up your boots. Once you get set in your ways, you're already part of history.

To get the most out of life you have to keep all your options open, keep your thinking and life flexible. You have to be ready to roll as the storm breaks – and by golly it always breaks when you least expect it. The instant you are established in a set pattern, you set yourself up for being knocked off-course. You might need to examine your thinking pretty closely to understand what I mean. Flexible thinking is a bit like mental martial arts – being ready to duck and weave, dodge and flow. Try to see life not as the enemy, but as a friendly sparring partner. If you are flexible you'll have fun. If you stand your ground you're likely to get knocked about a bit.

> TRY TO SEE LIFE NOT AS
> THE ENEMY, BUT AS A
> FRIENDLY SPARRING
> PARTNER

RULE 7

We all have set patterns in life. We like to label ourselves as this or that and are quite proud of our opinions and beliefs. We all like to read a set paper, watch the same sorts of TV programmes or movies, go to the same sort of shops every time, eat the sort of food that suits us, wear the same type of clothes. And all this is fine. But if we cut ourselves off from all other possibilities, we become boring, rigid, hardened – and thus likely to get knocked about a bit.

You have to see life as a series of adventures. Each adventure is a chance to have fun, learn something, explore the world, expand your circle of experience and friends, and broaden your horizons. Shutting down to adventure means exactly that – you are shut down.

The second you are offered an opportunity to have an adventure, to change your thinking, to step outside of yourself, go for it and see what happens. If this thought scares you, remember that you can always go back into your shell the second it's over, if you want to.

But even saying yes to every opportunity isn't set in stone as a rule, because that would be inflexible. The really flexible thinkers know when to say 'no' as well as when to say 'yes'.

If you want to know how flexible your thinking is, here are a couple of tests. Are the books by the side of your bed the same sorts of books you've always read? Have you found yourself saying anything like 'I don't know any people like that' or 'I don't go to those kind of places'? If so, then perhaps it's time to broaden your mind and take the shackles off your thinking.

RULE 8

Take an interest in the outside world

You may be wondering why this Rule is here and not in with the ones in the section about the world. Well, this one is about *you*. Taking an interest in the outside world is about developing you, rather than for the world's benefit. I'm not suggesting you have to watch the news constantly, but by reading, listening and talking, we keep abreast of what is happening. Successful Rules Players don't get bogged down by the minutiae of their own lives, they don't live in a tiny bubble. Make it your mission to know what's going on in the world – in current events, music, fashion, science, movies, food, transport, even TV. Successful Rules Players are able to hold a conversation on pretty well everything and anything because they are interested in what's going on. You don't necessarily have to *own* the latest everything but you should have a rough idea of what is changing, what's new and what's happening, both in your community and on the other side of the world.

And the benefits? Well, for starters it makes you more interesting as a person and it also keeps you young. I met an elderly woman in the post office the other day who was going on about PIN numbers, 'Pin numbers, pin numbers, what do I want with pin numbers at my age?' The short answer is that of course she needs them, she can't get her pension money without them. But it's more than that. It is terribly easy to sink into the, 'I've never done this before, I don't need to do it now' mentality. If we do this, we stand a good chance of really missing out.

The happiest, most well-balanced, most successful people in life are those who are part of something. Part of the world, not cut off from it. And the most interesting, stimulating people to be around are those who take a great interest in what's happening around them. Listening to the radio the other morning, the head of the American prison service was being interviewed and was talking about penal reform, a subject I have no interest in personally (I don't know anyone inside, over there). You could argue that I didn't need to know about the American prison service any more than the old woman needed to know about PIN numbers, but I felt more stimulated and alive and interested for it. And that can't be bad.

> TAKING AN INTEREST IN THE OUTSIDE WORLD IS ABOUT DEVELOPING YOU, RATHER THAN FOR THE WORLD'S BENEFIT

Be on the side of the angels, not the beasts

Every single day of our lives we are faced with an immense number of choices. And each and every one of them usually boils down to a simple choice between being on the side of the angels or the beasts. Which are you going to pick? Or did you not even realize what was going on? Let me explain. Every action we make has an effect on our family, people around us, society, the world in general. And that effect can be positive or detrimental – it's usually our choice. And sometimes it is a difficult choice. We get torn between what *we* want and what is good for others; personal satisfaction or magnanimity.

Look, no one said this was going to be easy. And making the decision to be on the side of the angels is often a tough call. But if we want to succeed in this life – and I measure success by how close we get to generating that self-satisfaction/happiness/contentment – then we have to consciously do this. This can be what we dedicate our lives to – angels and not beasts.

> WE GET TORN BETWEEN WHAT *WE* WANT AND WHAT IS GOOD FOR OTHERS

RULE 9

If you want to know if you have already made the choice, just do a quick check of how you feel and how you react if someone cuts in front of you in a line of traffic in the rush hour. Or when you're in a big hurry and someone stops to ask you for directions. Or if you have teenage children and one of them gets into trouble with the police. Or when you lend a friend money and they fail to pay it back. Or if your boss calls you a fool in front of the rest of your colleagues. Or your neighbour's trees start to encroach on your property. Or you hit your thumb with the hammer. Or, or, or. As I said it is a choice we have to make every day, lots of times. And it has to become a conscious choice to be effective.

Now, the problem is that no one is going to tell you exactly what constitutes an angel or a beast. Here you are going to have to set your own parameters. But come on, it can't be that difficult. I think an awful lot of it is self-evident. Does it hurt or hinder? Are you part of the problem or the solution? Will things get better or worse if you do certain things? You have to make this choice for yourself alone.

It is your interpretation of what is an angel or beast that counts. There is no point in telling anyone else that they are on the side of the beasts, as they may have a totally different definition. What other people do is their choice and they won't thank you for telling them otherwise. You can of course watch, as an impassive, objective, observer and think to yourself: 'I wouldn't have done it like that.' Or 'I think they just chose to be an angel'. Or even, 'Gosh, how beastly'. But you don't have to say anything.

Only dead fish swim with the stream

Life is difficult. And the Rule is to thank God* it is so. If it was all fluffy and easy we wouldn't be tested, tried, forged in the fire of life. We wouldn't grow or learn or change, or have a chance to rise above ourselves. If life were a series of lovely days, we'd soon get bored. If there was no rain, then there wouldn't be any feeling of great joy when it finally stopped and we could go to the beach. If it was all easy we couldn't get stronger.

So, be thankful it is a struggle some of the time, and recognize that only dead fish swim with the stream. For the rest of us there will be times when it's an uphill, upstream struggle. We will have to battle waterfalls, weirs and raging torrents. But we have no choice. We have to keep swimming or get swept away. And each flick of our tail, each surge of our fins makes us stronger and fitter, leaner and happier.

There is a statistic that suggests that for a lot of men, retirement is a really bad idea. Lots of them die within a relatively short time of handing in their briefcase.** They have ceased to swim against the current and get swept away. Keep swimming, little fish, keep swimming.

Try to see each setback as a chance to improve. They make you stronger, not weaker. You only get burdened with as much as you can carry – although I do appreciate that at times it may seem as if it's a whole lot more. And of course the struggles don't come to an end, but there are lulls in-between times – backwaters where

---

* Or whoever or whatever you choose to so thank. Don't write in.
** I don't know if this affects women just as adversely. You may write in.

RULE 10

we can rest for a while and enjoy the moment before the next obstacle gets thrown our way. And that's what life is, what it is meant to be; a series of struggles and lulls. And whatever situation you're in now, it's going to change. So what are you in? Lull or struggle? Rain or going to the beach? Learning or enjoying? Dead fish or healthy salmon?

> AND THAT'S WHAT LIFE IS,
> WHAT IT IS MEANT TO BE;
> A SERIES OF STRUGGLES
> AND LULLS

Be the last to raise your voice

For me this is a really hard one. I do love to have a good shout. I came from a big robust family where shouting was a way of life and the only way to get yourself heard, get any attention or to make a point. Dysfunctional? Yes. Noisy? Yes. Helpful? Probably not.

One of my sons has inherited the shouting gene and he is very good at it. The temptation is to join in. Luckily this Rule is *be the last to raise your voice*, so I do have a get-out clause. If he shouts first, I'm allowed to shout back. But I do try really hard not to. For me, shouting in any form is a bad thing, a sign that I have lost control, lost the argument. The son of a vicar once saw his father's sermon notes and in the margin he had pencilled, 'Shout here, argument weak'. I think this just about sums it all up.

But I have shouted at various times and invariably I regret each and every occasion. I know I've dined out on the time I was very shouty in a well-known high street electrical chain over a damaged video player. At that time I did get my own way, but the reality is that it was a bad thing and deep down I'm quite ashamed of myself.

> SHOUT HERE,
> ARGUMENT WEAK

RULE 11

So what do you do if you too have inherited the shouty gene like me? I find that I have to walk away to stop the inevitable decline into shouting in a challenging situation. Tough one, especially if you know you're right. There are so many things that make us shout, so many situations where we feel that a judicious loss of temper will get us our own way. But we are dealing with real live human beings who have their own feelings and shouting is not justified – even if they start it first.

There are two situations where people lose their temper – justified and manipulative. The first is where you run over their foot with your car and refuse to apologize or acknowledge you have done anything wrong. In this situation they are allowed to shout. The second situation is where people use anger to get their own way – a sort of emotional blackmail. You are allowed to ignore them, or to be assertive to control the situation. You are not allowed to shout back.

I know, I know, there are all sorts of situations where shouting seems appropriate – the dog is stealing the Sunday dinner; the kids won't tidy their room; your computer has crashed again and the repair department won't fix it quickly enough; the local hooligans are adorning your wall, again; after going through the umpteen options over and over again you fail to get through to the switchboard after holding for 20 minutes; they put up the closed sign just as you get to the counter; someone is clearly being stupid and deliberately choosing to misunderstand you.

And on and on and on. But if you take this Rule as a simple 'I don't do shouting', it becomes an easy benchmark to stick to. You get known as someone who is incredibly calm no matter what is happening. Calm people get trusted. Calm people get relied on. Calm people get looked up to and given responsibility. Calm people last longer.

RULE 12

Be your own adviser

Deep down within all of us is a fount of wisdom. This is called intuition. Listening to your intuition is a slow learnt process. It starts by recognizing that tiny inner voice or feeling that will tell you when you've done something you shouldn't have. It's an incredibly still, quiet voice and needs silence and concentration to hear it properly to begin with.

You might like to call it your conscience if you like, but deep down you know when you've done something bad. You know when you've got to apologize, make amends, put things right. You know. And I know you know. I know because we all know. There's no getting away from it.

> YOU KNOW. AND I KNOW
> YOU KNOW. I KNOW
> BECAUSE WE ALL KNOW

Once you start listening to that inner voice or feeling the feeling, you'll find it can help. It will become more than a mindless parrot perched on your shoulder, chanting 'You messed up again' after the event. The key is when you hear your intuition telling you whether something is the right thing to do or not – *before* you do it.

Try running stuff past your inner you, before doing things and see what reaction you get. Once you get used to this, you'll find it easier. Imagine, in any situation, that you have a small child standing at your side and you have to explain things to them. Imagine they ask questions – 'Why are you doing that? What's right and wrong? Should we do this?' – and you have to answer. Only in this situation, you ask the questions and you answer yourself. And you'll find you already know everything there is to know and everything you'll ever need to know.

Listen, and it's all there. If you are going to trust any adviser, who will it be? It makes sense for it to be *you* because you have all the facts, all the experience, all the knowledge at your fingertips. No one else has. No one can get inside you and see exactly what's going on.

Quick point of clarification here. When I say listen, I don't mean listen to what goes on in your head. Now that really is where madness lies. No, I mean a stiller, quieter voice. For some it's more a feeling than a voice – what we sometimes call gut instinct. And even if it is a voice, a lot of the time it doesn't speak at all – unlike our mind which babbles on incessantly – and if it does, you can miss it in the torrent of words that our mind produces.

This isn't about predicting what's going to happen. You won't discover which horse will win the 3.30 at Chepstow or who'll score in the Cup Final. No, this is the important stuff. What we're about to do, big decisions we have to make, why we are behaving in the way we are. You already know the answer, if you ask yourself.

No fear, no surprise, no hesitation, no doubt

Where does this come from? It's from a seventeenth-century samurai warrior. This was his four point key to successful living – and swordsmanship.

No fear

There should be nothing in this life that you are afraid of. If there is, you might need to do some work on overcoming that fear. Here I have to confess to a certain fear of heights. I avoid high places if I can. Recently, owing to leaky gutters, I had to crawl out on our roof – three floors up with a very long drop on one side. I gritted my teeth and kept repeating, 'No fear, no fear, no fear', until the job was done. Oh yes, and of course I didn't look down. Whatever your fear, face it head on and defeat it.

No surprise

Life seems to be full of them doesn't it? You're going along swimmingly and suddenly something huge rears up ahead of you. But if you look carefully, there were clues all along the way that it was going to happen. No surprise there then. Whatever your situation now, it is going to change. No surprises there. So why does life seem to surprise us then? Because we are asleep half the time. Wake up and nothing can sneak up on you.

RULE 13

No hesitation

Weigh up the odds and then just get on with it. If you hang back, the opportunity will have passed. If you spend too long thinking, you'll never make a move. Once we have looked at the options, we make a choice, a decision and then go for it. That's the secret. No hesitation means not waiting around for other people to help out or make up our minds for us. No hesitation means if there is a certain inevitability about a situation then just throw yourself in head first and enjoy the ride. If there is nothing to be done then waiting doesn't help.

No doubt

Once you have made your mind up about something, don't go over it again and again. Stop thinking and enjoy – relax and let go. Stop worrying. Tomorrow will come along as certainly as it can. There is no doubt about life. It just is. Be confident. Be committed. Be sure of yourself. Once you have committed yourself to a set course, a path, a plan, then follow it through. Have no doubt it was the right thing to do and no doubt that you will succeed. Get on with it and trust your judgement completely.

I wish I'd done that – and I will

Regrets, I've had a few . . . You might be expecting me to say there's no room for regrets or 'if onlys'. As it happens, they can be very useful – if you choose to use them to make a difference going forward.

There are three types of 'I wish I'd done that' scenarios. The first is when you genuinely feel you didn't capitalize on an opportunity, or that you missed out on something. The second is when you see somebody who's done something great and you wish it had been you. The final type is not you, but the others – the people who hang around with a sort of permanent 'I could have been a contender' mentality. If only I'd had the chances, the lucky breaks, the opportunities. For this last group, the bad news is that even if Lady Luck had come up and bitten them on the bum they'd still have missed it.

When it comes to looking at what others have achieved, this world is divided into those who look at others enviously and those who look at others as a motivational tool. If you find yourself saying, 'I wish I had done that/thought that/been there/seen that/experienced that/met them/understood that', then you need to learn to follow it up with a 'And now, I will . . .'

In many cases the thing you wished you'd done might not be out of the question – even if it's not exactly as you would have done it previously. For example, if you're thinking 'I wish I'd taken a year out before university and travelled to China like so and so did', then you're clearly not going to be able to reverse time. But could you get a sabbatical for six months and go now? Could you take a longer than usual holiday and go (with family if necessary)? Or

THE WORLD IS DIVIDED
INTO THOSE WHO LOOK AT
OTHERS ENVIOUSLY AND
THOSE WHO LOOK AT
OTHERS AS A
MOTIVATIONAL TOOL

how about making firm plans that when you retire you'll put this at the top of your 'to do' list?

Obviously, if the regret is that you didn't win an Olympic 400m gold medal, because you gave up athletics at 14, it's not going to happen if you're now 34. What you can do is resolve not to let any more opportunities pass you by. So you can choose to book those scuba diving lessons and in doing so, ensure that you won't be saying 'I wish I'd learned to dive' in another 20 years' time.

Count to ten – or recite 'Baa baa black sheep'

Every now and then someone or something is really going to get your goat. But you're a Rules Player now and you're not going to lose your temper any more. How, exactly? The answer is in fact one of those old pearls of wisdom. You get in the habit of counting to ten under your breath while you hope and pray that the feeling of impending rage will subside. It invariably does for me, and gives me those vital seconds to regain my composure and remember where I am and who I am. Once I have collected my wits and calmed down, I can find an appropriate response.

> ONCE I HAVE COLLECTED MY WITS AND CALMED DOWN, I CAN FIND AN APPROPRIATE RESPONSE

But that counting to ten is essential. 'Old hat', I hear you say. Yep, but it works. You don't like it? Then you are most welcome to find something else to recite under your breath. A poem perhaps, but it has to be a short one. That's why I suggested 'Baa baa black

RULE 15

sheep'. Or you could try 'I must go down to the sea again, to the lonely sea and the sky, I left my pants and socks there and I wonder if they're dry'.* That might make you laugh as well as calming you down.

Someone asks you a question and you're not sure of the answer. Take ten before you answer. They'll all think you incredibly wise and considered and thoughtful. (Don't tell them if you are actually reciting 'Baa baa black sheep'.) It's a variant on 'engage brain before opening mouth' too – that extended pause can save endless trouble.

If you find yourself in a confrontational situation, taking a quiet ten can help enormously. I was once in a rough part of a town but very hungry so I ventured into a fish and chip shop. As I was being served, the 'rough diamond' behind me whispered that I should be very careful when I left the shop. I asked why and he said that I would be relieved of my food when I got outside by the local lads who were all sitting on a brick wall. 'Saves waiting in the queue', he confided.

I left the shop with trepidation – no wait, it was actually fear. But I buttoned up my coat, took a deep breath and stood there looking at the youths. I counted to ten slowly while we all eyed each other up and then I walked towards them very purposefully. As I got to them, still counting, they turned away and I was left alone. God, those fish and chips tasted wonderful!

---

* Big apology to John Masefield for that but due credit to Spike Milligan.

Change what you can change, let go of the rest

Time is short. This is another of those facts you can't escape; it's a given. If time is short then it makes sense not to go wasting any of it, not a single lovely drop of it. It's my observation that the successful people in this life are the ones who wring every last ounce of satisfaction and energy out of life. They do that by practising this simple Rule. They pay attention to what, in their life, they have some control over and they simply, economically (time-wise), let go of the rest.

If someone asks you directly for help, then that's something you can do – or not as you choose. If the whole world asks you for help, then there is very little you can do. Beating yourself up over it is counter-productive and such a waste of time. Now I'm not saying to stop caring about things or to walk away from those in need. In fact quite the opposite in many ways, but there are areas in which you can make a personal difference and other areas where you'll never even make a dent.

If you waste time struggling to change stuff that is obviously never going to be changed, then life will whizz past and you'll miss it. If, on the other hand, you dedicate yourself personally to things you can change, areas where you can make a difference, then life becomes richer and more fulfilled. And the more rich it is, curiously, the more time you seem to have.

Obviously if lots of us get together we can change pretty well anything, but this is a Rule For You – these are your personal set – and thus this is about what you can change.

If you have the ear of a President or Prime Minister, you might be able to shape policy that affects the entire nation. If you have the

---

DEDICATE YOURSELF PERSONALLY TO THINGS YOU CAN CHANGE, AREAS WHERE YOU CAN MAKE A DIFFERENCE

---

ear of the Pope, you might have a hand in shaping the next Papal Bull. If you have the ear of a General, you might avert a war. If you have the ear of an Editor, you might get your name in print. If you have the ear of the Head Waiter, you might get the best table. And so on and so on. So whose ear have you got? What influence do you have and what change can you effect by using that influence?

Often the only ear we have is our own. The only definite influence we have is over ourselves. The only thing we can really, really change is exactly that – ourselves. Wonderful. What an opportunity to do some good. What a chance to make a real contribution. Begin with ourselves and let it spread outwards. This way we don't have to waste time preaching to those who won't listen. We don't have to waste effort or energy or resources on things over which we have no control and no certainty of any success. By changing ourselves though we can be assured of a result. Result.

Aim to be the very best at everything you do – not second best

Wow. What a tall order. This is a seriously difficult thing to aim for – and deliberately so. If you go to work, then do your job as well as is humanly possible. If you are a parent, be the very best parent possible. If you are a gardener, be the very best gardener you can be. Because if you aren't, then what are you aiming for? And why? If you set out to do something, anything, and you are deliberately aiming for second best, how sad is that? This Rule is really simple, really easy. Let's take parenting for example. What is the very best way of parenting possible? There are of course no right or wrong answers here, it's entirely a subjective assessment. What do *you* think the very best parenting means? Good. Now are you going to aim for less than that? Of course not.

And the same is true for everything you do. You aim to be the very best that *you* think is possible. Once you become the judge, the panel of experts, it is very easy to live up to those expectations because they are entirely yours. No one else can say whether you have failed or succeeded. No one else can set the criteria for what you are about to embark on.

Look, maybe this is a trick. If only you can judge whether you have succeeded, then obviously you are going to score 10 out of 10 every time. Aren't you? Probably not. It is amazing how tough we are on ourselves, when no one is looking. If we are only cheating ourselves, then we realize there simply isn't any point to it.

The most marvellous thing about setting your own standards is that no one else can judge; no one else can get their sticky little fingers on what, for you, is right or wrong, good or bad. How

RULE 17

liberating is that? Infinitely. Having established that you'll aim for the very best and you've set the standards of what that is, all you have to do is periodically check back to that standard to see how you are doing.

None of this has to be incredibly detailed. For instance, your view of being the best parent could be as simple as 'I'll always be there for them'. You don't have to provide details, even if it is just for yourself, of how many times a day you'll tell them you love them, or whether you make sure they wear clean socks every day. No, your aim is simply 'To be there for them, always', and that is your very, very best. Now if you fail it is only because you weren't there for them. Failing is fine. Aiming for second best isn't.

All you have to do is consciously think about what you are doing and then aim for that, the best. The secret is to be aware of what you are doing and have some sort of benchmark where you, and only you, monitor your performance. Make your goals, your aims simple and obviously attainable. Make sure you know what is, for you, best and second best.

> FAILING IS FINE. AIMING FOR SECOND BEST ISN'T

Don't be afraid to dream

This may seem incredibly obvious, incredibly easy but you would be surprised how many people seriously limit their dreams. They're *your* dreams for heaven's sake. There should be no limit to them. Plans have to be realistic; dreams don't.

> ## PLANS HAVE TO BE REALISTIC; DREAMS DON'T

I worked in the casino business for many years and was always intrigued that 'punters' (what we should really call 'customers') could never see it; that they would always lose because they wouldn't limit their losses but would always limit their winnings. Don't ask me why. I guess addicted gamblers are seriously not well. They'd go in with the right attitude – 'I'll just lose this fiver and then pack it in'. Result: They'd lose the fiver and cash a cheque to chase it. Then another to chase the lost cheque. And another.

I'm not advocating gambling by the way – not now, not ever, it's really not a good idea, believe me. The point is that people limit their dreams the way they limit their winnings. And yet dreams

RULE 18

are at worst harmless. Don't limit them! You are allowed to dream as high, as wide, as big, as extravagant, as impossible, as wacky, as silly, as bizarre, as unrealistically nonsensical as you want.

You are allowed to wish for anything you want as well. Look, wishes and dreams are all private affairs. There are no wish police, no dream doctors who are on the rampage looking out for unrealistic demands. It is a private thing between you and . . . that's it. Between you and absolutely no one else at all.

The only note of caution here – and I do speak from personal experience – is be very careful of what you do wish for, what you dream of, it might just come true. And where would you be then?

A lot of people think their dreams have to be realistic to be worth dreaming about. But that's a plan and that is something quite different. I have plans and I take logical steps to make them come to fruition. Dreams are allowed to be so improbable that they are never likely to come true. And don't go thinking you'll never achieve anything by sitting around day-dreaming all day. Some of the most successful people have also been those who have dared to dream the most. It isn't a coincidence.

Don't dwell on the past

Whatever the past was, it's gone. There is nothing you can do to change anything that has gone before and so you must turn your attention to the here and now. It is hard to resist the allure of dwelling on what has gone before. But if you want to be successful in your life, you have to turn your attention to what is happening for you right now. You might be tempted to dwell on the past because it was awful or because it was wonderful. Either way, you have to leave it behind because the only way to live is in the present.

If you're revisiting the past because of regrets, then you need to be clear that you can't go back and undo what you've done. If you hang on to guilt, you're only damaging yourself. We've all made bad decisions that have adversely affected people around us that we professed to love but whom we treated disgracefully. There isn't anything you can do to wipe the slate clean. What you can do is to resolve not to make such bad decisions again. That's all anyone can ask of us – that we acknowledge where we messed up and are trying our hardest not to repeat the pattern.

If the past was better for you and you hanker after your glory days, then learn to appreciate the memories but also move on and put your efforts into finding a different kind of good time right now. If it truly was better back then (take off those rose-tinted spectacles for a minute), maybe you can analyze exactly why – money, power, health, vitality, fun, youth. Then move on to find other avenues to explore. We all have to leave good stuff behind and find new challenges, new areas to inspire us.

Every day that we wake up is a fresh start and we can make of it what we want, write what we want on that blank canvas. Keeping that enthusiasm going can be tough – a bit like trying to take up exercise. The first few times are impossibly hard but if you persevere, then one day you find you're jogging, walking, swimming without conscious effort. But getting going is really tough and requires immense powers of concentration, enthusiasm, dedication and perseverance to keep at it.

Try to see the past as a room separate from the one you live in now. You can go in there but you don't live there anymore. You can go visit but it isn't home any more. Home is here now. Each second of this present is precious. Don't waste any drops of precious time by spending too much time in that old room. Don't miss what is happening now because you were too busy looking back, or later you'll be busy looking back at this time and wondering why you wasted it. Live here, live now, live in this moment.

> ## LIVE HERE, LIVE NOW, LIVE IN THIS MOMENT

RULE 20

Don't live in the future

Blimey, if you thought the previous rule was tough, try this one . . . But the future is where it's all going to happen, I hear you cry. The future is where I'm going to be successful, happy, rich, beautiful, famous, in love, in work, out of this crap relationship, out on the town, surrounded by friends, surrounded by the finest wines money can buy. Yep, those might be plans or dreams or whatever. But again, this here and now is where it is actually at. This is the moment you've been waiting for all your life. This is the moment you must appreciate without all those other things you long for. Look, longing really is the sweetest thing. Having those dreams is brilliant. Don't let anyone ever tell you dreaming is a bad thing. But appreciate that it is the you *right now* that is doing the dreaming. Enjoy the wishing and the longing. Enjoy being alive and having the strength and vitality to do all that dreaming.

Living in the moment doesn't mean throwing away all your responsibilities and cares; it doesn't mean taking off and being a total pleasure seeker; it doesn't mean sitting cross-legged and breathing deeply – although all and any of these things is fine if you want. It just means taking a moment or two every now and then to appreciate being alive and to aim to act like today matters and live life to the full, right here, right now.

We can't project all our future happiness into the future – 'Oh if only I were richer/younger/healthier/happier/more in love/less in this relationship/had a better job/had nicer children/had a better car/were slimmer/taller/fitter/had more hair/better teeth/more clothes' – the list is endless. If only this or that was changed everything would be perfect, wouldn't it? Unfortunately not – it just doesn't work like that. When this and that gets changed there will always be something else, waiting its turn and putting off that happiness until some later date. If you were to suddenly find that you were slimmer/fitter or whatever, then you'd probably find yourself wanting to be richer or that your partner was more loving. You'd find other things to wish for to make you happy.

Forget bigger and better and richer and thinner. The key is to appreciate what we've got right now and yet still dream and plan. That way we'll be a little happier now than if we're constantly looking to the future, where happiness apparently lies.

And don't go thinking it's all right for me, it's not. I too need to lose a few pounds, certainly get fitter, get more stuff (and how we all love stuff). But I also value the way I am and appreciate what I've got right now because – and this is the secret – it is real. The me that is now is the real me, the future one isn't yet born and may not happen (you mean I might not lose that extra weight or get fitter? Yep, right). And the stuff I have now is at least real, tangible, solid. Dreams are great but reality is fine too.

> # DREAMS ARE GREAT BUT REALITY IS FINE TOO

RULE 21

Get on with life – it's whooshing past

Every day, every second, life is whooshing past at an alarming rate. And it goes on getting faster and faster. I once asked an 84-year-old man if life slowed down as you got older. His reply was unprintable but he explained to me in no uncertain terms that no, it didn't. It carried on getting faster. I sometimes wonder if we aren't picking up speed for take-off, if you know what I mean – a sort of run-up before we leave. But the Rule, if you want your life to be successful, happy, fulfilled, meaningful, jam-packed with adventure and reward, is to simply get on with it. And I'm sure you do or you wouldn't be reading this.

So, how do we get on with it? Well, the easiest way is the same way we would get on with anything else we knew we had to do. We start with setting a target (a goal, an objective), make a plan, formulate a set of actions to take you towards the target and then, well, get on with it.

Imagine you were a project manager for a big company and they wanted you to organize, say, an exhibition. You would begin with clarifying what you wanted from the exhibition, what it was supposed to achieve (for example, to sell 100 items or to give away free gifts or to drum up 20 new customers). This gives you something to aim for. Then you would formulate your plan – booking the stand, arranging the staff, getting stuff printed, etc. With the plan in place, you would work out what you needed and then get on with it.

Life isn't so different. It's a project – albeit on a vast scale and much more important than an exhibition stand.

I'm sure you get the idea. You have to get on with life, but it is so easy to wallow if you don't have a goal (or goals) and a plan. It's very easy for the days to blur into each other if you've no idea where you are going or what you want to achieve.

None of this, by the way, need take away any spontaneity from life if that's what you're thinking. I don't regard life like a work project, honestly. I do see it as a challenging, rewarding, exciting, rich and diverse, unexpected and rather fantastic experience. But you have to give it a bit of thought if you want to get the best out of it. Without that thought, the days will blur. Without that thought, it's easy to find yourself adrift – floating downstream.

> YOU HAVE TO GIVE IT A
> BIT OF THOUGHT IF YOU
> WANT TO GET THE BEST
> OUT OF IT

I used to think that whatever turned up would be fine. I was a sort of adventurous fatalist – I would be ready for whatever challenge was thrown my way. But increasingly I see the huge advantage of having a goal and working towards that rather than to drift aimlessly. It makes it so much easier for good things to happen.

Dress like today is important

Today is important. Today is the only day you've got that has some reality to it. Why shouldn't you treat it as important? It is. So dress like it matters. And no, I don't mean in the way my mother always used to tell me, 'Make sure you've got clean underwear on, you never know when you'll get run over by a bus.' I loved this as a kid. I couldn't see how important clean underwear would really be when you were lying there in the road. And I used to imagine how, if they got you to the hospital in time and stripped away your torn and blood-soaked trousers, they'd look down and gasp in horror, 'Don't look! This kid has got yesterday's pants on – get him out of here.'

Look, a lot of these Rules are about *conscious* choice, *conscious* decisions, *conscious* awareness. Those I have observed who seem to have got a handle on this thing called life are conscious people. They are awake and aware. They know what they are doing and where they are going. If you too want your life to be more than a set of random events that happen to you and instead make it a series of stimulating challenges and rewarding and enriching experiences, then you too have to be conscious.

And you do this by greeting each day as if it is important. You get up and shower/wash/shave/put on make-up/comb hair/clean teeth etc. and basically do all those things to make you look good, feel good, smell good. And then you dress smartly, cleanly, snappily, stylishly, as if you were going to a job interview or a birthday party or on an outing. If you dress for each day expectantly, importantly, smartly, then each day will become that.

People will react differently to you if you dress as if it matters – and you'll react differently to that different reaction. It's an upward spiral. I have to stress we're not talking formal here, you don't have to be buttoned up and uncomfortable. Just dress as if it matters.

> ## PEOPLE WILL REACT DIFFERENTLY TO YOU IF YOU DRESS AS IF IT MATTERS

But what about weekends, I hear you ask, surely we can relax then? Of course, but it doesn't mean you should let yourself go. At weekends you're going to see friends and/or family (unless you spend every weekend totally alone) and they too deserve to see you looking good, and as if they matter. Hey, not even your friends want to see you slovenly, dishevelled, untidy, uncared for. But this bit is really about you. If you greet each day as if it is important, then it will do wonders to *your* self-esteem, *your* self-respect, *your* self-confidence.

But, hey, I don't want you taking anything on trust. Try this and see what happens. If you don't perk up and feel completely different within a fortnight, then go back to your old ways and to hell with this Rule. But I can guarantee you'll feel great and face each day livelier and more energetic and happier.

If you adopt the conscious approach to living, you'll find it quite hard to consciously dress down.

Have a belief system

No, no, no, this isn't where I begin a religious rant or a New Age indoctrination process to welcome you into a strange cult. This is where I simply say that those who have a belief system to sustain them through times of crisis and trouble do better than those who don't. It's that simple.

Now what do we mean by a belief system? Ah, that's harder to put into words. I guess a belief system is what *you* think the world is all about, the universe and everything. It's what *you* believe will happen to you after you die. It's what or who *you* pray to when the night is dark and you are in trouble. Those who have a handle on this curious thing called life seem to be the ones who have worked out, satisfactorily for themselves at least, what they think it's all about. And it doesn't seem to matter what it is they think that is. You could believe in a God or many gods or you could believe in something or someone else – maybe that we're all the product of some weird alien experiment, or you might be a fervent flat earther – it doesn't matter. Well, I guess it will to you, but as long as you have a belief system you will do better than those who don't. Being a seeker is not conducive to having a happy life.

'I know you're going to say, 'But what if I haven't been able to find an answer and don't have a belief system? What am I supposed to do then?' Why, carry on looking I guess but do try to wrap this one up pretty quick as it's an important Rule. Put aside some time to think about it and make sure you put it high on your list of priorities.

I hope you notice I'm not giving you any advice here as to what sort of belief system to have. Any one will do as long as it supports you in times of trouble, answers your questions about your life and what you mean to the universe, and gives you comfort. You have to be comfortable with your belief system; it's no good having one in which a vengeful and violent deity watches your every move and terrifies you into submission (sorry, if you've already got one like that you might need to re-think it).

You might want to think about whether your belief system makes you feel guilt-ridden or unhappy, asks you to cut bits off your body or in any way mutilate or change your appearance, excludes anyone else on the basis of their race or sex, or needs any formal ritual to bring you the comfort it promises. For some the ideal belief system won't have any sort of figurehead who needs either worshipping, obeying or submitting to in any way, shape or form. This is personal, but it's worth thinking about what you are OK with.

A belief system has to be that – a belief. You don't have to prove it to anyone else, justify it, even show it (*see Rule 1*), convert anyone else to it, or preach to the world in general. You may feel free to take bits from all other belief systems to build your own. But if you can, have something.

> ## YOU DON'T HAVE TO PROVE IT TO ANYONE ELSE, JUSTIFY IT, EVEN SHOW IT

RULE 24

Leave a little space for yourself each day

Most people think they get this but most people might be wrong. You may think you have a little quality time each day for yourself but I bet you don't. You see, even in our time alone we spend so much of it worrying about others, caring for our family, friends and loved ones, that there is very little left over entirely for ourselves. What I am proposing isn't revolutionary or difficult or extreme. In fact it's pretty easy. Just leave a little space for yourself each day. Perhaps only ten minutes (ideally half an hour) put aside and devoted entirely to yourself. Selfish? You bet. Of course it is and justifiably so – you are the captain, the engine, the driving force, the motivator, the rock. You need that time to regenerate, renew, invigorate yourself. You need that down time to recharge and repair. If you don't, you aren't taking on fresh fuel, your engine will run down and so will you.

So what are you going to do with that time? Answer: absolutely nothing. And I do mean nothing. This isn't time for lying in the bath, sitting on the loo, meditating, reading the newspapers, or sleeping. This is a little space for you, a breather, a time to sit still and do absolutely nothing. Just breathe. I find ten minutes sitting in the garden just breathing is a fantastic boost a couple of times a day. I sit there, not thinking, not doing, not worrying, just being, while I appreciate the pleasure of being alive.

I discovered this Rule when I was a teenager. I found it invaluable as a way of purging myself of angst and worries. My mother used to call out to me, 'What are you doing?' To which the reply was inevitably, 'Nothing'. And she would always reply, 'Well come in here and I'll find you something to do.' She also used to say: 'You'll never amount to anything by having your head stuck in a book.'

> ## IT IS THE LITTLE SPACE JUST FOR YOURSELF WHILE YOU DO ABSOLUTELY NOTHING

And the one I loved the most: 'No one needs to think as much as you do.' How do you answer that?

I find time spent doing nothing really important and as soon as I complicate it, it loses something. If I add a cup of coffee to my solitude, then it's a coffee break and not a space just for me. If I listen to music, then it's a music break. If I have a companion with me and I chat, then it's a social occasion. If I read the papers, then I have moved away entirely from the concept of a little space for me. Keep it simple. Keep it bare. Keep it pure.

Have a plan

You've got to have a plan. A plan is a map, a guide, a target, a focus, a route, a signpost, a direction, a path, a strategy. It says that you are going to go somewhere, do something, be somewhere by a certain time. It gives your life structure and shape, gravitas and power. If you allow life to turn up any old thing you'll be floating downstream as quick as you like. OK, so not all plans work out, not all maps lead to the treasure. But at least you're in with a better chance if you have a map and a shovel than if you just dig at random – or, like most people, don't dig at all.

A plan indicates you've had a bit of a think about your life and aren't just waiting for something to turn up. Or, again like most people, not even thinking about it but going through life perpetually surprised by what happens. Work out what it is you want to do, plan it, work out the steps to take to achieve your goal, and get on with it. If you don't plan your plan, it will remain a dream.

> IF YOU DON'T PLAN YOUR
> PLAN, IT WILL REMAIN
> A DREAM

So what happens if you don't have a plan? Well, you reinforce, to yourself, your sense of being 'not in control'. Once you have a plan everything else falls into place. Once you have a plan, the logical steps to achieve that plan also become available, accessible. A plan isn't a dream – it's something you intend doing rather than something you want to do. And having a plan means you've thought through how you're going to do it.

Of course, just because you have a plan doesn't mean that you have to stick to it, to follow it, to obey it to the letter come hell or high water. The plan is always up for review, for improvement, for changing as and when you need to. The plan shouldn't be rigid. Circumstances change, you change, your plan changes. The details of the plan don't matter. Having one does.

Having a plan gives you a fall-back position. When life gets hectic – and boy does it do that sometimes – it is easy to forget what we are here for. Having a plan means that when the dust settles you can remember, 'Now what was I doing? Oh yes, I remember, my plan was to . . . ' And off you go again, back on course.

Have a sense of humour

How important this is. As we struggle through this life – and it can be a struggle – we need to keep a sense of proportion about it. What we do and what we take seriously can often be so far removed from what it is actually all about that it is laughable. We get bogged down in trivia, lost in irrelevant detail to such an extent that our life can whizz past and we don't even notice. By letting go of things that really aren't important we can put ourselves back on the right track. And the best way to do that is through humour – laughing at ourselves, laughing at our situation, but never laughing at others, they're just as lost as us and don't need to be laughed at.

We get bogged down in things like worrying what the neighbours will think, concerns over stuff we don't have, or things we haven't done: 'Oh no, I haven't washed the car for two weeks and it's filthy and next door did theirs yesterday so it looks like we are really slovenly'. If we ever think we're getting like that then we do need to have a laugh about it. Life is for living, enjoying the sunshine, big things – not getting in a terrible state because you dropped some eggs on the supermarket floor.

Laughing at yourself and situations you find yourself in has a double positive effect. Firstly, it diffuses tension and helps regain a sense of proportion and secondly, it has real physical as well as mental benefits. Laughter causes the release of endorphins, which make you feel better as well as giving you a better perspective on life.

This isn't about telling jokes all the time, or cracking witty puns. It's more being able to see something funny in whatever life throws at us along the way – and there is always some humour in everything. I once came round after being unconscious from a serious car crash. I was in a cubicle in a hospital and in great pain. As I regained consciousness I let out a couple of choice words to describe my condition and, as I did so, the nurse arrived and opened the curtains only for me to find a nun sat outside.* I was mortified and immediately apologized. She looked at me most gravely, winked, and quietly said, 'It's OK, I've said worse myself.'

If you observe any aspect of human behaviour, you can see the ridiculousness in all of it. Learn to find the funny side of everything. It's the best technique for instant stress relief and dissolves anxiety and doubt. Try it.

> ## SEE SOMETHING FUNNY IN WHATEVER LIFE THROWS AT US ALONG THE WAY

---

* Nothing to do with me, she was quietly waiting for another nun who was being checked out in for a splinter in her finger, I later discovered.

RULE 27

Choose how you make your bed

Every action you take, every decision you make, everything you do causes an immediate effect on those around you – and on you. And this is the important bit. There *is* such a thing as instant karma. It is your bed and you are going to have to lie in it. Your actions will dictate whether in general your life is going to run happily or badly, smoothly or as if the wheels have fallen off. If you are selfish and manipulative it will rebound on you. If you are generally loving and thoughtful you will get your just rewards – and not in heaven (or the next life or whatever you believe) but right here, right now.

Trust me. Whatever you do and how you do it will come back to you in spades. This isn't a threat, merely an observation. Those who do good, get good. Those who do bad, get bad.

I know we can all point to people who seem to have it made and are still pretty vile. But they don't sleep at night. They have no one to really love them. Inside they are sad and lonely and frightened. Those who go around sharing a bit of love and kindness get rewarded with the same coming back.

It's a bit like the old adage that 'You are what you eat'. You are what you do. Look at the faces of those who spread joy and you will see laughter lines and smiles. Look at those who like to bully and get their own way and are arrogant or demanding or vicious and you will see etched lines of misery and fear, and frowns where there ought to be lightness. These lines won't ever be taken away by face creams or suntans or plastic surgery. They are what they do and you can see it in their eyes. And the state of their bed of course.

So be careful how you make your bed. What goes around, comes around. There is instant karma. What you sow you reap. Better to stand up and be counted right from the start. Do the right thing, every time. You know what it is. Then when you get in the bed you've made, not only will you be able to sleep at night, but you'll sleep the sleep of the just.

> ## DO THE RIGHT THING, EVERY TIME. YOU KNOW WHAT IT IS

Life can be a bit like advertising

Someone once said that half of the money he spent on advertising was wasted but he didn't know which half.* His point was of course that if you can't tell which half, then you have to keep on doing the whole lot, fully aware that not all of it will produce rewards. Life is a bit like that. Sometimes it seems so unfair. You put in loads of effort and get nothing back. You're polite to people and everyone seems rude back. You work up a sweat and others cruise it. Well, you have to keep on doing the 100 per cent because you don't know which bits will pay off. I know it isn't fair but then life isn't. Your efforts will be rewarded eventually but you'll probably never know which efforts are being rewarded – or for what – and which aren't.

We tend to think we are being lucky sometimes when actually we are just being rewarded for some bit of effort long ago that we have forgotten about. We have to keep going. You can't give up on the grounds that you've had a setback or two because you don't know which setbacks are the ones which count and which ones aren't. I suppose it's like the number of frogs you have to get acquainted with before you find your prince (or princess). Or the pile of oysters you'd have to open to find a pearl.

But whatever you do, don't lose heart because things don't seem to be panning out. Only by keeping up the effort will rewards come in eventually – and you'll never know from which bits comes the best reward.

---

* Lord Leverhulme I believe.

> ## YOU'LL NEVER KNOW FROM WHICH BITS OF EFFORT COMES THE BEST REWARD

Most well balanced and happy people will also tell you that sometimes you have to work at something without looking for a pay-off – apart from the immediate pay-off that we are being kept busy and thus can't get into trouble. Always looking for success, rewards, a pay-off, can be detrimental to our wellbeing when things don't pan out. Sometimes it's OK to do things just for the sheer enjoyment of doing them. I love painting miniature water-colours – tiny, tiny landscapes. Once in a while someone will come along and suggest I put them into an exhibition or sell them commercially. And every time I do it fails miserably and I give up for a while. Once the dust has settled I always go back to them and I have learnt it is a personal thing and no longer will I try to sell them or show them. They are a not-for-profit part of my life and immensely rewarding. No, you can't see one.

Get used to stepping outside your comfort zone

Be prepared to be a little bit brave every day. Why? Because if you don't you'll grow stagnant and mouldy or curl up and wither. We all have a comfort zone where we feel safe and warm and dry. But every now and then we need to step outside and be challenged, be frightened, be stimulated. It's this way that we stay young and feel good about ourselves.

If we grow too attached to our comfort zone, chances are it will either start to shrink, or something will come along and dismantle it. Fate, or whatever it is that runs things, doesn't like us to get too complacent and every now and then gives us a great big cosmic kick up the backside to wake us up. If we have practised stretching the boundaries of our woolly cocoon occasionally, that kick won't have too much impact – we're ready for it – it's much easier to cope.

But it's more than that. Expanding your comfort zone makes you feel good about yourself. It gives you extra confidence. And the best bit is that you can do it oh so gently. You don't have to go hang-gliding or fire-walking or have sex with a stranger just to test your comfort zone. It might be as simple as volunteering for something that you've never done before and that you feel slightly nervous about. It could be taking up a new sport or hobby. Maybe it will involve joining something. It could be doing something alone that you've only ever done in company before or speaking up for yourself when you would usually keep quiet.

We impose a lot of restrictions on ourselves that limit us, hold us back. We think we couldn't do that, wouldn't feel happy with that. Taking the challenge of expanding our comfort zone brings us out of ourselves and keeps us learning and growing. You can't grow mould if you're growing experience.

> ## EXPANDING YOUR COMFORT ZONE MAKES YOU FEEL GOOD ABOUT YOURSELF

Learn to ask questions

Look, you may not like the answers but at least you'll know. Most of the world's problems can be laid firmly at the feet of *assumptions*. If we assume (no, I'm not going to do that dreadful 'it makes an ass out of u and me' stuff*) then, in effect, we think we know but we don't. We assume that our bit of faulty information is a fact and things go on getting worse. We assume that other people like our plan but they don't and it all goes pear-shaped. Better to ask questions right from the start and know what's what.

Questions help clarify the situation. Questions put people on the spot, which means they have to think – and thinking is always a good thing for everybody about everything. Questions help people clarify their thoughts. Questions demand answers and answers require the situation to be thought through, to its logical conclusion.

> ## QUESTIONS HELP PEOPLE
> ## CLARIFY THEIR THOUGHTS

As someone very wise and very dear to me once said: 'The better you understand the beliefs, actions, desires and wants of others,

---

* I know I did but that was a joke.

the more likely you are to make the right response, alter your own thinking where necessary and generally be successful.'

Asking questions gives you time to think, buys you breathing space. Rather than flying off the handle because you think you know the situation, it's better to ask a few questions and find out the truth. You'll be better equipped to respond logically, calmly and correctly.

You can always tell the real Rules Players; they're the ones asking questions while others are reacting, panicking, misinterpreting, assuming, losing control and generally behaving badly.

Ask questions of yourself constantly. Ask why you think you're right – or wrong. Ask yourself why you are doing certain things, want other things, follow a particular course of action. Question yourself firmly and rigorously because maybe there isn't anyone else doing it. And you need it. We all do. It keeps us from assuming we know what's best for ourselves.

And of course there is a time to stop asking questions; of others and of ourselves. You have to know when to back off. All this takes a long time to learn and we all make mistakes as we go. Any questions?

Have dignity

I've spent years watching successful people, and I don't just mean successful as in having lots of money or a big-shot career. In fact one of the most successful people I ever met lived incredibly frugally and simply and reclusively and yet had cracked it in a really big way – happiness, peace, contentment. This was a person you couldn't have wiped the inner smile off even if you had tried.

Almost all successful people have a sense of their own dignity. Now what do I mean by this? Well, they are all pretty solid in themselves, they have worked out who they are and what they are about. They don't need to show off, brag about what they have or who they are. They don't need to draw attention to themselves because they aren't particularly interested in what we think – they are too busy getting on with things in their own lives. They maintain decorum (lovely old-fashioned word that) not because they are frightened of making a fool of themselves or falling flat on their face but because they simply can't be bothered with attention-seeking stuff.

It is important – if you want to be a successful Rules Player – to show poise, gravitas, be a bit separate from the herd, have good manners, be polite and considerate and to be someone others might like to look up to. You don't have to be all aloof and stand-offish, serious and grown-up. You can still have fun – just don't go making a prat of yourself. You can still let your hair down – just don't let go of control completely. You can still relax – just don't fall off the edge.

Dignity is about showing self-respect and having quiet self-esteem. It's amazing how others will respect you and hold you in greater esteem when you start the ball rolling.

> # DIGNITY IS ABOUT SHOWING SELF-RESPECT AND HAVING QUIET SELF-ESTEEM

It's OK to feel big emotions

If we're busily maintaining dignity and being peaceful, it's tempting to think that we're detached and so there's no place for big feelings and such like. Well, the good news is, it doesn't work like that. It is OK to feel emotions. It is OK to feel angry when someone really hacks you off. It is OK to feel huge sadness and grief when you lose a loved one. It is OK to feel tremendous joy. It is OK to be scared, anxious, relieved, excited, apprehensive and all the others.

We are human beings and we have emotions. This is all quite natural. It is quite natural to feel big things deeply and it's OK to let it all show. We don't have to be ashamed of our feelings. It is OK to cry. Sitting on our feelings isn't a good idea. They just get squashed that way. Far better to let them out, deal with them and then get on with things.

> ## SITTING ON OUR FEELINGS ISN'T A GOOD IDEA. THEY JUST GET SQUASHED THAT WAY

If we go through trauma, upsetting experiences and difficult times, it certainly doesn't help to be thinking all the time that we have to keep a lid on it or people will think us weak or out of control. I know it might look as if it contradicts keeping our dignity, but feeling emotion is not undignified unless we express it inappropriately or at the wrong time.

Sometimes even getting angry is totally appropriate – as long as we remain in control and don't do anything we might regret later. Getting angry reminds people that we aren't a pushover and that they have hurt/offended/threatened us deeply and seriously and that their actions have caused us great pain. Of course we shouldn't get angry over silly things – instead we choose to show anger only when it is needed, and needed seriously. Likewise it's not good to get angry and take it out on innocent people – if you can't express the anger appropriately, then you need to find a way of letting it out that isn't going to hurt anybody else. But let it out you must. Bottled anger eats away at you.

It's not just anger that shouldn't be permanently restrained. Neither should fear or anxiety or great joy or any of the other emotions. Just because we are feeling big emotions doesn't mean we are out of control. We can be quite emotional and still be in charge of what we are expressing. You wouldn't be human if you didn't feel stuff – and feel it big time. It is natural and you shouldn't even make any attempt to stifle it. Of course you can make sure it is let out at an appropriate time and place, but that is within your control. But then again if you do respond badly, you can always feel guilty about it afterwards – and that's OK too.

RULE 33

Keep the faith

> ". . . 'We have kept the faith!' we said;
> 'We shall go down with unreluctant tread.
> Rose-crowned into the darkness!'"

This is from a poem by Rupert Brooke called *The Hill*, which is about friendship (I think). It may of course be about something entirely different, it's always so hard to tell. But for me it is about the friendship between two lovers, two friends. It is about keeping faith, keeping your promise to support, trust, believe in. It may of course be about keeping faith as a religious thing, but knowing Brooke's poems I somehow don't think so.

Keeping the faith is about sticking to your promises, going down into darkness rose-crowned, proud, unreluctant, knowing you've done the right thing, stuck by your friends in times of trouble. These are perhaps old-fashioned values – honour, loyalty, trust, pride, support, fidelity, reliability, dependability, strength, seeing things through, constancy – but no less worth having for all that. We live in a throw-away society and keeping your word, being there when you said you would, being dependable and reliable, makes you stand out as a person of some value, some worth. This is a good thing.

We fight shy of being 'good' these days in case people mistake us for 'goody-goodies'. But that's another thing entirely. Keeping the faith is something you do. Being a goody-goody is when you try to convert others. Having your own values and keeping them to yourself (sticking to Rule 1) is fine. Trying to make everyone else do the same as you is a bad thing. That makes you a goody-goody. No, it doesn't apply to me because I'm only giving out information, not trying to convert you. It is entirely up to you whether you pick up this information and run with it. But I can guarantee you I shall keep the faith and the information I give you today will be the same information I would give you in 20 years' time. Old-fashioned values don't ever go out of style (perhaps they've always been out) and I shan't let you down.

> ## KEEPING THE FAITH IS SOMETHING YOU DO. BEING A GOODY-GOODY IS WHEN YOU TRY TO CONVERT OTHERS

Here's another bit from the same poem:

"... *Proud we were,*
And laughed, that had such brave true things to say."

You'll never understand everything

Look, we are tiny complex humans in a huge complex world (and even bigger universe). It's all so unimaginably, fantastically strange that believe me we'll never be able to understand everything . And that applies at all levels and in all areas of life. Once you grasp this rule you'll sleep easier at night.

There are likely to be a few things going on around you right now, as there always will be, that will remain just slightly outside of your comprehension. People will behave oddly and you won't understand why. Things will go unexpectedly wrong – or right – and it won't make sense. Spend all your time desperately trying to work it all out and you'll drive yourself crazy. Much better to just accept that there is always stuff that we won't understand and let it go at that. How simple that is.

> **PEOPLE WILL BEHAVE ODDLY. THINGS WILL GO UNEXPECTEDLY WRONG – OR RIGHT**

It's the same principle for the big stuff – why things happen to us, why we are here, where we go afterwards, that sort of thing. Some of it we'll never know, some of it we can try and work out, but I have a sneaking feeling it won't turn out to be anything like we think.

It's as if our lives are an enormous jigsaw and all we get access to is the bottom left hand bit. And from that we make these huge assumptions: 'Oh, it's a . . .' But when the veil gets taken away we see that the jigsaw is massive and that the one tiny bit we were scrutinizing was actually something else, and there we are looking at an entirely different picture to the one we'd imagined.

We are now collecting information faster than any human, or any computer, can process it. We can't understand it all. We can't even begin to understand a tiny fraction of it. Same with our lives. Stuff is going on around us at such a rate we'll never get to the bottom of it. Because as fast as we try, picture changes, new information comes in and our understanding alters.

Be curious, ask questions, wonder to yourself, talk to other people if you like – but know that this won't always give you a clear and concrete answer. People don't always make sense. Life doesn't always make sense. Let it go and discover the peace of mind that comes with knowing that you'll never understand everything. Sometimes it just is.

Know where true happiness comes from

No, I'm not about to reveal the secret people have sought since the beginning of time – where true happiness comes from. But I do know where it *isn't* to be found. And I do have an inkling where it might be. Let's take a scenario. You go out to buy a new car/house/suit/computer/whatever turns you on. You have the money (no, I have no idea where you get it from, this is just an example) and you buy whatever it is, and it makes you feel incredible/happy/excited/fantastic. Now imagine whoever it was who built/made/created whatever it is you bought. When they made it, where did they fit that feeling in? I think you might have brought that feeling with you.

> ## I THINK YOU MIGHT HAVE BROUGHT THAT FEELING WITH YOU

Now imagine you fall in love. It is again, incredible. You feel fantastic, happy, excited. You go to meet your new love and when you see them, that feeling spills out in all directions. You feel amazing because you are with them and they are generating that feeling. Right? Wrong. Again you brought it all with you. You may look to them to trigger it but even if they go to the other end of the planet, you'll still have that feeling and they're nowhere near you.

You get fired. Ghastly. You get given your papers. You walk away devastated. You feel like nothing. Now where in that documentation is that feeling you now have? Nowhere, that's right. Again you brought it all with you. We all go to work every day with the potential to have that 'I've just been fired' feeling. We all meet new people with the 'I've fallen head over heels in love' feeling.

But no amount of falling in love, buying new stuff or getting sacked is going to keep that feeling going for longer than it takes us to get over it. People get addicted to buying new stuff or falling in love or whatever because they just love that feeling without realizing that they already have it. They have to keep having their 'fix' because they think it's the only way to get that feeling going. The secret is knowing how to trigger it without anyone else or anything else being involved. No, I don't know. You have to find that one for yourself. Clue: It's the one place you'd never think of looking, yep, right inside you.

Know when to let go – when to walk away

Sometimes you have to just walk away. We all hate to fail, hate to give up, hate to give in. We love the challenge of life and want to keep on until whatever we are trying to 'win' has been overcome, vanquished, beaten, won. But sometimes it just ain't going to happen and we need to learn to recognize those moments, learn how to philosophically shrug and walk away with our pride intact and our dignity high.

Sometimes you really want to do something, but it is unrealistic. Instead of knocking yourself out, cultivate the art of knowing when to walk away and you'll find it a lot less stressful.

If a relationship is coming to its end, instead of playing out long and complicated – and potentially hurtful – end games, learn the art of walking away. If it's dead, leave it. This isn't a Rule that should be in the relationship section – it's here because it is for you, to protect you, to nurture you. This is nothing to do with 'them' but all to do with you. If it's dead, don't go digging it up every five minutes to check if there's a pulse. It's dead, walk away.

You may want to get even – don't get mad, walk away. This is much better than getting even because it shows you have risen above whatever it is that is driving you crazy. And there can be no better way of getting even than to ignore something so completely it can be left behind.

Letting go and walking away means you are exercising control and good decision-making powers – you are making your choice rather than letting the situation control you.

> IF IT'S DEAD, DON'T GO
> DIGGING IT UP EVERY FIVE
> MINUTES TO CHECK IF
> THERE'S A PULSE. IT'S
> DEAD, WALK AWAY

I don't want to be rude but your problems – hey, my problems too – won't even warrant a footnote in the history of the universe. Walk away now and look back after ten years and I bet you'll be hard pushed to even remember what it was all about. No, this isn't a 'time is the best healer' crusade, but putting space and time between you and your troubles does give you a wider view, a better perspective. And the way to do that is to walk away, put that space there. Time will put itself there, in time of course.

Look after yourself

You are the Boss, the Captain, the Driving Force. If you are sick, who is going to run the ship? There is no one else. It makes sense to look after yourself. And I have no intention of getting all preachy here and telling you to go to bed early, eat your greens and take loads of exercise – that would all be pure hypocrisy because I don't do any of those things. Doesn't mean you shouldn't, however. They are all a good idea.

An occasional quick body service might be a good idea, a regular check-up to nip any potential problems in the bud. I have an annual one. I would also suggest that some foods are like dynamite and they fill you with energy, speed your metabolism and make you feel great. Other foods make you sluggish, get stored as fat and slow you down. They might also do you long-term damage in the way of clogging up bits. Now the choice is entirely yours but the machine that is you runs better on high-energy food and worse on junk food.

Same with sleep. Going without makes you tired. Having too much makes you lethargic. Getting the right amount makes you feel good. Going back to sleep makes you feel blurry. Getting up straight away makes you feel good – and noble. Nothing better. But of course all this is entirely up to you. No one is going to stand behind you anymore and make sure you've washed behind your ears or check your shoes are clean and polished. You're a grown-up and on your own now. Fantastic. But it means you have all the responsibility too.

YOU'RE A GROWN-UP AND
ON YOUR OWN NOW

Rules Players eat well, sleep well, relax a lot, take exercise (and no, computer games don't count). They also stay away from potentially harmful situations. They know how to say out of danger, avoid threatening encounters and generally take care of themselves.

Looking after yourself is exactly that. Not relying on anyone else to make sure you are fed on time and fed well, washed and ready to go, comfortable, tidy, healthy and let out regularly for your walk. It's great being a grown-up. You get to stay up all night partying if you want to, but you can also choose to take care of yourself if you want to.

RULE 38

Maintain good manners in all things

In her wonderful book *Watching the English*,* Kate Fox observes that in any small transaction, like buying a newspaper, there will be around three pleases and two thank-yous – and that's a minimum. Yes, the English (and a few other nationalities besides) are terribly polite but what's wrong with that? We have to interact with a whole host of people every day and a little politeness has to be a good thing. The Rules Player maintains good manners in all things. And if you don't know what good manners are, then we are in trouble.

You're probably thinking that you have good manners already. Most of us believe we do. However, the more you hurry and the more stress you are under, the more manners are likely to slip. All of us, if we're honest, will admit to forgetting to properly express gratitude for something when frazzled by life, or feeling a huge temptation to push in front of somebody doddery when rushing to catch a train.

However rushed and fraught you are (and following the Rules should make you less so), you should always make the effort to show these good manners:

- queuing without jostling
- complimenting people when you need to (and when they deserve it, no use throwing compliments around if they aren't justified and earned)

---

* *Watching the English: The Hidden Rules of English Behaviour* by Kate Fox (Hodder & Stoughton, 2004).

- not sticking your nose in where it isn't wanted
- keeping a promise
- keeping a secret
- keeping basic table etiquette (oh come on you know this stuff: no elbows, no talking with your mouth open, no over-stuffing your mouth, no flicking peas with your knife)
- not shouting at people who get in your way
- apologizing when you get in someone else's
- being civil
- not swearing or being religiously profane
- opening the door ahead of people
- standing back when there's a rush
- answering when spoken to
- saying 'good morning' and such like
- thanking people when they've looked after you or done something for you
- being hospitable
- observing manners of other communities
- not grabbing the last piece of cake
- being courteous and charming
- offering visitors refreshment and going to the front door to say goodbye to them.

No matter how many small interactions with people you have each day, don't let the manners slip. They cost nothing and yet can generate so much good will and make everyone's life that much more pleasant.

Prune your stuff frequently

Why? Because collecting clutter clutters your home, your life and your mind. A cluttered home is symbolic of cluttered thinking. Rules Players are clear and direct in their thinking and don't collect junk. If only. We all do of course. All I am suggesting is that occasionally clearing some of it out might be a good idea or it overwhelms you emotionally and gets more and more cobwebby.

Pruning your stuff gives you a chance to get rid of anything that is useless, broken, out of date, un-cool, un-cleanable, redundant and ugly. It was, after all, William Morris who said not to have anything in your home that wasn't useful or beautiful. Having a good clear-out refreshes you, revitalizes you, makes you conscious of what you are collecting – and anything that makes us conscious is a good thing in my book.

Again I have noticed a difference between successful people and those who seem to labour in a backwater never really getting their lives off the ground. Those who are punchy and getting on with things are also those who have an amazing ability to prune stuff, clear the clutter, sort the wheat from the chaff. Those who are having trouble getting lift-off are those running along the tarmac still clutching black plastic sacks full of useless stuff they bought from the charity shop and have never thrown away – or opened since they bought them, cupboards full of junk that is just taking up space, drawers full of broken things and wardrobes full of clothes they can no longer get into or which have so long gone out of fashion they may be worth something as collector's items but will never be worn again.

RULE 39

There is an 'unburdening' effect that comes with pruning. You have more space in your home, a feeling of being more in control, and you get rid of that slightly overwhelmed feeling that comes with having piles of stuff accumulating everywhere. You don't have to live in a spotless house full of designer furniture and minimalist styling. All I'm suggesting is that if you want to find out what's holding you back, try looking in the cupboard under the sink or under the bed or on top of the wardrobe in the spare room.

> CLUTTER OVERWHELMS
> YOU EMOTIONALLY AND
> GETS MORE AND MORE
> COBWEBBY

Remember to touch base

Before you can touch base you have to know where base is. Base is home. Base is where you belong. Base is where you feel comfortable, secure, loved, restored and trusted. Base is where you feel strong and in control. Base is anywhere you can kick your shoes off, metaphorically and physically, and rest your head safe in the knowledge you'll be looked after.

We all lead increasingly busy, frenetic and frantic lives. We all get caught up in the hurly-burly of life to such an extent that we lose sight of where we thought we were going and what we thought we were going to do and what we were going to achieve. Base is going back to where you dreamed it all, planned it all out. Base is where you were before you got lost.

> ## BASE IS WHERE YOU WERE BEFORE YOU GOT LOST

Base camp might well be rediscovering our roots – essential in an age when we all move around so much. Knowing who your family is, where you come from, what your real background is. It's OK to have ambition and move on from our roots, but it's also important to know who we are and where we came from. You can sometimes

RULE 40

sense it in celebrities who have become incredibly famous or rich. Often they try to deny their past and pretend to be something else and in the process they come across as shallow and fake.

For you, base might be a place where you grew up, where you're reminded of the feelings of growing up – the hopes and fears, the younger you. Or it might be a person who provides the base – a best friend from many years ago who can remind you of how you were before it all got so confusing.

Of course, we might not all know where we come from and we have to make allowances for that. You might be adopted, but you were raised somewhere. Whatever your circumstances, you will have something that makes you feel grounded if you look for it. It doesn't have to be where you were born and raised. If you are really struggling, then it's possible to create yourself a new base. Anywhere that makes you feel secure is fine.

We all need time with people or in places where we can be ourselves, where we don't have to explain, justify, provide background or give a good impression. That's the joy of touching base – being somewhere you are accepted without question and everything around you reminds you of what's really important. Touching base is something that when we do it, we wonder why on earth we left it so long.

Draw the lines around yourself

Personal boundaries are the imaginary lines you draw around yourself that no one should cross either physically – unless invited in – or emotionally. You are entitled to respect, privacy, decency, kindness, love, truth and honour, to name but a few rights. If people cross the lines, blur the boundaries, you are entitled to stand up for yourself and say, 'No, I won't put up with this.'

But you have to draw the lines first. You have to know what you will stand for and what you won't. You have to set the boundaries in your own mind before you can expect others to respect them, stick to them.

The more secure you become with your boundaries, the less power other people will have to affect you. The more clearly defined your boundaries, the more you realize that other people's stuff is more to do with them and less to do with you – you stop taking things so personally.

You are entitled to basic self-respect. You can't except others to respect you unless you respect yourself. You can't respect yourself until you have formed a clear picture of who you are and what you are. And setting boundaries is part of this process. You have to feel important enough to set those lines. And once set, you have to be assertive enough to reinforce them.

Setting personal boundaries means you don't have to be scared of other people any more. You now have a clear idea of what you will put up with and what you won't. Once someone crosses the line between appropriate and inappropriate behaviour, it gets really easy to say, 'No, I don't want to be treated like this/spoken to like this.'

Probably the best way to start this is with your own family. Over the years we get set in patterns of behaviour. Say, for example, if you are used to going to visit your parents and coming away feeling bad because they put you down or made you feel inadequate. You can change things by saying to yourself, 'I won't put up with this any more.' And then don't put up with it. Speak your mind. Say you don't like being criticized/told off/made to feel small, you are an adult now and entitled to respect and encouragement.

> # SETTING PERSONAL BOUNDARIES MEANS YOU DON'T HAVE TO BE SCARED OF OTHER PEOPLE ANY MORE

Setting personal boundaries enables us to resist pushy people, rude people, aggressive people, people who would take advantage of us, people who would use us unwisely and unwell. Successful people know their worth and don't get messed around. Successful people are the ones who can recognize emotional blackmail, people playing games with them, people on the make, people who themselves are weak and needy, people who dump on others, people who need to make you look small to make themselves feel big. Once you've got those lines drawn around you, it gets a whole lot easier to stay behind them and be firm, resolute, strong and assertive.

Shop for quality, not price

I have to admit my wife taught me this one, for which I am eternally in her debt. To me it seemed a natural thing to shop for price. Perhaps this is what chaps do. I would work out what I wanted and then go and buy the cheapest items I could and feel really pleased with myself for saving money. And then I was always dissatisfied with what I had. Stuff broke or didn't work or wore out quickly or looked shoddy after a very short time. I was living in a mess – and a cheap one at that. What I needed to learn was the art of quality shopping.

Basically:

- Accept only the very best – second best is not for you, ever
- If you can't afford it, don't buy it *or* wait and save until you can
- If you have to have it, buy the very best you can afford.

There, that's pretty easy isn't it? Well, for me it wasn't as easy as that. It took me quite a long time to really get to grips with this one. It isn't that I don't – or didn't then – admire quality or appreciate excellence; it was that I was impulsive. If I thought I needed something, I wanted it right then and there. And if I couldn't afford the very best, I would settle for the cheapest. In fact, in a very English sort of way, I thought that 'getting a bargain' was what it was all about. We don't like to talk about money and we don't like to brag about how much something cost, too tacky by far – better to buy tacky in the first place. I think not.

RULE 42

> ## IF YOU CAN'T AFFORD IT, DON'T BUY IT

Going for quality doesn't mean we're stuck up or a load of toffs or living beyond our means – if you can't afford it, don't buy it. Going for quality means you appreciate the finer things, can see the sense in buying well-made, well-produced things as they will:

- last longer
- be stronger
- not break so easily.

And this means they will not need to be replaced so often, which means you might actually be saving money. They will also make you look and feel better.

Now that I've latched on to this Rule I really enjoy that anticipation before I buy something. I make sure it really is the quality I am going for and not just the price. I still shop around for a bargain though – it's just now I look for the quality items but I'm prepared to find them at the lowest price.

It's OK to worry, or to know how not to

The future is uncertain, scary, hidden. We wouldn't be human if we didn't worry about things at times. We worry about our health, our parents/kids/friends, our relationships, our work and our spending. We worry that we are getting older, fatter, poorer, more tired, less attractive, less fit, less mentally alert, less everything really. We worry about things that matter and things that don't. Sometimes we worry about not worrying.

Look, it really is OK to worry. Just so long as there is something real to worry about. If there isn't, then all you're doing is putting wrinkles in your brow – and that makes you look older you know.

The first step is to decide whether there is something you can do about whatever it is you are worrying about, or not. There are usually logical steps to take to eliminate that worry. I worry that

> . . . ALL YOU ARE DOING IS PUTTING WRINKLES IN YOUR BROW – AND THAT MAKES YOU LOOK OLDER YOU KNOW

RULE 43

people aren't taking those steps, which means they are choosing to hang on to their worries rather than be free of them.

If you are worried then:

- get practical advice
- get up-to-date information
- do something, anything as long as it is constructive.

If you are worrying about your health, go and see a doctor. If you are worrying about money, set a budget and spend wisely. If you are worrying about your weight, go to the gym – eat less, do more. If you are worrying about a lost kitten, phone the vet/police/local animal rescue. If you are worrying about getting older, there is simply no point – it's happening whether you worry or not.

If there is nothing you can do about your worry (or if you are a persistent worrier, even bordering on the neurotic), then distraction is the only answer. Get absorbed in something else. A man with the rather impressive name of Mikhail Csikszentmihalyi identified something called 'flow', where you are so absorbed in a task you are doing, so fully immersed, that you become almost unaware of external events. It's a pleasurable experience and it completely banishes worry. He also said: 'The quality of our lives improves immensely when there is at least one other person who is willing to listen to our troubles.'

Worrying may be a symptom that you don't really want to *do* something about the problem. It might be easier just to carry on worrying – or looking concerned and appearing to worry – rather than doing something about it. It is OK to worry properly, profitably, usefully. It is not OK to worry pointlessly or needlessly. Or at least, it is OK but it's a colossal waste of life.

Stay young

I did say earlier that if you were worrying about getting older, you should stop as there wasn't anything you could do about it. It's inevitable. So why a Rule saying *Stay young*? Well, growing older physically (and temporally) is something we all have to do and putting it off by endless surgery and the like is pointless. Better to stay young. And by this I mean mentally and emotionally. Billy Connolly made a wry observation in one of his shows when he bent down to pick something up and made a noise, a sort of bending grunt that oldies make. And he said he didn't know when he had started to make that noise but it had crept up on him and he made it now. That's what I'm talking about – all those noises and actions we make to indicate we're old. All that wrapping up well when we go out in case we catch a chill. All that making sure we take our coat off when we come in, even if we're going straight out again or we won't feel the benefit. All that 'I'd rather just have a cup of tea if it's all right with you' stuff. All that 'We're going to the same place we always go on holiday – you know what you're getting.'

I was reading yesterday about a chap who had just taken his father backpacking in the Greek islands. His dad is aged 78 and he said he had trouble keeping up with him. Now that's staying young. I know a woman in her sixties who describes how she feels the same inside now as she did when she was 21. And it shows outside. That's staying young.

Staying young is trying new things, not grumbling or saying all the things you know people say as they get older. It's not going for the safe option; it's staying abreast of what is happening; not giving up stuff like cycling because you think you're too old for it (if you are very young, by the way, I do apologize for all this but you will need it one day, believe me).

Staying young is trying out new tastes, new places to go, new styles, keeping an open mind, not getting reactionary (hmmm, I should read this again) or being disapproving of more and more things, not settling for what you've always had or always done. Staying young is about keeping a fresh vision of the world, being interested, being stimulated, being motivated, being adventurous.

Staying young is a state of mind.

> **STAYING YOUNG IS TRYING OUT NEW TASTES, NEW PLACES TO GO, NEW STYLES**

Throwing money at a problem doesn't always work

Years ago when I worked in one particular industry, whenever something was going wrong my boss would always sigh and say, 'Well, I guess we can try the "American solution".'* What he meant, basically, was throw money at it until it went away. At work this approach often works wonders but problems in life tend to need a more hands-on approach, a more delicate touch. We tend to think that if we just chuck enough money at things they'll get sorted out, instead of finding ways to really sort them out that require time and attention and care.

Let's go back to that getting older thing again. You might think that throwing money at it in the shape of cosmetic surgery might be the answer but it isn't, it only delays things and can create worse problems than it solves. How much better to work on one's mental approach to aging and come to terms with it in a dignified and graceful way instead. If somebody you care about seems distracted, tense, not themselves, then buying them a present might well cheer them up, but the better (and cheaper) option is to make time to take them out for a walk and ask them about themselves, give them the opportunity to talk.

We tend to think that if we spend more money on something it will solve the problem. Maybe sometimes we need an old-fashioned approach of time and attention and finding out. Like our grandparents, who didn't throw things away and get a new

---

* This in no way is meant to be derogatory towards Americans or their solutions. Look, it works. I have no gripe with this method at work, it's just in our personal life it isn't so efficient but I don't mean to be rude.

one when something had stopped working – they patiently sat down and tried to sort out what it was that had gone wrong and if there was a way to put it right again. That went for relationships as well as for watches or kettles.

Throwing money at things makes us feel powerful and grown-up when instead we might need to stand back and see if we couldn't do better by changing the situation another way. I know I'm as guilty of this one as anybody. It happens to me most with cars. I buy a car – usually an expensive, temperamental, costly to fix model. Then when it goes wrong, as it invariably does, I pay the garage to come out and take it away and spend a fortune having it put right. How much simpler my life would be if I could stand back and see that the car was unsuitable in the first place, basically a mistake. Throwing money at it now doesn't alleviate the problem, it merely delays it, puts it off until the next time when it goes wrong again. And it will. Oh believe me, it will, it always does. In this case the American solution most definitely doesn't work.

> THROWING MONEY AT IT DOESN'T ALLEVIATE THE PROBLEM, IT MERELY DELAYS IT

Think for yourself

You'll think this one's so obvious you'll be wondering what it's doing in here and I do apologize if it seems patronizing, simplistic or downright rude. I don't mean to offend or insult and I do appreciate that you do think for yourself. I guess what I mean by this Rule is that we need to be incredibly clear about our opinions, grounded in our own sense of identity, and very assertive about being *us* so that we aren't easily swayed by what other people think of us. It's tougher than it looks at first glance. We are all vulnerable inside. We all have fears and concerns. We all want to be loved and accepted. We all want to blend in, be one of a crowd, be acknowledged. We all want to belong. The temptation is to say 'I'll be whatever you want me to be.'

Being original or creative or different can make us think we stand out too much and will get shunned. But truly successful people aren't shunned, they instead become pack leader because of their

> WE ALL WANT TO BLEND
> IN, BE ONE OF A CROWD,
> BE ACKNOWLEDGED. WE
> ALL WANT TO BELONG

originality, their difference. If you are obnoxious or rude or hurtful, you will indeed be shunned. But if you are kind, thoughtful, caring and respectful you will be loved and accepted. If you are also original in your thinking, you will be looked up to, respected and admired.

To think for yourself you have to be pretty sure of who you are and be clear in your thinking as well as doing it for yourself – there's no point in thinking for yourself if it's all muddled and woolly.

I have a friend who is very intelligent and astute but all her opinions come from reading a particular national newspaper. Whatever line it takes on a particular issue is the same line she will come out with. She trusts her paper implicitly and is unable to see how predictable her views are – seeing as they are always based on what she has read. She will argue her case articulately, force-fully and in a well reasoned way, but always absolutely in line with her paper's views. Sometimes we can all be a bit like that and need to change where we get our information from occasionally to make sure we stay fresh and original.

Of course, to think for yourself means you have to (a) have something to think about and (b) actually do the thinking. Look at a selection of people you know. If they are at one with their own life, I bet they are doing both. If they are badly adjusted and generally struggling, I bet they're not doing either.

You are not in charge

Sorry if this comes as a shock but you're not, no matter how much you want to be, no matter how much you think you are, no matter how much you deserve to be. If you are not in charge, it doesn't mean anybody else is either. We may all be on the same runaway train with no driver or there may indeed be a driver (the driver may be insane, drunk or asleep but that's another thing entirely).

Once you accept that you are not in charge, you can let go of so much stuff it's very liberating. Instead of complaining, 'Why isn't it like this?' you can accept it isn't and let it go. Instead of metaphorically bashing your head against a metaphoric brick wall, you can walk away whistling with your hands in your pockets – you are, after all, not in charge and therefore not responsible.

Once you get your head around the wonderful concept that you are here to enjoy and not here to run things, then you are free to sit in the sunshine a bit more often, take time off.

Look, stuff happens. Good stuff and bad stuff. There may or there may not be a driver. You can blame the driver if you want. You can accept that if there isn't a driver, the journey will sometimes be scary, sometimes exhilarating, sometimes boring, sometimes beautiful (actually whether there is or isn't a driver the same holds true). We have to have both the good stuff and the bad stuff. That's a fact. If you or I were in charge, we'd probably interfere too much and get rid of most of the bad stuff and the human race would die out ever so quickly due to stagnation, lack of challenge, lack of motivation and lack of excitement. It is, after all, the bad stuff that fires us up, makes us learn and gives us a reason for living. If it was all good it would be awfully fluffy and boring.

A slight condition to this one though. You might not be running the show but that doesn't discharge you of all responsibilities. You still have obligations – you still need to be respectful of the world you live in and the people you live in it with – it's just that you don't have overall responsibility for the whole show and everything in it.

Seeing as you are not in charge you can watch it like a movie and cheer at the exciting bits, cry at the sad bits and hide during the scary moments. But you are not the director or even the projectionist. You are not even the usherette.* You are the audience, enjoy the show.

> ## ONCE YOU ACCEPT THAT YOU'RE NOT IN CHARGE YOU CAN LET GO

---

* There's probably a frightfully modern PC word for this job. Please don't write in.

Have something in your life that takes you out of yourself

I have a friend who swears by her adopted greyhounds. No, I don't mean she stands next to them and curses, although I'm sure she does from time to time. But what I mean is that no matter how miserable she is, no matter how hard she's been working, no matter how annoying life has been, no matter how fed up, cross, or what sort of a bad hair day she's had, when she gets home and gets that incredible greeting from her rescued dogs it all then becomes worthwhile. The gloom is lifted and she is instantly restored, calm, happy and loved. It's a bit sad but there you go (only joking).

For me it has to be my children and where I live. Although my kids drive me insane at times, there is still something incredibly magical about the way they view the world and how they grow. As for where I live, I only have to think about going home to feel lifted and invigorated.

For every one of us there will be something different that does it, that pushes our button in a very positive way. And I find the wonderful thing about this Rule is that it invariably isn't the things that cost money that have this power. The things that lift us are usually magical in some way – a particular view or person, a pet or a child, a favourite book or film that we turn to, to help us recharge. It might be a state of mind that we arrive at through some ritual such as going to a place of worship or meditating. It might be a certain piece of music that lightens our heart. For some it will be reorganizing their stamp collection, for others it will be doing charity work or being a volunteer (there's nothing like doing something for others or for a greater good to take you out of yourself). Whatever it is, make sure you have it, know it and use it. No good it being a piece of music that always lifts your mood if you don't play it occasionally.

> NO GOOD IT BEING A PIECE OF MUSIC THAT ALWAYS LIFTS YOUR MOOD IF YOU DON'T PLAY IT OCCASIONALLY

I guess we all need something in our life that takes us out of ourselves and perhaps, stops us taking ourselves too seriously. Whether it's a dog, a child or a chat with a lonely person at a day centre, there needs to be something that makes you realize that all the stuff that's getting to you isn't that important and reminds you of the simple pleasures in life.

Only the good feel guilty

Bad people don't feel guilty, they are too busy being bad. Good people feel guilty *because* they are good and they feel they have done wrong, let somebody down, made a mistake or screwed up somewhere. Good people have a conscience. Bad people don't. If you do feel guilty, that's a good sign. It shows you are on the right track. But you have to know how to deal with it, because guilt is a terribly selfish emotion. It is wasteful and pointless.

> ## IF YOU DO FEEL GUILTY THAT'S A GOOD SIGN

We have two choices: put it right or dump the guilt. Yes, we all make mistakes. We all screw up from time to time. We don't always do 'the right thing'. And if we've got a conscience, we will feel guilty sometimes. But guilt is utterly pointless unless it is acted on for the better. You would be better off feeling something else* if you aren't going to act on your guilt. If you hang around feeling guilty but don't do anything about it, then it's a waste of time and life.

---

* Self loathing, fear, panic – all good substitutes for guilt if you really must. But better just to let it go.

The first thing to do is to assess whether you really need to feel guilty. It could just be an overdeveloped conscience or sense of duty. If you are the kind of person always to volunteer, but just this once you say 'no', then there is no need to feel guilty. You'll know deep down if you've earned this one off. If you've a choice between doing something or not, then it's simple: do it or don't do it but without guilt. Make the choice with that in mind. Not doing it and feeling guilty is not an option.

If you *do* have cause to feel guilty, then if you can, put it right. That's the simplest course of action. And what if you can't put things right? Then learn the lesson, make a resolution, dump the guilt and move on. If it keeps on gnawing away at you, you have to find a way to put it behind you.

If you can't say anything nice, don't say anything at all

It is very easy to moan, to complain, to criticize. It is much harder to always find something nice to say about a situation or a person. But think of it now as a huge challenge. Saying something nice is hard because our natural inclination is to moan. If someone asks how the weekend camping went, it's easier to start on the bad weather and the problems with the campsite and the annoying behaviour of the people in the next-door caravan, than it is the joy of being with people you wanted to be with and in a fantastic setting. When a friend asks how you're getting on with your boss, the things they do that really annoy you usually spring to mind before the upsides.

No matter how horrid someone is, there is always something about them that is good. Your job is to find that good bit and highlight it, speak about it, draw attention to it. Same with a situation that seems troublesome. I remember reading once of someone who was on the Metro in Paris during a major strike. It was chaos and people were shoving and pushing and it was pretty horrendous. There was a woman with a small child there and it could have been quite scary. She bent down to the child and said quite brightly, 'This, my dear, is what they call an adventure'. It has become a pet phrase of mine in times of crisis and trouble.

When asked your opinion of someone, something, somewhere, you need to find something good to say, something flattering and positive. There is ample evidence that being positive has many benefits but the most noticeable is that people will gravitate towards you and not even know why. That positive air about you is attractive. People like being around those who are upbeat,

> # THIS, MY DEAR, IS WHAT
> # THEY CALL AN ADVENTURE

positive, happy and confident. We need to bite our tongue more and say good things more often.

Obviously if you are only going to say good things, then this cuts out back-biting, gossiping, slagging off, telling tales, being rude about people, complaining (you are allowed to point out defects or problems but in a constructive way). And that could leave you with a big gap to fill.

Before opening your mouth, try – just for a week – to find something good to say. It's one of those things that will amaze you by how it improves your life, but don't take my word for it – just try it. And if all else fails, and you really can't think of anything positive to say at all, then don't say anything. At all.

PARTNERSHIP RULES

We all need to love and to be loved. Most of us want the comfort of a relationship and the closeness of companionship that such a relationship brings. We aren't islands and we do need to share together with someone very dear and close to us. 'Tis human nature. We wouldn't be the fantastic people we are without that need to give and to be given to.

But, and this is a big but, (does my but look big in this?) human relationships being what they are, this is an enormous area in which to make mistakes, fall flat on our face and to generally make a dog's dinner out of the whole business. We need Rules here like they are going out of style. We need all the guidance we can get. Right, that's enough about me.

But seriously we do all need help and sometimes it pays to come at the subject from a slightly different angle. What follows are some unusual Rules to get you thinking about your relationship from a new perspective.

None of this is revolutionary, but these are the Rules I've noticed those who have successful, productive, sustaining, long-lasting and nurturing relationships have about them. They are also the ones having exciting, stimulating, extremely close and powerful relationships.

RULE 51

Accept the differences, embrace what you have in common

'Sugar and spice and all things nice . . . slugs and snails and puppy dogs' tails' – isn't that how the rhyme goes? So which are you? The slugs and snails or the sugar and spice? Chances are, you're a bit of both. Look, it's true that men and women have differences. We would be fools if we didn't accept and recognize that. But we're not so different than we are separate species – or from separate planets, as some would have us believe. We actually have more in common than we have different. If we embrace those things we have in common and accept what is different, we might get on a whole lot better instead of treating each other as if we were separate species.

A relationship is, if you like, a team made up of initially two people (later the team may get swamped by lots of junior team members) who both bring talents and skills and resources to the relationship. Every team needs different people with different qualities to achieve things and to make the project work. If you are both strong leaders, quick decision makers and impulsive hotheads, then who is going to see to the detail and finish off projects? Who is going to do the work instead of just generating the ideas? Never mind just accepting the differences – see the benefits! Try to view differences in the light of them being special talents – differences that could be used effectively to make your team function better.

And what of the things you have in common? It can be great (shared views, shared tastes) but it doesn't always make life simple (shared love of being right, shared need to be in control). If you are both genuine leaders, you might both be wrestling for the

> # WE MIGHT GET ON A WHOLE LOT BETTER INSTEAD OF TREATING EACH OTHER AS IF WE WERE SEPARATE SPECIES

driver's seat. Instead, agree to take it in turn to lead. The things in common should be celebrated and used – in combination or alternately – to really fire you both up and make the relationship special and successful.

Look, you're in this together – whatever 'this' is – and you need to work together to make it successful. If you combine the talents you have in common, you will get a lot further and have an easier time of it than if you both pull in different directions. Strip away the layers and we are all human, all frightened, all vulnerable, all trying to make some sort of sense out of our lives. If we focus on the differences and make a big deal out of them, we risk losing the input and contribution of somebody who can help to lighten our load and make the journey more fun. All those crass internet jokes – if a woman was a computer she would be this, and if a man was a car he'd be that – really don't help. Real life isn't like that.

Allow* your partner the space to be themselves

It's a funny old thing but we often fall in love with someone because they are independent, forceful, powerful, in charge, in control and very much out in the world. Then, the second we've captured them, so to speak, we try to change them. We come over all jealous if they carry on being as independent; as if being in a relationship with us somehow limits them, ties them down, cuts their wings off.

Before we met them, they managed quite well without us. The second we meet them, we start giving them advice, restricting their choices, limiting their vision and dreams, curtailing their freedom. We need to stand back and give them the freedom to be themselves.

A lot of people say that the magic of their relationship has worn off, that there is no sparkle there any more and that they have grown apart. And then when you look into it a bit more deeply you find two people locked in a symbiotic relationship of mistrust, oppression and niggling encroachment. They don't give each other any space at all, let alone space to be themselves.

So what can we do? Firstly stand back and see your partner as they were when you first met them. What attracted you? What was special about them? What turned you on?

Now look at them. What is different? What has gone and what has been replaced? Are they still the same independent person or have

---

* Yes, yes I know I said 'Allow'. It is a joke, don't write in . . .

> ## WHAT ATTRACTED YOU? WHAT WAS SPECIAL ABOUT THEM? WHAT TURNED YOU ON?

you eroded their space, confidence, independence, vitality? Maybe not, that seems a bit harsh, but unconsciously we do tend to rein them in a bit and they do lose their sparkle.

You have to encourage them to step outside of the cosiness of the relationship and rediscover their energy and vitality. They may need to spend some time rediscovering their talents and skills at independence. And you may need to sit on your hands at times to avoid reining them in again. So encourage, stand back, sit on your hands, push and be there. Tall order. Most successful relationships have an element, and a big one, of independence. The couple spend time apart to bring something back to the relationship with them. This is healthy. This is good. This is grown-up.

RULE 53

Be nice

It is very easy in the hurly-burly of modern life and the complex sparring of a day-to-day relationship to forget that we are dealing with a real live human being here and not just someone we bounce off as we go along. It is easy to start to take someone for granted, to think we've thanked them or praised them or said 'please', when instead we ignored them, were rude by the guilty sin of omission, disregarded them and generally behaved like they were pond life by default.

To make the relationship go with a zing, you have to go back to square one and start being courteous again in the old-fashioned sense of the word. You have to reintroduce yourselves to each other as respectful, tactful individuals who are going to start again being pleasant, kind, civil and polite. From now on you will say 'please' and 'thank you' no matter how many times a day it is necessary. Be thoughtful. Be complimentary. Give gifts without there being any reason for it. Ask questions to show you are interested in what your partner is saying.

> ## GO BACK TO SQUARE ONE AND START BEING COURTEOUS AGAIN

Be solicitous of their health, welfare, dreams, hopes, workload, interests and pleasure. Take time to help them. Take time to focus on their needs and wants. Take time to just be there for them, not to have to do anything except listen, show an interest, show that you still love them. Don't allow benign neglect to ruin your relationship.

We treat strangers exceedingly well and usually reserve our best attentions for people we work with. Our partner gets missed, lost in the bustle of it all. In fact we should treat them better than anyone else. After all, they are supposed to be the most important person in the world to us. It makes sense to show them this is true.

Of course, if you already do all this you must excuse me reminding you to.

I was reading about a chap who kept buying his wife new handbags – always unsuitable ones, not big enough or tough enough for her needs. She tried explaining that she was quite happy to buy her own bags as she was a grown-up, but he had got it into his head that his idea of 'style' was so much better than hers. In the end she bought him a bag and that shut him up for a bit. I thought this a wonderfully Zen solution. She didn't get cross or yell at him, but just gently poked fun at him. Brilliant.

You want to do what?

Just because we come together to be a couple for however long, doesn't mean we are joined at the hip and have to think the same, do the same, feel the same, react the same. I have noticed that the most successful relationships are the ones where the couple is strong together but also strong apart. The best relationships are the ones where both are supportive of each other's interest even if they aren't their own.

Being supportive of your partner and what they want to do means you have to be very centred yourself not to feel jealous or mistrustful or resentful. You have to be prepared for them to be independent, strong, out in the world separate from you. It can be hard. It can ask a lot of you. It can be a real test of how much you care and how protective you tend to be.

The more freedom you give/allow/tolerate/encourage, the more likely they will be to reciprocate and return. If a partner feels they

> YOU HAVE TO BE PREPARED
> FOR THEM TO BE
> INDEPENDENT, STRONG,
> OUT IN THE WORLD
> SEPARATE FROM YOU

are encouraged and trusted, they are much less likely to 'stray' or want out because they feel hemmed in or caged. The more supportive you are, the more they will feel they are being treated kindly and that is a good thing.

But what if you disagree with what they want to do? Then you have to look at your own stuff I'm afraid. You see, they are a separate human being and entitled to do pretty well whatever they want to do – assuming it isn't hurtful to you or in any serious way jeopardizes the relationship (such as sleeping with other people or committing crimes) – and it is your role to be supportive. You may need to question what it is about what they want to do that you find hard to go along with. This might be more about you than them.

Ask yourself – if they do this, if they go ahead, what's the worst that can happen? They make a mess of your floor, ruin part of the garden, spend money on something you don't really want, aren't around much for a week. Now compare that to the thought of them leaving or living with you frustrated and unhappy. Which is worse?

Of course, just because they say they want to do something doesn't mean they will. Some very stubborn types will however be more likely to go ahead and do it just because you're objecting to everything they mention. Say 'yes' and they might well never bother anyway.

If you look ahead to Rule 64, you will read about how you should treat your partner *better* than your best friend, and being supportive is part of this. We forget that our partner is a separate entity. We forget that they too have dreams and plans and unfulfilled ambitions. It is our job to encourage them to find their path, to realize those ambitions, to stretch themselves to their fullest extent, to be complete and satisfied and fulfilled. It is not our job to put them down, ridicule their dreams, belittle their plans or laugh at their ambitions. It is not our job to discourage them, put them off, place obstacles in their path or restrict them in any way. It is our job to encourage them to soar.

RULE 55

Be the first to say sorry

Don't care who started it. Don't care what it was about. Don't care who is right and who is wrong. Don't care whose game it was. You are both behaving like spoilt brats and should go to your room at once. No seriously, we all fall out from time to time, that's human nature. From now on, if you want to be a committed Rules Player, and I can see from the glint in your eye you do, you will be the first to say sorry. That's it. End of Rule. Why? Because that's what Rules Players do. We are the first. We take great pride in being first because we are so firm in our own sense of ourselves that we don't feel any loss of pride if we say sorry. We don't feel threatened or challenged or weak. We can say sorry and still be strong. We can say sorry *and* retain our dignity and respect.

We will say sorry because we *are* sorry. We are sorry to have become embroiled in an argument of any sort and have by the very nature of arguing forgotten at least five Rules.

You see, if it has got as far as a falling out, no matter how trivial or minor, we have already committed a few cardinal mistakes and

> ## WE CAN SAY SORRY *AND* RETAIN OUR DIGNITY AND RESPECT

RULE 55

thus should be the first to say sorry because we are in the wrong no matter what the argument is about. Arguing is what we are saying sorry for. Never mind *what* it was about, we are saying sorry first because we are noble, kind, generous in spirit, dignified, mature, sensible and good. I know, I know, gosh we have to be all these things and still say sorry. Tough call, tall order. Just do it and see how good it makes you feel. The view is always fantastic from the moral high ground.

And what if you are both reading this book? Heavens. Then you must not tell each other you are – Rule 1 – but then race to be the first to say sorry. Could be interesting. Let me know how you get on.

Saying sorry has many benefits, even if it does stick in your throat a little. Not only does it give you the moral advantage, but it also diffuses tension, gets rid of bad feelings and clears the air. Chances are that if you say sorry first, they will probably be humbled into apologizing also. Maybe.

Always remember you are not apologizing for the sin or crime or faux pas you have committed – you are apologizing for being so immature to have argued in the first place, apologizing for losing your rag, apologizing for forgetting Rules, apologizing for being boorish or argumentative or stubborn or rude or childish or whatever. You can come out of your room now.

PARTNERSHIP RULES   117

Go that extra step in trying to please them

What? You have to be the first to say you are sorry, encourage and support them, give them freedom, be supportive, be nice, and now I am saying go that extra step in trying to please them as well. Strewth, anyone would think you were doing this out of love. You'd think this was for someone you adored and worshipped and respected and had great affection for – someone you really cared about. Precisely. That is exactly what it's about. This is about going an extra step to please the person who means the most to you in all the world, the person you love and cherish and care about, the person who is the most important human being in your life. This is about your love, your companion, your treasure, your soul mate, your lover and friend. So what's your problem? Why wouldn't you want to do this? Why wouldn't you be doing it already?

> WHY WOULDN'T YOU WANT TO DO THIS? WHY WOULDN'T YOU BE DOING IT ALREADY?

So if we want to, what is it we are supposed to be doing? Easy, thinking ahead. Planning birthdays that are more than just a present, a card, some flowers and a couple of drinks down the pub – and that's if they're lucky this year. It's thinking about what they would like, what they might want, for birthdays, special treats, days off, long weekends and anniversaries. It's thinking of extravagances, luxuries, indulgences. It's going out of your way to find out what they would really, really like and then giving it to them. And I'm not talking money here. This is about surprising them, finding little things to delight them and show that you have thought of them. Arranging things in advance to let them know how special they are and how much you care and how important they are.

This is finding ways to delight them beyond the normal, way beyond what is expected, further than anyone else would. This is a fantastic opportunity to be creative, adventurous, wacky, unusual, caring and loving all at the same time. Haven't got the time? Then you must check your priority list. What could be more important than delighting your lover and partner and friend (yes, it is the same person, not three people).

Always have someone – or something – that is pleased to see you

We're back to the woman and her greyhounds here. When she comes home her dogs are always pleased to see her, but then dogs always are. No matter how badly you have treated them* they always go nuts. Of course, you want your partner to behave in just the same fashion, to go nuts when you come home. And I'm sure they do, don't they? And of course you do when they come home, don't you? No? Why not? Yes? Well done.

We all need someone who is pleased to see us. It makes us feel it is all worthwhile. I love it when I have to go away for work for a day or two and then when I get back my children all stand there, like children do, with their hands outstretched with that lovely, 'Have you brought me something back?' look on their faces.

> WE ALL NEED SOMEONE
> WHO IS PLEASED TO SEE
> US. IT MAKES US FEEL IT
> IS ALL WORTHWHILE

---

* Not taking them on a long enough walk because you've been so busy, forgetting biscuits, stuff like that. I don't mean treating them really badly, who would do that?

Or when they get back from school and you ask if they've had a good day and they grunt at you. So refreshing. But you are still incredibly pleased to see them – for them you are their someone or something.

And no, the red light of the TV standby button isn't enough. You do need a person or a pet. One of my sons claims his gecko is always pleased to see him but I have tried hard to detect any emotion on its face and so far failed – the gecko's not my son's.

Having someone or something who is pleased to see you is important because it gives you someone who needs you and this gives you a purpose, stops you getting self-absorbed, gives you a reason for getting on with life. But what if you live alone and don't have pets or children? Well, voluntary or charity work is a very good way to quickly get in the situation where somebody is pleased to see you. Then again, it could be right on your doorstep.

Even living alone in a part of London where nobody really talked to their neighbours, a friend of mine discovered there was a disabled retired man who lived a few doors down from her. She noticed that he found excuses to 'just happen to be at his door' as she walked past on her way back from work most days. He was clearly a bit lonely and really valued a quick chat (or a longer one if possible). He was pleased to see her. Who is pleased to see you?

RULE 58

Know when to listen and when to act

I don't know if it's harder for us chaps to learn this one but I find it tough. Whenever anyone has a problem, I want to rush off and *do* something. Doesn't really matter what, just so long as I am doing something, anything.

In actual fact what is often required of me is that I sit down and listen. I am not being told troubles and problems just so I can be all macho and rescue someone or leap to their defence or single-handedly take on the world for them (in fact be a hero). What is needed is a sympathetic ear, a shoulder perhaps to cry on, an 'Oh, that must be awful for you' sort of response, a counsellor's approach and a full and rapt attention with eye contact. That's the tricky bit. As soon as I've heard the problem I've switched off, or rather I've switched to working out what the solution must be.

But for me, when I have a problem I don't want to hear sympathetic noises and encouraging sounds. I don't want a heart space where I can share. I just want a solution, an offer of help, an extra pair of hands, a stout length of rope and a screwdriver.*

But then all my problems are object related and need practical solutions – a chap's sort of thing. All the problems that I find the hardest to just listen to are person related and need a completely different approach. Knowing when to listen and when to act is an extremely useful skill to develop. I still constantly need to sit on my hands though to stop someone sharing a problem with me by saying, 'Hold it right there, I can see exactly what this needs' and then rushing off to fetch my tool kit.

---

* Or whatever it takes to fix my particular problem.

Of course, some problems don't actually have solutions, that's not why we're being told them. We are being told so we can be part of the process, and that may be sympathy, grief, shock, empathy, kindness, emotional advice, hand holding. Knowing when to offer tea and sympathy or a tool kit and a stout rope instead is the skill to learn and a good Rules Player gets it right. (Yes, yes, I know, I still get it wrong far too often.)

> **KNOWING WHEN TO OFFER TEA AND SYMPATHY OR A TOOL KIT AND A STOUT ROPE INSTEAD IS THE SKILL TO LEARN**

Have a passion for your life together

So you two met and fell in love and resolved to spend your lives together. And you are I hope. But at what level? I'm not being funny here but serious (for once). Just sort of living together, going through the days, not really connecting isn't good enough I'm afraid. You have to have a passion for your life together. A what? A passion. Being together has to be a strong bond, a common sharing of experience, a dream-fulfilling romance that carries you both along. Love isn't for the half dead, the sound asleep (or even the merely dozing off), the can't be bothered to make the effort any more. You have to make the effort. You have to stay awake, in touch, in tune. You have to share dreams and goals and ambitions and plans. You have to have passion for being with each other.

Look, I know that all relationships go through peaks and troughs. I know we get complacent and even a little bored at times. But you are dedicating your life to someone else's happiness in a way, and that requires focus, strength, passion, drive, enthusiasm and effort. What's that? You're not dedicating yourself to someone

> . . . YOU ARE DEDICATING YOUR LIFE TO SOMEONE ELSE'S HAPPINESS

else's happiness? Then what are you doing? That's what a relationship is all about in a sense. And if you're not doing that, what do you think you are doing?

You have to really care, to still be in love, to want your partner to be fulfilled, successful, happy, complete.

In an ideal world you only get one crack of the whip at this (I know that lots of people have several partners over a lifetime but I assume the aim is always to stay together for life and not to get divorced). This is your chance to have a really good strong relationship based on mutual trust, responsibility, shared happiness, drive and the pursuit of excellence. It isn't? What is it then? It has to be if you are going to get the maximum out of it. Your partner isn't just there for someone to chat to when you get a bit fed up and want some company. They are there because they love you and you them. They are there for you both to have a relationship. If that isn't as much as anyone needs as an incentive to live life to the full and have a passion, then I don't know what is.

Make sure your love making is making love

So! We get to talk about sex now? Well, actually no, what I'm going to talk about is love. If you are in love and being loved, it is part of the natural process to make love and this is both fun and fraught with all sorts of problems. In a relationship, as successful Rules Players, we have to be kind, courteous, reverential, stimulating, creative, respectful, thoughtful, considerate and sexual. Within that sexual relationship we have to be all those things as well – respectful, kind etc. We have to take our partner's needs and wants into consideration without subjecting ourselves to anything we wouldn't want to do or find embarrassing or difficult. We have the right to privacy. We have the right to respect. We have the right to be held in high esteem.

And so does our partner. Consideration has to be the key word. We have to be considerate of what they need, like, want, are capable of doing. We have to be courteous.

> ## WE HAVE THE RIGHT TO PRIVACY, TO RESPECT, TO BE HELD IN HIGH ESTEEM

RULE 60

And yes, within all this there is a space and a place for passion, for excitement, for rude raunchy sex. We don't have to be tame to be considerate, we don't have to be inhibited to be kind, we don't have to be tame just because we are being respectful. This isn't about being unexciting or dreary or boring just because we are taking our partner's safety, privacy, health, intimacy into account. Even the most passionate lovers can be kind to each other while tearing each other's clothes off and having very physical sex – the two can go together.

Having sex with someone you love – making love if you like – is an honour in a way. (For me, just having someone these days who is prepared to take their clothes off at the same time as I do is an honour . . .) Making love is as close as we are ever going to get to another human being, as intimate as it is ever going to be. If we don't move respectfully in this arena, then what are we doing? And respect grows out of knowledge – knowledge of not only what our partner likes best but of the whole process. We should be as skilful as possible and if we aren't, it is something we can spend a bit of time learning about. There is no shame in learning. We can't all be born the best drivers and the best lovers in the world.

Keep talking

Yep, gotta keep talking. When there is trouble afoot it's talking that will get us out of it. When we are going through bad patches, it is talking it out that will see us through. When we are optimistic and excited, it is talking that will help our partner share it.

If we aren't talking there is something wrong. If we aren't talking, what are we doing? Talking helps us understand, listen, share, communicate.

> IF WE AREN'T TALKING THERE IS SOMETHING WRONG. IF WE AREN'T TALKING, WHAT ARE WE DOING?

Lots of people assume that silence means there's a problem, something wrong. Of course, we don't need to fill all the silences but there are some pretty basic rules of etiquette when it comes to talking to each other:

RULE 61

- Acknowledge that your partner has spoken to you – and no, a grunt or a sigh isn't what I mean
- Make some recognition every few seconds that you are still awake, alive, in the room, interested, paying attention – this may be a nod, a yes or no, a noise of encouragement (hmm, oh)
- Be aware that talking is part of your duties as a lover/partner and you should be good at it
- Good talking leads to good sex – if you aren't talking you aren't flirting, holding hands, seducing. By talking we are committing the act known as foreplay
- Talking helps resolve problems, silence only amplifies them
- Talking keeps you together – it's what you used to do when you first fell in love, remember?

There is obviously a time and a place for silences (*see Rule 58*) – but talking is healthy, productive, companionable, friendly, loving, kind and fun. Silences can be boring, unhelpful, destructive and threatening. Obviously there is quality talking and there is rabbiting on. Make sure you don't just chatter away to fill the silences with meaningless trivia. Talking has to have some purpose although gossiping is fine. Just wittering isn't. So talk sensibly now.

Respect privacy

'I want to be alone . . .' Each and every one of us has a God-given right to respect, privacy, trust, honesty. But of all of them, it is privacy that is the most sacrosanct, inviolate, untouchable.

You must respect your partner's privacy as they must yours. If you don't, you have to question all those other things – trust, respect, honesty – as well. If they are all missing, what you've got there isn't a relationship and quite frankly I don't know *what* it is, except it belongs in the morgue. So we'll assume you have a good and healthy relationship. This means you have respect for your partner's privacy. In all areas.

If they choose not to discuss something with you, then that is their right and you do not have the right to:

- wheedle
- threaten
- emotionally blackmail
- bribe
- withhold privileges
- try and find out by underhand means and methods.

And no, charming them out of it counts as a no-no as well. Privacy isn't just about not opening someone's post or listening to their telephone messages or reading their emails when they're not looking. Privacy is also making sure they can carry out their ablutions on their own – we all need a certain degree of grace and dignity in our lives and separate bathrooms is the standard bottom line actually. One bathroom between two isn't desirable,

RULE 62

let alone using it at the same time. Ugh, how horrid. It is impossible and unhelpful and unnecessary. Don't do it. Winston Churchill said the reason he managed to stay married for 56 years – or however long it was – was separate bathrooms. So keep yourself to yourself in your ablutions and make sure you don't intrude on anyone else's privacy. You can extend this Rule to everyone else in the entire universe, not just your partner.

If you feel a need to intrude on someone else's privacy, you have to take a long hard look at yourself and fathom out why. The truth may be unpalatable but you have to know it.

> IF YOU FEEL A NEED TO INTRUDE ON SOMEONE ELSE'S PRIVACY, YOU HAVE TO TAKE A LONG HARD LOOK AT YOURSELF AND FATHOM OUT WHY

Check you both have the same shared goals

When we first meet and fall in love, we think we know pretty well everything we can about our love. We have so much in common. It all seems so easy, so intuitive, so natural. Of course we want the same. Of course we are two sides of the same coin. Of course we are going to share life's highway together.

Wrong, wrong, wrong. The highway will diverge at times and if you aren't on the ball you will lose sight of each other completely and forever. You have to keep checking that you are both singing from the same map so to speak, both heading for the same destination, both going in the same direction even.

So what are your shared goals? Where do you both think you're going? No, don't guess here. Don't make them assumed goals or even guessed goals. You have to *know* what your partner thinks are the shared goals – and what you think. They might be a world apart. Or then again they might be very close. You'll only know if

> YOU HAVE TO KEEP
> CHECKING THAT YOU ARE
> BOTH SINGING FROM THE
> SAME MAP

you ask, discreetly of course, don't want to frighten the horses here.

And you have to differentiate between shared goals and shared dreams. We all have dreams – the cottage by the sea, the trip round the world, the Ferrari, the second home in Malibu, the purpose-built wine cellar (fully stocked of course), the Olympic-size swimming pool – but goals are different. Goals are to have children (or not); to travel a lot; to retire early and live in Spain; to bringing up the children to be happy, well-adjusted people; to stay together (!); to move to the countryside/town; to downsize together and work from home; to run your own business together; to get a dog. I guess dreams are things you aim to get one day and goals are what you are doing together. Dreams are acquisitions that either of you could want and goals are shared aims that you need each other for because without the other the goal is pretty meaningless.

This Rule is about reviewing. To review, you have to talk to your partner about where it is you both think you're going and what you're doing. It doesn't have to be heavy. This can be a light review just to touch base and check that you are both on the same track. It doesn't have to be too detailed, just simple questions to confirm a general similar direction, rather than trying to map out an A-to-Z of your future life together.

Treat your partner better than your best friend

I was talking to a friend about this Rule the other day and she disagreed with me emphatically. She said you had to treat your friends better because you knew them better and you owed them more loyalty. I then went on to talk to another friend and she said that wasn't the case. You treated your partner better because you knew them less well. Intriguing. My point is you should treat your partner better than your friends because your partner is both lover *and* friend. And ideally *best* friend.

If they're not, then who is? And why? Is it because they are the opposite sex and you need a same-sex best friend? Or are they the same sex and you need an opposite-sex best friend? Is it because you don't see a lover as a friend? (If you do answer yes to this, what *do* you see your partner as . . . what is their role or function in being your partner?)

Again all this is about being conscious. Treating your partner better than your best friend means you have given it some thought and made a conscious decision to do so – or not if it's the case.

I would have thought treating your partner better than your best friend would have been a given. This means not interfering, respecting their privacy, treating them like independent grown-ups. You only have to look around to see couples who treat each other like small children, nagging, scolding, arguing, criticizing, nit-picking. They wouldn't do it with their friends, so why do they do it with the one person who is supposed to mean heaven and earth to them?

RULE 64

> ## WHAT YOU DO SEE YOUR PARTNER AS . . . WHAT IS THEIR ROLE OR FUNCTION IN BEING YOUR PARTNER?

I'll give you an example. You are a passenger in a car being driven by a friend. They make a foolish error (though not a dangerous one). You would probably start teasing and laugh a lot. Now imagine the same scenario but with your partner who has messed up. Do you:

- Make them feel very small?
- Not let them forget it in a long while?
- Tell everyone else?
- Take over the driving for a while on the grounds they're not to be trusted?
- Treat them the same as you would a friend and laugh a lot?

Hopefully the last one, but watch other couples in similar situations and see what they do.

RULE 65

Contentment is a high aim

If you ask a lot of people what they want in life, they say, 'Oh, just to be happy I guess.' Same goes if you ask what they want for their children, 'I don't mind what they do as long as they are happy.' You'd be better off wishing that you or your children could be astronauts or brain surgeons – at least you're in with a sporting chance then. You can train. They can qualify.

Happiness is such an illusory thing that spending too much time chasing it is not very worthwhile. Happiness is one end of a spectrum – misery being the other end. It is a state of extreme, just as misery represents the other end. If you check back at the times in your life when you've been happy – or thought you might have been – I'll bet there were other extreme feelings involved. The birth of a child? Excitement yes. Wonder yes. Relief at a successful birth. Yes. But happiness? I'm not sure.

People think they'll be happy on holiday when they mean relaxed or stimulated or freed from their cares – and indeed they are. Aiming for happiness is one of those 'bigger is best' things. You're never going to make it because there is no top end limit. You just have to go on aiming for even bigger all the time. Instead of aiming for happy, it's better to aim for contentment. Now that's attainable. That's a worthy goal.

This applies especially to relationships – both to the quest to find Mr or Mrs Right and in what happens when you do. Most of us want to fall madly head-over-heels in love. Big chemistry – fireworks, butterflies, unbelievable feelings. It's brilliant. It's extreme. But that intensity can't and won't last. You have to go back to reality sometime. You have to get on with your life. No one can live at that intensity, that lofty altitude all the time. Contentment is what you hope for after the elation has worn off and you settle back into a relaxed and happy simplicity. In fact, contentment is the worthier aim, because it lasts.

And so if you find you are with somebody where there is no big firework display, palpitations and extreme of feelings but there is a baseline contentment and warmth and love – be happy with that.

> CONTENTMENT IS WHAT YOU HOPE FOR AFTER THE ELATION HAS WORN OFF

You don't both have to have the same rules

Lots of couples make the assumption that everything has to be the same for both of them – that you have to have the same set of rules for both partners. Not true. You can operate under different rules for important areas. The happiest relationships, the most successful, the strongest, are where both parties see the need for flexibility in their rules and adjust their relationship accordingly.

> ## THE HAPPIEST RELATIONSHIPS ARE WHERE BOTH PARTIES SEE THE NEED FOR FLEXIBILITY IN THEIR RULES

I expect you want an example? Of course you do. Let's suppose one of you is fanatically tidy and the other fanatically messy (whatever that is). Normally you would have one going on at the other all the time about how messy/tidy the other is. There would be rows and problems. That's because you are both trying to work to the same rule – we both have to be tidy/we both have to be messy. How about a different rule? I can be messy; you can be tidy. I can have areas where I can be messy and you have areas where you can be tidy. Now we don't row because we have a different rule. I don't have to be tidy when it isn't in my nature and you don't have to be messy when it isn't in your nature.

Another example? My wife hates being teased and she hates being tickled. Me? I'm not bothered. She has the rule that she is not to be tickled – or teased – and my rule is I can.* You may be the kind of person who wants to know where your partner is, whereas they're not bothered about where you are and doesn't expect you to report on it. You can then have a rule where your partner tells you where they're going, to reassure you, but you don't need to keep them completely in the picture as they don't worry about it.

Your partner may need constant reassurance that you love them and may need to be told several times a day. You might prefer to be told less frequently but when it's genuinely felt – so you would have a rule that you'd mention it often but they didn't have to say it back every time. Different strokes for different folks.

---

* No, this is only for my wife. Of course you can't come round and tickle or tease me.

FAMILY AND
FRIENDS
RULES

If you imagine yourself as the centre of your own universe, then you are the very hub. The next circle around you is your lover, your partner; this is your closest, most intimate relationship. The next circle to that is your family and friends. These are the people you love the most, choose to spend most time with, love you the most. These are the people you can relax with, kick off your shoes and be yourself. But there are still Rules. There is still a right way to treat them and a not-so-right way. You still have to behave with honour, dignity, respect. You have responsibilities towards both your children and your parents. You have a duty to your siblings. You have obligations, that have to be taken seriously, to your friends.

You have a whole raft of hats to wear – parent, friend, child, brother/sister, uncle/aunt, godparent, niece/nephew, cousin – and a whole set of rules and duties to perform. The next section is guidance on how best to wear all these hats.

As we go through this life we have to interact with other people. We rub up against them (emotionally) all the time and we have to have rules to govern our behaviour so we do right by them, to steer us through tricky situations, new experiences and ongoing close relationships.

If we want our relationships with our family and friends to be successful and for them to think the very best of us, then we do need to give those relationships some thought – a conscious approach rather than sailing on asleep at the wheel like most people. By consciously being aware of what we are doing we can improve those relationships, iron out the problems, encourage others and generally spread a bit of warmth and happiness as we go. What could be finer?

If you are going to be a friend, be a good friend

Being a real friend is a tremendous responsibility. You have to be loyal, honest (but not too honest), sincere, reliable, dependable, friendly (stands to reason really), pleasant, open, sociable (not much point having friends if you're not going to be sociable is there?), responsive, welcoming and gracious. You also have to be forgiving at times, be prepared to offer help, support and sympathy. At the same time you don't want to be taken advantage of nor have the wool pulled over your eyes. And you may have to be brutally candid at times and be prepared to risk the friendship by being so. Yet equally there are times you need to hold your tongue and keep your opinion to yourself. They are your friends, not clones of you – they do things differently. You have to be counsellor, confessor, priest, helper, companion, friend, confidant(e) and comrade. You have to offer the friendship enthusiasm, dedication, determination, creativity, interest, passion and drive.

And this is all what *you* have to do. What do they have to do? Well, in an ideal world the same. If they fail to do any of this, you will still carry on being their friend, being forgiving, being supportive and being there.

And I guess if you have to take anything away from this Rule, the most important bit is being there. You are there when they are going through it and not just there for the good times. You will be there when they need you in the early hours, the dark days, the times of trouble and stress. You will be there to hold their hand, let them cry on your shoulder, lend them a hanky, pat them on the back and make them endless cups of tea. And you will tell them to cheer up, not to worry, stop being such a fool, whatever it takes to get them up and at it again.

RULE 67

> ## THE MOST IMPORTANT BIT IS BEING THERE . . . AND NOT JUST FOR THE GOOD TIMES

You will be there to give them good advice. You will be there just to listen at times. You will be there when you don't want to be. You will be there when all their other friends have fallen by the wayside. You will be there no matter what.

Someone once said that a real friend is someone you can be having a conversation with as they get on a plane, you don't see them for ten years and when they arrive back they carry on the conversation as they get off the plane like a moment hadn't passed. That's exactly how it is between good friends.

Never be too busy for loved ones

It is very easy in the rush of living to overlook people close to us. I do it. I have brothers who are very special, very close to me and I forget to phone, forget to stay in touch. Not because I don't care but because I am too busy. Unforgivable. Every now and then I'll complain that I haven't heard from them. But of course it is me not staying in touch just as much as it is them. We have to make time, because if we don't, time slips past so fast that a few weeks become months, and then years are added on before we know it.

It's the same with children. Parents all harbour a secret fantasy of, 'Wouldn't it be nice to return to the Victorian ideal of seeing them for an hour before bedtime when nanny has them all bathed and pyjama-ed and ready with the muffins and jam?' sort of thing. Well, I know I do even if you don't. But the more time we put into our relationships – with children, siblings, parents, friends – the more we get out of them. It has to be us to make the move, to phone, to stay in touch. And what if they don't also do this? Fine. You're now the Rules Player.

> THE MORE WE PUT INTO OUR RELATIONSHIPS, THE MORE WE GET OUT OF THEM

RULE 68

This is what you do. You become incredibly successful at handling your life, at processing guilt (you don't have any because you phoned, you wrote, you stayed in touch), at forgiveness (they didn't phone or write or stay in touch), at relationships in general. You take the moral high ground and be the first to offer the hand of friendship, be the first to forgive and forget (and I don't care how serious the squabble was, Rules Players don't carry grudges, ever . . .).

No matter how busy your life is – and hopefully these Rules will eliminate some stress and free up some time – you have to make time. You have to make quality time (sorry, I hate that expression as well) for all those around you to whom you make a difference. Those that love you get repaid in time – it's a fair exchange. They love you and you give them something of yourself, something precious. Yep, your time and attention. And you do this willingly, not as a chore. You do this with dedication and commitment and wholehearted enthusiasm – or you don't do it at all. There is no point spending quality time with your kids, for example, and using that time to catch up on work or read the paper or get tomorrow's lunchboxes ready. You have to be there entirely for them or they'll know your attention is elsewhere and they'll feel cheated.

So when the phone rings and it's your mum, grandmother or your old friend but you're really busy doing something, don't keep them on the phone making 'uh huh' noises while you simultaneously finish searching the web or writing that letter. Either put everything down and give them your full attention, or ask if you can call them back later – and make sure you do. One day they might not be there – and then you will so desperately wish you'd actually listened. But then it'll be too late. So make time for the people who matter – today.

Let your kids mess up for themselves – they don't need any help from you

I have children and I naturally want them to be happy and well adjusted and successful. But do I also harbour secret plans for them? Do I want them to be doctors? Lawyers? Diplomats? Scientists? Archaeologists? Palaeontologists? Writers? Entrepreneurs? The Pope (look, someone has to be the Pope and it may be some parent's ambition somewhere to see their child as the Pope)? Astronauts?

No. I don't think so. Hand on my heart, I can say I haven't ever had such ambitions for them. I do hope they're not listening but I can say that I've been disappointed on the odd occasion when their career choice has seemed a bit unusual – not their sort of thing at all. But you have to let them make mistakes. You can't steer them right all the time or they'd never learn for themselves.

> YOU CAN'T STEER THEM RIGHT ALL THE TIME OR THEY'D NEVER LEARN FOR THEMSELVES

RULE 69

And this is what this Rule is all about – giving your kids the space to mess things up. We've all done it. I was given immense freedom to screw up and I did it big time, magnificently, spectacularly. Result? I learned pretty quickly what worked and what didn't. I have a cousin who wasn't given anything like the same freedom and was much more protected and he didn't screw up anywhere nearly so badly. But later in life, and he'd be the first to agree with this, he managed his life in such an unfortunate way that his screw-up really was spectacular. We all have to make mistakes. Better to make them while we're young and have the resiliency to bounce back.

Being a parent is about 75 per cent making it up as you go along. You too have the freedom to make mistakes. Trouble is that if you get it wrong as a parent, your mistakes can really affect someone's life adversely. That's why it can be really hard to stand back and watch our children make bad choices. We want to run to them and protect them, nurture them a bit more and keep them from harm. But they have to learn by getting it wrong. If we think they'll only learn by us telling them, then we are making a big mistake. They have to do life for themselves to really get to grips with it. It's real and they can't learn it from a book or from us or from the television. They can only learn it by getting their fingers burnt. Your job is to stand by with the elastoplast and the antiseptic and a kiss to make it better.

You are of course allowed to ask leading questions: Are you sure that's a good idea? Have you thought this one through? And what happens after you've done that? Can you afford to take that much time off? Won't it hurt a bit? Didn't you try something like this before? You can also do this with friends as well when you can see they are about to make a big mistake but you don't want to be the killjoy. Try not to make your questions sound too judgemental or moany or they'll ignore you and go ahead just to be stubborn.

Have a little respect and forgiveness for your parents

This one may or may not affect you. Personally, as I am now technically an orphan, it shouldn't affect me. But it does. Big time. I was brought up with two major dysfunctional attributes. A missing father and a difficult mother. I have siblings with the same background. We have all handled it differently. I found it easier to come to terms with my mother once I too had children and could see what a difficult job it is. I could then also see that some people are intuitively, naturally good at it. And some people are, to be brutally frank, utterly useless at it. My mother fell into the latter category. Was that her fault? No. Should I blame her? No. Can I forgive her? There is nothing to forgive. She embarked on a life path for which she was ill equipped, received no help, was lacking in any skill, and found extremely limiting and difficult. Result? She treated her children appallingly and we probably all need therapy. Or forgiveness and respect. Why should she be blamed for doing a difficult job badly? Hey, there are lots of areas in all our lives where we aren't very efficient or skilled or even enthusiastic.

Your parents do the best they can. And that might not be good enough for you but it is still the best they could do. They can't be blamed if they weren't very good at it. We can't all be fabulous parents.

And the absent father? That's OK too. We all make choices that others can judge as bad or unforgivable or just plain selfish and wrong. But we aren't there. We don't know what weaknesses people have or what drives them. Or indeed what is even going through their head. We can't judge until we too have to make the

RULE 70

> HEY, THERE ARE LOTS OF
> AREAS IN ALL OUR LIVES
> WHERE WE AREN'T VERY
> EFFICIENT OR SKILLED OR
> EVEN ENTHUSIASTIC

same choice. And even then if we choose a different way, then that's fine, but we still can't judge or blame.

So, for the fact they brought you into the world, have a little respect and forgiveness. If they did a good job, then tell them. If you love them (and there is nothing that says you have to), then tell them. And if they were appalling at parenting, then forgive them and move on.

As offspring you do have a duty to be respectful. You have a responsibility to treat them kindly and be more than they are by being forgiving and non-judgemental. You *can* rise above your upbringing.

RULE 71

Give your kids a break

We'll talk in a bit about what good parenting is – what your role as a parent is. First, let's look at this Rule – give your kids a break means support and encourage your children. In fact this should be support and encourage *all* children, not just your own. Children get a pretty poor deal of it. They get it in the neck from all directions and the word that figures most in their lives is 'no'. No, you can't do this. No, you're not old enough for this. No, you can't have that. No, you're not going there. No, you can't see that film.

Cast your mind back and see if it wasn't the same for you.

'No' is terribly easy for us to say. It's the word that trips so readily off the tongue. But to give support and encouragement we do have to train ourselves out of it. We have to learn to say 'yes'. Obviously we need to qualify our 'yes', depending on the age or skills or development of the child. But a resounding 'yes' gives

> THEY GET IT IN THE NECK
> FROM ALL DIRECTIONS
> AND THE WORD THAT
> FIGURES MOST IN THEIR
> LIVES IS 'NO'

them a great boost even if it is followed by a 'but not at the moment', or 'when you are old enough' or 'when you have saved up'.

It is also easy to say to a child, 'You're not very good at that', or 'I wouldn't do that if I were you, you'll only fail'. Better to encourage them and let them learn that they might fail than to set the idea running in their mind beforehand. I know we all want to protect them from harm, from failure, from disappointment. But sometimes we have to push them forwards and shelve those worries for the moment.

Truly successful parents are the ones saying, 'Go on, you can do that, you'll be great at that, you'll be terrific'. By voicing such positive enforcement, our children get to believe in themselves and can do more, be more, achieve more. If we just say 'no', they'll grow up with low self-esteem and lacking in confidence.

A friend recalls how she desperately wanted to be a ballet dancer when she was 6 years old. She was already showing the signs of being destined for her current 6 ft tall, large feet, athletic build – as far from a ballet dancer as you can imagine. Her parents must have been able to see this, and could have told her that really she should do something else. Like all-in wrestling for kids. But instead, they found her a ballet class. It didn't take long for her to realize that ballet wasn't right for her and she stopped going because it made her legs hurt. However, it was her choice to stop. And she left with her self-esteem intact. (She only wishes they hadn't taken the photos.)

Whatever they want to do, it is not your job to edit their dream, stand in their way, voice your concerns, limit their hopes or discourage them in any way. Your job is to give guidance while supporting and encouraging. Your job is to give them the resources to achieve whatever it is they want to. Whether they do or don't achieve is by the by. If they had the chance, that's everything.

Never lend money unless you are prepared to write it off

The full title of this Rule should actually be: Never lend money – to a friend or your children or siblings or even parents – unless you are prepared to write off either the money or the relationship.

There is a lovely story told, I think, about Oscar Wilde (correct me if I've got the wrong person) who borrowed a book from a friend and forgot to return it. His friend turned up and demanded the book back by which time young Oscar had lost it. His friend asked Oscar if he wasn't jeopardizing the friendship by not returning the book. Oscar Wilde merely replied, 'Yes. But aren't you also doing the same thing by demanding it back?'

If you lend money – or a book or anything else – don't do it unless you are prepared for it to be lost, forgotten, not returned, broken, ignored, whatever.

IF YOU ARE PRECIOUS ABOUT IT, THEN DON'T LEND IT IN THE FIRST PLACE

If you are precious about it, then don't lend it in the first place. If it means a lot to you, keep it safe. If you do lend anything, including money, then don't expect to get it back if you value the friendship – or relationship. If you do get it back then that is a bonus. If you don't, well you were prepared for that in the first place.

Lots of parents make the mistake of lending money to their children and then getting all hurt and disappointed when they don't get repaid. But they have spent the child's entire life giving them money and then as soon as they get a bit grown up and go away to university or whatever, the parents suddenly start saying it's a loan and demanding repayment. Of course the child isn't going to repay it. They haven't been trained to. It is unrealistic to expect them to do so. If they do, count your blessings and be grateful for the bonus.

Same with friends. Don't lend them anything if the non-return is going to matter to you. It is your choice after all. You don't have to lend anything to anyone. If you choose to do so, be prepared to write it off or don't do it. Obviously if the money means more to you than the friendship, then of course demand it to be repaid – and add interest as well.

And the same goes for siblings or parents (goodness don't ever lend money to them, they'll never pay it back). So who should you lend money to? Strangers of course. And they won't pay it back either.

There are no bad children

A certain phrase once crept out of Southern California and made its way to the UK. It made my blood boil: 'They're a good child who's done a bad thing.'

How it made me cringe. I hated it. I railed against it. This was the most awful bit of New Age PC-speak I had ever heard. But I have to now apologize. I have taken this one on board and, while I may never actually say 'They're a good child, who's done a bad thing,' I do endorse the sentiment. You see, there are no bad children. Yes, there may be children who do bad things. There may be children who do appalling things. But they are not bad. No matter how naughty my children are, they are not bad. They may make me climb the walls with their behaviour at times but when they have gone to sleep and you peep in at them, they are angelic little cherubs, utterly good, utterly perfect. Yes, what they do during the day, to get my dander up, may be naughty, may be bad behaviour, but they remain intrinsically good.

The only reason the behaviour is bad is because they are exploring the world and learning where the boundaries are. They have to make mistakes in order to find out what's what. It is only natural and quite normal.

The same goes for any other behaviour that is out of the ordinary. There are no clumsy children, only clumsy behaviour. There are no stupid children, only stupid conduct. They are no spiteful children, only spiteful acts. There are no selfish children, only selfish actions.

RULE 73

They don't know any better and it is your job to teach them, educate them, help them, encourage them. You start off on the wrong foot if you start off believing they are bad. You're almost bound to fail if you believe them to be faulty. You can't change a bad child but you can change bad behaviour. If you believe the child is good, you're on to a winner immediately. All you've got to do is change the behaviour and that is an attainable goal.

It is awfully detrimental to say to a child, 'You are a bad child'. It sets something up in their mind that is hard to shift. Better to say, 'You've done a naughty thing', or 'You've been naughty'. This they can do something about. But if you tell them they are bad, there is nothing they can do about that and it affects them.

> YOU CAN'T CHANGE A BAD
> CHILD BUT YOU CAN
> CHANGE BAD BEHAVIOUR

Be up around people you love

Your job from now on, as a Rules Player, is to be up around people you love. No more moaning. No more complaining. No more grumbling. These things will no more issue from your lips. You are, from now on, the positive one, the perpetually cheerful, always up one around whom good things revolve and happen.

When asked how are you, instead of saying, 'Can't complain, mustn't grumble,' in future you will say, 'Fine, good, marvellous'. No matter how crummy you feel, no matter what sort of a day you've had, no matter how low, down or fed up you are. And do you know, the interesting thing is that when you do say 'Marvellous', even if you don't feel it, you'll find something positive to say to follow it up with. Whereas if you'd said 'Been better', then the follow-up thoughts would be all negative. Try it – honestly, it really works.

In future, right from today, from this very second, you have to become the one who is always jolly, up, cheerful. Why? Because someone has to, or everybody will want to end it all. This life is hard and treacherous. Someone has to lift the burden, lift the spirits, lift the gloom. So who's it going to be? You, that's who.

I know, I know. You'll be sitting there reading this, thinking, 'Why me? Why lay this burden on me?' Because you can do it, that's why. But do it secretly (remember *Rule 1*), without fuss or bother. Just a simple change of heart, change of direction. From now on you cannot be anything but up around those you love. OK, moan to strangers. But loved ones get the full treatment. Up, up and away.

SOMEONE HAS TO LIFT THE BURDEN, LIFT THE SPIRITS, LIFT THE GLOOM

Successful people, those who have got it licked, are invariably cheerful. They care more about what people around them are going through, feeling, suffering than their own petty problems. They invariably want to know what's wrong with you rather than moaning about their day. They think positively, act positively, project confidence, verve and enthusiasm.

I had a friend who went to live abroad in a country where he spoke very little of the language. But he said his mood lifted whenever he was there because he didn't know the words for fed up or miserable or down. When someone asked him how he was, he could only say 'Happy', because that was the only word he knew to reply with. He found that when he said it, he felt it.

RULE 75

Give your kids responsibilities

Children grow up and leave home. They go from helpless babies to mature adults who have sex and drink beer while your back is turned. The secret is to try and keep pace with them. As they grow you have to back off more and let them do more. You have to resist the urge to do everything for them and let them fry eggs* or paint dustbins** for themselves.

> ## AS THEY GROW YOU HAVE TO BACK OFF MORE AND LET THEM DO MORE

---

* This one comes from my own son who, when he was asked what being a grown-up meant, said it was being able to fry eggs as he wasn't allowed to – he was about 8 at the time. I felt so mean I got him cooking breakfast every day for a month until he was sick of frying eggs.

** This came from a friend who was always angry with his father. When I asked him about his relationship, he complained that as a kid he was never allowed to do anything to help. He finally lost it with his father when his father was painting a dustbin and the kid wanted to help and his father said, 'No'. But why? It wouldn't have hurt. Why the father was painting a dustbin in the first place remains a mystery.

It's a delicate balancing act. You can't give them more responsibility than they can handle but at the same time you can't hold them back. And when you do let them fry eggs or paint dustbins for the first time, they are going to make a mess – yolk on the cooker, paint on the garage floor. It's the mess most often that makes a parent say, 'No, you can't'. But we have to break a few eggs (ha ha) to be able to fry one. We have to gloop a bit of paint if kids are going to be able to carry out any DIY job for themselves when they are grown up.

When they are tiny and learning to drink from a cup for the first time we expect spillage. We stand there with kitchen roll in our hand prepared to mop up. But by the time they are teenagers we've forgotten the art of hiding the kitchen roll behind our back waiting for them to spill stuff. We expect them to be able to keep their room tidy first time. But they've never done it before. They don't know how to do it. They have to learn and part of that learning process is not doing it, doing it badly, doing it differently from how we, as adults would do it. Our job is to help them. To hand them responsibility slowly, bit by bit, but with guidance.

We expect them to do everything right first time, no spillage, no broken eggs, no paint on the floor. It is our expectations that are unrealistic. Growing up is a messy business.

Your children need to fall out with you to leave home

They've never tidied their room. They've played their music long and loud and driven you mad. The two of you are about at breaking point and you wonder where you went wrong as a parent of a sullen, moody, dressed-in-black teenager. They are monosyllabic, depressed (but miraculously cheer up when their mates come round), always hungry, rude, mercenary, troublesome and unrelentingly embarrassed by you. And you blame yourself. It is all your fault. You have somehow failed them. Rubbish. This is all good stuff.

Look, your kids have got to fall out with you to be able to leave home. If they loved you too much they couldn't leave. You've nurtured them, wiped their bum, dressed them, fed them, doled out money for all of their life. And they don't want to feel grateful. They want to leave, to drink too much, have sex and use grown-up swear words. They don't want to be your darling little angel any more. They want to be spiky and daring and rude and adult. They want to discover and explore and get into trouble all by themselves. They need to break the chains, rip the parental ropes off and run over the hill shouting that they are free at last. How on earth can they do that if they are still in awe of you, still feeling so attached to you, still loving you so much? They have to break free by *not* getting on with you before they can come home again as something more than just your child.

It is all natural and you should welcome it and be glad to see the back of them. Chuck 'em out early I say and then they'll be back all the sooner. You can't ruffle their hair ever again or tuck them in or read them a story, but you will find a grown-up friend comes back and you can share a whole new relationship with them.

THEY HAVE TO BREAK FREE BEFORE THEY CAN COME HOME AGAIN AS SOMETHING MORE THAN JUST YOUR CHILD

Hold them back and they'll resent you for longer. Take it personally and they'll take longer to return because they'll feel guilty.

And you can show this to your teenager: Don't give your parents too hard a time. They are feeling just as threatened by this new relationship as you are. Give them a break, they're making it up as they go along, just as much as you are.

RULE 77

Your kid will have friends you don't like

'Oh no, not Mickey Brown – again!' This was my mother's cry, every Saturday morning. She hated Mickey Brown. Loathed and detested him with a vengeance. Why? I have no idea. She disliked most of my friends but she saved up all the venom for poor Mickey Brown, whom she took against before she ever met him.

Look, your children will sometimes have friends you don't approve of. It's natural. Live with it. As kids we are attracted to other kids who are different from us. It's our way of finding out. We go for the very poor kid or the very rich kid because we have no experience of it and want to know what it is like. We go for the ruffian or the spoilt princess or the kid from a different ethnic background to ours or the ragged urchin who smells or the autistic kid or the one from the gypsy encampment or the smug middle-class one whose parents are accountants.

Whatever it is, we will be tempted to disapprove. It's human nature but we mustn't. We must be supportive, encouraging, welcoming and open. Why? Because if our child is hanging out with other kids that test our tolerance, it's a good thing. It shows we are bringing them up not to be prejudiced or judgemental. And if they aren't being, nor should we.

The funny thing is that Mickey Brown's parents couldn't stand me either. He wasn't allowed to play with guns and I was always smuggling them into his house when his parents weren't looking. I didn't like guns particularly – and we are talking cap guns here – but I did love getting him into trouble . . .

> # IF OUR CHILD IS HANGING OUT WITH OTHER KIDS THAT TEST OUR TOLERANCE, IT'S A GOOD THING

One of my own children had a birthday party and insisted on inviting a kid in his class who had serious adjustment problems (what we used to call a 'naughty child' but you can't do that any more – *see Rule 73*). When his parents came to collect him they were quite tearful, as it was the first birthday party this poor kid had ever been invited to. What's that? His behaviour? Oh he was a little angel and didn't put a foot wrong. In your dreams. He behaved true to type and I was heard muttering, 'Never again, he never comes here again', for many weeks afterwards. No, seriously he played up a bit and wrecked the place but no more than any of the others did. One of the others, a supposedly good kid, was caught filling one of my wellington boots with cheese sandwiches and jelly – second hand if you get my drift.

Your role as a child

So, you're a grown-up now and probably don't recognize yourself as a child. But you are still a child, although you'll get strange looks if you park in a 'parent and child' space if you happen to go shopping with your mother or father.

Until both of your parents are passed on and you have been promoted, so to speak, you remain a child. And you have a responsibility. You have a duty – now you are a Rules Player – to be courteous, thoughtful, patient and co-operative towards your parents.

> ## YOU HAVE A DUTY TO BE COURTEOUS, THOUGHTFUL AND CO-OPERATIVE TOWARDS YOUR PARENTS

Yes, yes, I know they drive you mad but from now on you have a role and it is simply this:

RULE 78

- To behave impeccably with them
- To look after them if that's what they want/need
- To back off if that's what they want/need
- To listen to them when they witter on, without losing your rag or sighing
- To appreciate that they have had a long and hard life and gathered a lot of experience – some of which may be of some use to you – and you won't know if you carry on shaking your head and ignoring everything they say
- To visit, write, phone, communicate more often than you think you should – but probably not as much as they think you should
- Not to bad mouth them in front of your children but to talk them up as being the greatest grandparents in the world
- To be pleased when they come to stay and happily let them watch whatever TV programme they want without complaining.

And why will you do all this? Because they gave you life, brought you up. Yes, yes, I know they made mistakes along the way but you forgive them all of them (*see Rule 70*) and you turned out fine. Oh yes you did.

Parents deserve decent treatment when they get old and need attention and someone to listen to them and take them seriously – and they make great baby/dog sitters (and usually free as well).

RULE 79

Your role as a parent

Gosh, this is a tough one. You have a role and it is important, but how do we define it, make it real for you, so that you can live by it, put it into practice?

Steve Biddulph, who wrote *Raising Boys** and other books about parenting, said in a recent newspaper interview that our job, as parents, is to keep our children alive until they are old enough to get help for themselves . . .

If you are crazy enough to take on the role of parent, then you are signing an invisible contract with your children to give and get them the very best of everything you can. And I don't necessarily mean material possessions. Your mission, should you choose to accept it, is to be all that the very best parenting requires. You will be encouraging, supportive, kind, patient, educational, loyal, honest, caring and loving.

You will have to make sure they eat the best food for developing children. You will supply them with the best education for their talents and skills. You will aim to develop their interests in all areas and not just the ones you are keen on. You will set clear boundaries so they know what's what, and what they can and can't do – and with clear and acceptable levels of discipline should they overstep the mark. You will adjust your degree of supervision to match their age – little ones need closer supervision than big ones. You will always provide a safe haven for them to come home

---

* *Raising Boys: Why Boys are Different – and How to Help Them Become Happy and Well-balanced Men* (Thorsons, 2003; 1st edn Finch, 1997).

RULE 79

> YOUR MISSION, SHOULD
> YOU CHOOSE TO ACCEPT
> IT, IS TO BE ALL THAT THE
> VERY BEST PARENTING
> REQUIRES

to – no matter how much trouble they've got themselves into in the big bad world outside.

You will be firm, loving, sharing, caring and responsible. You will set them standards and be a role model to them. You won't do or say anything you wouldn't be proud of them knowing. You will stand up for them, protect them and keep them safe. You will stretch their imaginations and feed them with stimuli so they grow up creative, excited about the world and raring to go.

You will approve of them, boost their self-esteem, improve their confidence and send them out into the world literate, educated, polite, helpful and productive members of society. And when the time comes for them to leave the nest, you will help them pack and keep giving that support while they find their feet (or should that be wings?).

Not much then, really.

SOCIAL
RULES

Every day we come into contact with real live human beings – at work, commuting, in shops, out and about – people we might have met before or often complete strangers. The world is full of people with whom we interact. Those interactions, small or large, can be life-affirming or deeply unpleasant. So, what follows are a few social Rules. These aren't set in stone. They aren't a revelation. They are a reminder.

We will look at some Rules for dealing with people at work. After all, that's where we spend an awful lot of our time and anything we can do to make our career more successful and our working life happier, more satisfying and productive, and most of all enjoyable, surely can't be a bad thing?

Social Rules are the fourth circle we draw around ourselves (the first is self, second is partner, the third is family and friends, the fourth is social relationships and the fifth is the world itself). It's terribly easy to see our own group, social class, or any level of community as the right one, the important one, the better-than-yours one. But each community sees itself as that. How much better to draw that fourth circle around ourselves so that it includes people from other backgrounds, other ethnicities, other communities, so that we feel part of the big community, the human one. It is better to include more than to exclude even one. And it is very easy to exclude for whatever reason, to assume that it is a 'them' and 'us' situation, when actually we are all 'them', we are all 'us'.

We have to treat everyone with respect or what's it all about? We have to care about everyone or the whole thing falls apart. We have to help each other no matter who they are, because if we don't there won't be anyone to help us when we need it. We have to be the first to put our hand out. Why? Because we are Rules Players.

We're all closer than you think

I have a friend. Not a good friend particularly, more of an acquaintance. He's a regular sort of a chap. Runs a computer business. Has a family. Normal, regular, 9 to 5, straight, nothing unusual about him. Or so he thought.

He is English, born and bred. He used to have a bit of a rant about immigration. Went on a bit about numbers but you always felt it was a bit deeper than that. He found out not long back that he was actually adopted. Nothing wrong with that – plenty are – but it set him to tracing his family. Yep, you've guessed it. His father was a foreigner.* Now you wouldn't know it to look at the man but he's only half as English as he thought he was. Interesting.

If you trace back anyone's history it's going to throw up a lot of different bits from different communities and ethnic groupings. None of us is in any way 'pure'. The whole thing has been melted, shaken and stirred and blended until any one of us would be hard-pressed to swear where we originated. Go back far enough and we all contain something a bit different. Apparently half of all European males carry a line that can be traced back to Genghis Khan – and he came from Mongolia.

My point? Don't judge others, because we are all human, all drawn from the same melting pot. We are all related if you go back far enough. There is no difference. We have to accept other

---

* That's his word, by the way, not mine.

> # THE DIFFERENCE BETWEEN US IS SO VERY LITTLE WHEN YOU WIPE AWAY THE VENEER WE ALL WEAR

communities, other cultures even if they are very different from ours because the difference between us is so very little when you wipe away the veneer we all wear.

Yes, we may wear different clothes and speak different languages and have different customs but we all fall in love, all want someone to hold and hug, to have a family, to be happy and successful, not to be afraid of the dark, to live a long time, die a good death, to be attractive and not to get fat, old or sick. What does it matter if we wear a suit, a sari or a grass skirt if deep down we all cry when we are hurt, laugh when we are joyful and our stomachs rumble when we are hungry? The veneer can be wiped away in a second and then we are all the same, all quite lovely and quite, quite human.

It doesn't hurt to forgive

It's easy to be angry. It's easy to get riled up and mutter or to make rude gestures and swear. It isn't so easy to be forgiving. And I'm not talking about turning the other cheek here or any of that stuff. I'm talking about seeing it from the other person's point of view. And being forgiving.

I had an incident recently on holiday which basically involved a very wet cyclist mouthing off because he thought someone (no, it wasn't me) had driven too close to him and nearly forced him into a ditch. He was loud, rude, aggressive, out of order and foul-mouthed. I tried to speak to him reasonably on behalf of the person he was being abusive to and he gave me a mouthful as well. Then he rode off and shook his fist at me which made his bicycle wobble and inside I laughed, a lot. I found it easy to forgive him not in any religious sense but because I could see he had chosen the wrong holiday.

He had obviously been persuaded that the cycling holiday would be fun but it was in hilly, really hilly, countryside, and it had rained all that day. He was tired, wet, aching and very unhappy. How could I not forgive him? If I had foolishly chosen that holiday, I too would have been grumpy, ready for a fight, fed up, tetchy and raw. I felt quite sorry for him and could sense a great deal of his unhappiness. Yes, he was in the wrong to use such foul language – especially in front of children. Yes, he was ready for a fight and intimidating and aggressive. But he was also me or you or anyone else in that situation, cold, wet, miserable. And who is to say we wouldn't have lost our temper if we too had chosen the wrong holiday?

Being forgiving doesn't mean we have to be pushed around or to put up with nonsense. We can stand our ground and say, 'Sorry I don't need to take that', but we can also make an attempt to forgive because we can see it from their point of view. Maybe the word is tolerant rather than forgiving. But either way we don't have to mistake forgiveness or tolerance or whatever with meekness. We can still be saying, 'Shove off with your bad language and sad bicycle and your mother smells of hamsters', while feeling sorry for the poor idiot at the same time. He was a good man who did a naughty thing.

Just bear in mind that anyone you come into contact with who hacks you off may have had a really bad time before they got to you.

> **BEING FORGIVING DOESN'T MEAN WE HAVE TO BE PUSHED AROUND**

It doesn't hurt to be helpful

We said in the previous Rule that the angry person you encounter may have had a bad day before they got to you. Let's try to make it a good day for all of them before they get to someone else. Let's spread a bit of goodwill around out there and then maybe, just maybe, mad cyclists won't be quite so ready to rear up and be abusive and aggressive. Perhaps no one had been kind to him that day. Perhaps no one had been kind to him for a very long time. See, it's all your fault. If only you'd been a bit nicer to him, he wouldn't have taken out his wet angst on the rest of us that day.

Always offering a hand and being generally decent to everybody is really easy once we get into the mindset that it's what we are supposed to be doing. It can become your 'default' behaviour. So your first reaction becomes 'Yes, sure, I can show you how to do that, no problem', rather than 'I'm very busy, can't you ask someone else?'

Try it as a different approach at work and see what it does for your reputation and career. Getting known as someone who is always ready to help does not get you known as a pushover. Quite the reverse in fact.

If you see someone in trouble – even if it's only that they've spilt their shopping getting it into the back of the car, you can always go up and say, 'Can I help?' If they want you to they'll accept and if not . . . well, you tried and that's the main thing.

This is all about going into every day thinking the best of people, being the first to smile, seeing where somebody might need a hand instead of bustling on past. It's about trying to see a situation

from their viewpoint, being sympathetic if they have problems –
you don't have to solve them all. It means taking the time and
trouble to make sure people around you are OK. And yes, this
does mean strangers as well. If we all took the trouble to smile
occasionally at strangers, the world might start each day on a
slightly less confrontational foot.

> THIS IS ALL ABOUT GOING
> INTO EVERY DAY THINKING
> THE BEST OF PEOPLE

Take pride in what we do collectively

I went to Iceland a while back – fabulous country, very friendly, educational and fun. One thing I did notice was the way they spoke about civic projects. I was in a taxi and we were held up at some road works in Reykjavik. I asked what the road works were about as they seemed to be lowering a road. 'Ah, yes, we are moving a road here because this road is bad in the winter.' When I was back in the UK I asked an English cab driver a similar question near Heathrow. 'Dunno mate, dunno what they are doing there, they're always digging up the ******* roads round here.' In Iceland they spoke of 'we' as in 'We are doing this'. In the UK it is 'they' as in 'They are doing this'. Interesting.

I'd never considered how we spoke of ourselves to be indicative of how we feel about our community. In Iceland they have a very strong sense of identity, belonging and community and they speak of 'we'.

To be supportive of our community, perhaps we ought to take an interest, find out what is going on, play some part, stop moaning and join in, try and change things from the inside. It's the same when a village shop shuts. Everyone moans and says it's a bad thing – and then carries on shopping at the big out-of-town supermarket. You can't have it both ways. If you want a community you have to be a part of it and support it or it stagnates and dies.

I'm not suggesting you run as a local councillor or join all the committees. But you can support by attending, by taking an interest and seeing what's going on.

> ## TO BE SUPPORTIVE OF OUR COMMUNITY PERHAPS WE OUGHT TO TAKE AN INTEREST . . . PLAY SOME PART

And you don't have to live in the countryside to feel part of a community. Most big cities are really a whole series of villages, each with a specific identity and clear boundaries. You can still support yours and feel part of it.

If your community – and this extends right up to the whole country – is doing stuff you disagree with, then only by voicing your feelings will things change. And I don't mean sitting in the pub moaning about them. You have to get involved in some way to make a difference.

What's in it for them?

We all want to win. At work and in most aspects of life, winning is good, and we don't like to lose. No one sets out to be a loser. But we do tend to think that if we are going to win then someone else, someone around us has to lose. But it doesn't have to be that way.

In every situation, the smart Rules Player weighs up the circumstances and asks: 'What's in it for them?' If you know what's motivating the other person, you can help steer the situation (and your actions) so you get what you want, but they feel they've got something out of it too. The 'win-win' mentality might have come out of the workplace, but it applies to pretty much every situation and relationship.

To work out what others are likely to want and need, take a step back and remain a little detached, so you're looking at the situation as if from outside. Suddenly it stops being *you* and *them*,

> YOU GET WHAT YOU WANT,
> BUT THEY FEEL THEY'VE
> GOT SOMETHING OUT OF IT
> TOO

and you'll stop thinking that *they* need to give way in order for *you* to win.

Dealing with somebody who's got the hang of this Rule is a rewarding experience – people will look forward to working with you, because there's an air of co-operation and understanding. Once you've learned to always look for the other person's 'bottom line' you'll become very fluid in your negotiations and will gain a reputation for being adult and supportive – and that's another bit of winning for you as well.

And it's not just in workplace negotiations that this win-win reaps rewards. Try it at home too. If you're debating where to go on holiday, and you desperately want to go horse riding in France, think 'what's in it for them?' – what is it about that holiday that will make *them* happy? Highlight those aspects and they're more likely to agree. If you're struggling to think of anything that will appeal to them, you need to think more broadly – maybe you can find a place where you go horse riding while they go fishing or sailing. You see how it works. Just asking the question 'what's in it for them?' helps you think it through.

Being a parent is another area where this works. If you just lay down the law without considering what your children want and need, they'll rebel, or at least be difficult to handle. But again ask 'What's in it for them?' and you'll see the situation from their perspective and handle it better. Winner.

Hang out with positive people

If you want to be successful in your life, at work, socializing, you need to be aware that there are two groups of people to hang out with. First, there are those who lift you up, are positive about life, have energy and enthusiasm, walk their walk, talk their walk and generally make you feel great to be alive. And then there are the moaners, who bring you down to their level of inactivity. The second group are not the group to hang out with if you want to make things happen and be happy.

So hang out with the positive, smart people. I mean people who feel life is an exciting challenge worth wrestling to the ground and having fun with. The sort of people who have interesting points of view, who make you feel good talking to them, who have positive things to say or suggest rather than moaning. The sort of people who tell you that you look fantastic rather than criticize you.

Earlier on we talked about clearing clutter out of your life – physical stuff (*see Rule 39*). Now maybe it is time to clear some people clutter (hmm that sounds terribly LA*). Let's have a look at the people you do hang out with.

Which ones can you honestly say make you:

● Feel enthusiastic about seeing them?
● Make you rise to every challenge?
● Make you laugh and smile and feel great about yourself?

---

* If this book is on sale in LA then I meant somewhere else entirely.

- Support you and nurture you and encourage you?
- Stimulate you with new ideas, new concepts and new directions?

And which ones make you:

- Feel depressed after you've seen them?
- Make you feel angry, dejected or criticized?
- Squash your ideas and pour cold water on your plans?
- Don't take you seriously?
- Don't make you feel as if you can achieve anything?

Hang out with the first group. Cull the second group – unless they are just having a bad day (and we all have those). Move on, get it done. Ah, but you'll say it is cruel to prune friends ruthlessly like that. Well, I suppose it is, but then I want to enjoy my friends not moan about them. If I find myself doing that, I prune them. No point hanging out with people who don't make you feel good – not unless you like being down.

> # NO POINT HANGING OUT WITH PEOPLE WHO DON'T MAKE YOU FEEL GOOD

Be generous with your time and information

As you get older – and probably not any wiser (*see Rule 2*) – you will learn a lot of stuff. Some of that stuff will be important to other people, often younger people, but not always. Share what you know with them. Don't hold on to information for the sake of it. Don't hold on to your time for the sake of it. What would you be doing with it that could be in any way more worthwhile?

If you have a special talent or skill, pass it on. I don't necessarily mean you have to spend all your spare evenings down at the local youth club teaching young tearaways all about whatever it is you do or know about.

But if the opportunity arises then go for it. I was recently asked to give a talk to a bunch of 6 year olds about what it means to be an author. At first I thought: 'But I'm not an author; I might just qualify, and only just, as a writer'. But an author sounded far too grand, too fiction, too grown-up for me. What on earth could I tell 6-year-olds about what I do for a living? But, remembering my own Rule, I warmly and graciously accepted and went along. I must say I had one of the most pleasurable mornings in a long time. They were fantastic. They asked brilliant questions, paid attention, chatted in a very adult way, were keen and interested and in general well behaved and marvellous. It would have been so easy to say no. And you never know what you might inspire in others, what flame you might fan, what encouragement you might give without even knowing.

This Rule especially applies at work. It's very easy to fall into the mindset that if you know stuff that nobody else does, then you have the upper hand. To believe that knowledge is power and you should hang on to every little bit of it. Actually, the most successful people in life are always looking to pass on what they know, to bring on others in their wake. Because if you don't, then who's going to replace you? You make yourself indispensable and you have just wedged yourself in a career rut.

If you're not passing on your talents and skills, what are you doing with them? What great secrets have you got that demand to be withheld from the world? Or is it laziness? Successful Rules Players say yes as often as possible because there is an incredible experience to be had in passing stuff on. And it is genuinely useful. Don't go thinking that what you know is of no use to anyone. I guarantee it will be quite the opposite because the second you say yes, you become one step up from all those that say no. That makes you important, successful, decisive and generous. And that makes you special.

> ## IF YOU HAVE A SPECIAL TALENT OR SKILL, PASS IT ON

Get involved

Get involved in what? Anything really (or at least almost anything). I guess what I mean by this is to take an interest in your world. Don't watch it on television but go out there and interact with it. Too many people are living their lives through the lives of others seen on that little screen. Or even living their life vicariously through the lives of others in the real world (gossip and tittle-tattle keeps them going). There is a great big wide world out there full of life, vitality, energy, experience, drive, excitement. Get involved means get out there and be part of it. Get out there and find out what it all means and how it works. Watching TV is warm and safe and comfortable. Being out there can be scary, cold, uncomfortable. But at least you know you're alive.

People are always complaining that life goes faster as we get older. But my experience is that the more we do out in the world, the more time seems to be stretched. If we watch TV, whole evenings can vanish before our very eyes.

Get involved means co-operating, contributing, taking part. Not watching from the sidelines while someone else has your life for you. Getting involved means rolling up your sleeves and getting your hands dirty but having an experience along the way, a real experience. Getting involved means joining in, offering help, volunteering, turning a theoretical interest into a real one, being out there and talking to people. Getting involved means having fun, real fun, not TV fun. Getting involved means helping other people appreciate and enjoy their lives a bit more than they would have done without you.

> # GETTING INVOLVED MEANS ROLLING UP YOUR SLEEVES AND GETTING YOUR HANDS DIRTY BUT HAVING A REAL EXPERIENCE ALONG THE WAY

I have noticed that successful people – and that is what this book is all about, and by successful I do mean content and happy rather than wealthy or famous – have outside interests that don't earn them any money or bring them any kudos. Stuff they do for the fun of it, to be helpful, to encourage others. They often find the time by doing it instead of watching more TV (seriously).

They become volunteers, mentors, school governors, local business advisers, charity workers. They join groups, associations, clubs, societies. They get out there and belong and have fun. They put themselves out there to make a difference or share an interest. They go to evening classes in ridiculous subjects. Maybe they laugh and poke gentle fun at themselves for doing it. Maybe they even sometimes wish they hadn't got involved as some things can creep up and take over your life. But they are part of something. Part of the world – in a full and proper sense.

Keep the moral high ground

Boy is this a simple one to say and a really difficult one to live up to. I do appreciate that it's a tough one, but I know you can do it. It takes a simple shift of vision, from being the sort of person who acts in a certain way to being a different sort of person who acts in a different sort of way. Look, no matter how rough it gets you are never going to:

- take revenge
- act badly
- be very, very angry
- hurt anyone
- act without thinking
- act rashly
- be aggressive.

That's it, the bottom line. You are going to maintain the moral high ground at all times. You are going to behave honestly, decently, kindly, forgivingly, nicely (whatever that means) no matter what the provocation. No matter what the challenge thrown at you. No matter how unfairly they behave. No matter how badly they behave. You will not retaliate in like kind. You will carry on being good and civilized and morally irreproachable. Your manners will be impeccable. Your language moderated and dignified. There is nothing they can do or say that will make you deviate from this line.

Yes, I know it's difficult at times. I know when the rest of the world are behaving appallingly, and you have to carry on taking it on the chin without giving in to your desire to floor them with a savage word, it's really, really tough. When people are being horrid to you it's natural to want to get your own back and lash out. Don't. Once this rough time has passed, you will be so proud of yourself for keeping the moral high ground, that it will taste a thousand times better than revenge ever would.

I know revenge is tempting, but you won't go there. Not now, not ever. Why? Because if you do you'll be sinking to their level, you'll be at one with the beasts instead of the angels (*see Rule 9*), because it demeans you and cheapens you, because you will regret it and lastly because if you do, then you're no Rules Player. Revenge is for losers. Taking and keeping the moral high ground is the only way to be. It doesn't mean you're a pushover or a wimp. It just means that any action you do take will be honest and dignified and clean.

> KEEPING THE MORAL HIGH GROUND WILL TASTE A THOUSAND TIMES BETTER THAN REVENGE EVER WOULD

Have a plan for your career

So where are you going at work? Have you a plan? A goal? Even a humble aim? If you don't have any of these, chances are you're going to drift. If you have a plan, you stand a better chance of getting to where you want to be. Knowing where you want to be is 90 per cent of the battle. Knowing where you want to be means you've sat down and thought about things, that you've been conscious about your future and have focused your attention on it.

Once you've looked ahead and decided where you want to be – and there is no right or wrong about where that is, you can be as determined and ambitious as you want – you can plan the logical steps you need to get you there. And once you have those steps, you can work out what you need to do to make each a reality. Is it further qualifications? Experience? To change jobs? To change the way you work? Whatever it takes for you to make those steps is what you have to do. Don't stagnate. Don't get stuck in a rut.

We all need to work to earn a crust. Staying at home watching daytime TV really isn't an option. Work keeps your mind fit, and active as well as gets you in touch with other people, and work also presents a daily challenge. Believe you me, we are better off with it than without it.

If you don't have a plan you could end up anywhere. Yes, sure that might be exciting but I doubt that many people end up happy and successful merely by chance. It's something you have to work at, consciously. And having a plan is part of that conscious effort. I know luck plays a crucial part in some people's lives, but only a very few. And formulating a plan and working hard while you're

> ## STAYING AT HOME WATCHING DAYTIME TV REALLY ISN'T AN OPTION

waiting for the luck to turn up doesn't mean that it won't, or that when it does you aren't free to throw away the plan completely.

If you're not busy planning and working towards the next goal, there is a real chance you can fall into a downward spiral of despondency and apathy. Successful people have 'get up and go' – and when they don't have it naturally, they artificially create it. They pretend to if you like, but the very act of pretending gets them up and about. Try it, it works.

Learn to see your community as part of a bigger picture

We all know about the nature of ripples. We throw a stone and it causes ripples. We say something and it causes ripples. We take action and it causes ripples. We belong to a community – small or large – and our behaviour in that community causes ripples. All those ripples affect other people. All those other people are throwing their stones as well, and their ripples are affecting us. Sometimes we need to stand back and look at all the stone throwing and the ripples and see it from the outside.

Your community has an impact on other communities and it is up to you – partly – what that impact is and how it affects other people. We have to take individual responsibility for our community. If it is behaving badly, adversely affecting other people, swamping folk with its ripples, we have to stand up and say so. We have to do something when we feel our community is overwhelming another one with its ripples.

It's no good pretending it isn't happening or thinking we have no power to make change. We have power all right. It's no good

> EVERYTHING OUR
> COMMUNITY DOES HAS A
> RIPPLE EFFECT

waiting for someone else to stand up and be counted. We have to do the standing and the counting. It's no good trusting others to make all the decisions for us and hoping they are going to be the right ones. We have to get involved, be part of the process, be proactive. If others are making the decisions for us, chances are we are being led like sheep.

Everything our community does – and by this I mean from tiny village to town to city right up to entire country – has a ripple effect that changes others' lives. If we want to shut our eyes to the plight of others caused by our own community's actions, we are fooling no one and will reap a bitter harvest. We have to take responsibility and see the bigger picture. We have to get involved and be a part of the process. We have to be a part of the solution and not part of the problem.

Look at the long-term ramifications of what you do for a living

Just as your community has an effect, so too does what you do for a living. It is no longer safe or responsible or ethical to carry on working without thinking about what we do and the effect it has. I'm not going to question you about what it is you do. That is entirely for you to do. As a writer, I am aware that a lot of good trees could die young because of me. Balanced against that are the positive effects (I hope) of what I write, and people who are employed as a result of the writing. Ah, but I have no control over their working conditions so I'm off the hook there. Or am I?

> AS A WRITER I AM AWARE THAT A LOT OF GOOD TREES COULD DIE YOUNG BECAUSE OF ME

So, for me it is dead trees, the electricity I use in my office and the pollution caused by trucks delivering books to book stores, to name but a few byproducts of my sitting here tapping away. What about you? Handled any hazardous waste lately? Or designed a missile guidance system? Or logged an entire rain forest? Or does your work provide an essential service or product; does it make people happier, wealthier or more successful?

What we do for a living has an impact. We can be working in an industry that pollutes, causes harm, is unpleasant and bad. Or we might be working to help others, to benefit people positively. Knowing that what we do causes an effect – for good or bad – doesn't mean we have to instantly chuck everything up and change jobs. Nor does it mean we can sit back and relax and think we're doing OK just because we work in a caring job.

Every job, every industry has some ramifications – good and bad. Everything we do at work can have great benefit or cause harm. We have to weigh it all up and check how we feel about it. And if we are unhappy we can leave, but not too fast because there's a great chance we can change things from the inside.

I worked in one industry for a while where I was aware that things were a bit dodgy, so I adopted the line of asking, 'What if the press get hold of this, what would that do to us?' I wasn't whistle-blowing or opposing anyone, merely asking. But it did draw attention to the fact that what was happening was slightly the other side of a fine line. Maybe you could do the same. Or maybe you can slowly, quietly use the influence that you have and the actions you are able to take, to change things ever so slightly for the better.

Be good at your job

How we behave at work has an effect on our colleagues. We need to have standards – and stick to them of course. We have to be moral and decent and honest and trustworthy of course. But here are a few others to help you become fantastically successful along the way.

> ## WE HAVE TO BE MORAL AND DECENT AND HONEST AND TRUSTWORTHY OF COURSE

- Treat your job as important and do it to the very best of your ability. Don't stand still but learn all the time, stay ahead of your industry and new developments. Put in extra hours if you must but don't be seen to be too hard-working – a laid-back approach gains you more respect

- Always be on the look-out for ways to improve the lot of everyone rather than just yourself. Think in terms of 'we' rather than 'I'. You are a part of a team and should fit in and be a part effectively and efficiently

RULE 92

- Try to spread a little happiness as you go. Don't badmouth people. Stick up for the under-dog. Compliment people and be genuine about it. Don't indulge in gossip or tittle-tattle. Keep your own counsel and be a bit aloof. It'll get you promoted

- Dress smartly and try to make a good impression. Maintain high standards and put in the hours. Try not to go to work to sleep or steal the pens or look for love. You are there to work, get on with it

- Try to be kind to colleagues, they are as lost as you once were. Give them a break, a chance, a bit of slack. Encourage them by example. Be a role model for junior members of staff. Try to understand your boss's point of view and to see things from the company perspective

- Understand the politics of office life – and don't get involved of course – but use it to your own advantage. Don't be frightened to put yourself forward or to volunteer (just so long as you know what you are volunteering for). There is no kudos in being work-shy. Be proud of being effective and efficient

- Know your boundaries. Know how to say 'no', and mean it. Don't let anyone take advantage of your good nature. Be assertive without being aggressive

- Enjoy what you do. Have a passion for your work. Have fun.

WORLD
RULES

There is an element of scaling-up here. In Partnership Rules we've looked at celebrating the things you and your partner have in common rather than highlighting the differences. This is true on a much larger scale. On a global level, we are all human, we all inhabit this wonderful planet together. We have so much more in common than we have differences, although you wouldn't always think so.

We all occupy a bit of land. On the big scale, there are differences – some of it is sunny, some of it is cold; some of it is wet, some of it is dry. But still we manage to fight over who has got the bigger bit, the best bit, the driest bit, the bit with the most oil, the bit with the least people. We are very sad. If we can't learn to share, it will be confiscated and we won't get any of it back.

And the bit of land we do have we keep pretty filthy – on the small scale right up to the big stuff. Not just the land either – we also find an amazing variety of stuff to chuck into the rivers and hazardous waste to throw into the ocean. The ocean gives us food and yet we try to make it so polluted we can't even swim in it. We empty our raw sewage into it. What sort of message does that give to those who live in it full time?

And then if we're not squabbling about land or making a mess over what bit we do have, we also manage to find conflict in our beliefs – really what's that all about? My deity is bigger/more powerful/more magic/more omnipresent than yours?

So that's what the World Rules are basically about. Cleaning up after us. Trying to stay friends with the other kids. Learning how to share and how to tidy up after us. Not being bullies.

Please feel free to skip them if you have someplace else to go, another planet to retreat to when this one gets too messy.

Be aware of the damage you are doing

This Rule doesn't mean, as yet, that you have to do anything. All it means is a conscious decision to evaluate what you are doing to the environment, the world, and whether it is a good thing or a bad thing. You might choose to change what you do in the light of this evaluation. Or you may not, either because you figure what the heck or because you figure you're pretty 'green' already and don't need to change anything.

The reason I say 'Don't do anything as yet,' is that it is all too easy to rush headlong into action without having all the facts in front of you. You need to know if the changes you are making are actually making things better or worse. For example, when my youngest child was born I was seriously concerned about the reports of the damage disposable nappies are doing. Apparently they take some 500 years to decompose. But I was also concerned that terry nappies take a lot of washing with all the usage of electricity, soap, water etc. And some argue they are both as bad as each other when it comes to damaging the environment. Trouble is, you have to use something or you risk damaging your carpets . . .

So you might like to consider what car you drive; what sort of heating you use in your house; how you get to your holiday destinations (planes aren't that environmentally friendly by all accounts); whether you recycle; if somebody else can use what you don't want – that sort of thing. I leave the details entirely up to you (heaven forbid that I should lecture anyone on these matters) but it's good to have a conscience about these things and to try and minimize the damage we are doing.

This goes back to the big theme underpinning all of the Rules, namely that we need to go through our lives with our eyes open, conscious and aware of what we are doing and the effect we are having on the environment and on other people around us. We don't have to become goody-goodies but we should be at least giving it some thought.

> WE DON'T HAVE TO BECOME GOODY-GOODIES BUT WE SHOULD BE AT LEAST GIVING IT SOME THOUGHT

I think the time for complacency is over and it really is time to consider the impact we make quite carefully. And once we have considered it, we might like to start making a few changes to improve things. If we all did a little bit, it would make a grand difference.

Be for the glory, not the degradation

We can work for the glory of humankind or we can try to bring it all crashing down into degradation. Shakespeare is for the glory, a crack house is for the degradation. A village fete on a warm summer's afternoon is for the glory, stealing someone's purse is for the degradation. And it doesn't have to be tame; a parachute jump for charity is for the glory, porn is for the degradation – but an erotic movie can be for the glory. Get the idea?

Anything that makes us more than we are, makes us strive for perfection, improves us, challenges us, excites us in a good way, makes us rise above our base nature and brings us out into the sunshine is for the glory.

So what are you going to be for? The glory or the degradation? Well for the glory of course. My fear is that you will think this is all about being good and that has a bad press. All our lives we have been told that being good is a bad thing, somehow dull, for the meek and namby-pamby, the sandal wearers, the holier-than-thou brigade. Being good hasn't had a lot going for it. As a kid at school if you tried to be good you got beaten up. At work if you try to be good they call you the boss's pet.

Well, being good, being for the glory is a private thing. You don't have to tell a soul. If you keep it quiet you are being good. If you brag about it you are a goody-goody. If you interfere with others and try to make them be good, you are a do-gooder. Just make a decision to be for the glory and say nothing.

JUST MAKE A DECISION TO
BE FOR THE GLORY AND
SAY NOTHING

Be part of the solution, not the problem

This goes further than just being good, being for glory not degradation. This is about positive, affirmative action. Look, if we don't take some action then this world, this fabulous planet of ours, is going to hell in a handcart. I was reading an article the other day about the Easter Islands and how they could stand as a perfect metaphor for our own sad predicament.

> ## LOOK, IF WE DON'T TAKE SOME ACTION THIS WORLD, THIS FABULOUS PLANET OF OURS, IS GOING TO HELL IN A HANDCART

The Easter Islands were settled by a Polynesian race around 500 years ago.* They found an island heavy with wildlife and heavily

---

* Don't write in if I got the facts vaguely wrong – it's a metaphor.

wooded with trees. Within a few short years they had eaten the way through the wildlife and chopped down all the trees. They also polluted the rivers and were on the verge of extinction. The only thing that has rescued them is tourism.

Planet Earth has no tourists. There is nothing going to rescue us so they can take our photo. We all have to start being a part of the solution now, and stop adding to the mayhem, the destruction, the problem. And we start to be part of the solution when we stand up and get counted. We stop the problem when we stop saying, 'I was just doing my duty,' or 'It was part of my job.' Come on, we have to stop the nonsense now or we're going to be relegated to being some vast amusement park for aliens – who aren't coming.

So the Rule is to start looking for ways we can personally contribute to the solution. We have to take part, get involved, find solutions, take action, get off our backsides and contribute. If you want your life to feel right, to be good, to be successful and mean something, you have to put something back. You have to pay back your loan. You have to reinvest in life and that means caring and wanting things to get better.

Check what history would say about you

So what is history going to say about you? What do you feel in your heart of hearts is going to be your epithet after you've gone? And I don't mean what is engraved on your tombstone but written in some great cosmic record of the universe. Personally, I don't think I'll even warrant a footnote. But if I do, I would like history to record that I had a go, made an effort, tried my best to make a difference. That I stood up for what I believed in, stood up to get counted and stood up for my rights. I would like history to say, maybe, that I got up off my backside and just stood up – it would be enough.

And you, my friend, what would you like? What do you *think* history will say? What would you *like* history to say? Is there a gap between these two? Can you bridge it? What do you have to do to make that gap connect? Think about both what it would say about you as a person, and about your deeds.

We have to care, if we want to be successful, that those who come after are going to inherit a better world than the one we found ourselves in. You remember all those books on self-sufficiency that were all the rage back in the 1970s?* Well a key thing they all seemed to have in common was they said if you had land, you had to make better use of it than the person who had it before you. You had to improve it. Same with this world. We have to consciously make the effort to improve it before we go. We have

---

* Yes, yes, I too was sold the dream and moved to the country to grow my own yoghurt, wear sandals and eat lentils. It didn't last long, not for me anyway.

to take responsibility for what we've been given and make a better use of it before we shuffle off and pass it on.

How will we point at the polluted oceans, the dried-up rivers, the melted ice caps and say to our metaphorical children, 'One day all this will be yours – oh and sorry about what we did with it.' I think they may be a little angry at us. History may indeed write us off as termite people. We have destroyed and polluted and slaughtered and made a pretty poor show of things. Individually we can make a difference. We must make a difference. Individually history must hold us accountable.

The trouble is there are so many people who won't change because they think they won't be held accountable. If there is no one watching, they think they can get away with murder. History will make short work of them.

> HISTORY MAY INDEED
> WRITE US OFF AS TERMITE
> PEOPLE

Keep your eyes open at all times

Rainforests in South America and other places are being decimated at an alarming rate. Countries wage war on each other and on their own people using weapons sold to them by richer countries. People starve to death because their leaders are too busy stripping money out of the country and into their own pockets. Floods happen because too much land has been badly used and houses built in the wrong place to profit some development company. Pollution is happening throughout the whole world. Things aren't getting worse, they've always been bad, but we are contributing to disaster much more. Each of us, individually, can do little. But if we come together collectively we can achieve great things.

Individually we can start by being conscious of what we buy, where it comes from, how it is made, who makes it, under what conditions it was harvested/built/made/grown. We can all do a little by boycotting countries that don't do nice things. We can all lobby our representatives to make changes. We have to have a voice and make it heard. We have to be conscious about where we live and how we live.

I love the people who buy houses in tiny villages that have a great main road running through them and then complain and start a campaign to have a bypass built. I find myself wondering why they bought them in the first place – it isn't like they didn't know.

I also look at things like pylons and think I would never live under or near one. I'm not surprised when evidence is presented that they are a health hazard and the people who do live under or near them are aghast. But what did they think they were doing?

> ## IF WE COME TOGETHER COLLECTIVELY, WE CAN ACHIEVE GREAT THINGS

What did they think the pylons were adding to their lives? Sorry if this sounds like a criticism, I don't mean it to be, but I am constantly amazed by how asleep people seem to be and they suddenly wake up and demand to know what is happening to them. Take control. Take responsibility. And turn the lights out in a room when there is no one in it.

Not everything can be green

I've just heard about a chap* who has invented shoes that recharge your mobile phone battery while you're walking. Brilliant. I want a pair but they all look like rugged walking boots – designed for areas where recharging equipment isn't available, such as jungles and deserts. I'll have a pair when they make them in Oxford brogues. Not everything can be green. Not everyone can be as organic and as green as we would have them be.

> ## NOT EVERYONE CAN BE AS ORGANIC AND AS GREEN AS WE WOULD HAVE THEM BE

OK, we've gone through the rant about the state of the world and what we're doing to it. Now I'm going to give you a tiny get-out clause. Not everything can be green. There has to be by-products. There has to be some pollution. There has to be some damage. We are vast in number – billions of humans living on the planet have to have an effect – and we have to live. There will always be some

---

[23] Trevor Bayliss – he also invented the wind-up radio.

damage. Our job is to limit it but it is unrealistic to attempt to eliminate it altogether. It's all a question of balance, of priorities.

It is unrealistic to demand the immediate elimination of all motor vehicles in the world; it's not going to happen. But we can do our bit by buying cars that use less fuel, emit cleaner exhaust fumes, use recyclable materials in their construction. But they won't be totally green, they can't be.

We might all rush off to disaster zones to lend a hand but we'll fly there and aircraft emit huge quantities of exhaust fumes. You see, we are making choices all the time. Driving to work, heating our homes, what we wear, what we eat. We can't expect everyone to be as green as we want to be. We can't expect everything to be as green as we would have it.

If we all manage to achieve a reduction it helps. If we all do our bit it helps. If we are all conscious about what we are doing it helps. But we can't expect perfection. We can't turn things around overnight. If you're trying so hard to be green that it's causing you a great deal of stress and your life is suffering as a result (just try to go food/household shopping and buy nothing at all in plastic and you'll quickly see what I mean), then stop. Make an effort but accept that it's never going to be totally perfect. Just so long as we are trying to do something, it helps.

RULE 99

Put something back

I firmly believe that none of us asked to be born and that this world doesn't owe us a living, or anything. But by the same token we are in hock up to our armpits. Sure, we didn't get a choice about being here, but once we *are* here we get fed and watered, entertained and amused, challenged and educated, awed and flabbergasted. It's all here on offer for us. We can do pretty much anything we want. We can take from this world all it has to offer. And this world has an amazing amount to offer all of us.

We can take and take and take. There is nothing to say we can't. What I am suggesting is that we sleep better at night if we put something back. After the show be one of the volunteers clearing up.

> WE SLEEP BETTER AT
> NIGHT IF WE PUT
> SOMETHING BACK

Be generous with everything. Be generous with your generosity. You don't have to give money but rather your time and care. If you have a special talent, use it to help others in some way. If you have facilities lend them to others who need them. If you have the power to effect change for the better. then use it. If you have influence, use it.

And if you don't? I'm sure that we all can make a difference in our own small way. We might have to look carefully or use our imagination a bit or be creative in how we define 'giving something back'.

We don't all have to become charity workers or missionaries but we could sponsor a child in need. We don't have to turn our house into shelter for the homeless but we could start a wildlife patch in our garden. We don't have to become totally organic but we could recycle a bit more or just ask questions about the companies we choose to buy from.

I guess we all have to ask ourselves: 'Is this world a richer place for me being in it? Will I leave it a better place than when I came into it? Have I made a difference to someone's life? Have I put something back?'

RULE 100

Find a new Rule every day – or occasionally at least

So, that's about it – 99 Rules for a successful and fulfilled life. Phew. But don't think it's over yet. There is no time to sit still, there are no tea breaks for Rules Players. As soon as you think you've got it sussed, you'll fall flat on your face. You have to keep moving forwards. You have to be inventive, creative, imaginative, resourceful, original. This final Rule has to be to keep thinking up new Rules, not to stand still, to carry on developing this theme, adding to, improving on, evolving and growing and changing these Rules. These provide a jumping-off point. They're not a revelation, more a reminder. These Rules are a starting point for you to pick up and run with.

> ## THESE RULES ARE A REMINDER. THEY ARE A STARTING POINT FOR YOU TO PICK UP AND RUN WITH

I've tried to avoid the pedestrian (Time is a great healer) and the humorous (Never tip anyone who isn't looking) and the impractical (Love everyone), the plain daft (Turn the other cheek – you get hit twice that way, better to run I say), the wibbly (Everyone's a rainbow), the obviously wrong (There are no victims) and the very, very difficult (Spend 35 years in a cave and you'll find the secret of the universe – and get a wet bottom). I've also avoided the trite (It'll be alright on the night – my experience is it never is) and the unpleasant (Don't get mad, get even).

I hope you too will follow a similar plan when you formulate new Rules for yourself. I guess the main thing is that you need to continually formulate your own Rules. When you learn something – from observation or just an illuminating moment – then absorb the lesson and see if there's a Rule there for future use.

Try to find a new Rule every day – or at least occasionally. And I am quite genuine about wanting to know what you come up with – if you want to share them. Being a Rules Player is a lot of fun and quite fascinating to try and spot other Players. Whatever you do though, don't go telling everyone about it. Keep it secret, keep it safe – but you can tell me: *Richard.Templar@RichardTemplar.co.uk*

Being a Rules Player requires dedication, hard work, perseverance, keenness, ambition, enthusiasm, devotion and sheer doggedness. Keep at it and you will live a fulfilled, happy and productive life. But go easy on yourself, we all fail from time to time and no one is perfect – I'm most certainly not. Enjoy and have fun and be good.

THE RULES OF WORK
A definitive code for personal success

"This is a definitive code for personal business success...Key points, concisely made, that can steer anyone through the minefield of office life."

Management Today

Some people seem to be just great at their job. They glide effortlessly onwards and upwards through all the politics, the back stabbing, the system, the nonsense that goes on. They always seem to say and do the right thing. Everybody likes them. They get pay rises and promotion. They get on with the boss. And somehow, they do all these without breaking much of a sweat or seeming to put in excess effort.

Is there something they do that we don't? Is it a natural ability or something we could all learn? The answer is a most definite and resounding yes. They know the 'Rules of Work'. These rules are about how you are seen to be doing your job – brilliantly and efficiently. They are about how you appear to others – successful and confident. If you want to be successful, and be regarded as a thoroughly decent person by your colleagues and bosses, then read *The Rules of Work*, these rules will help you to rise up the ladder of success.

Richard Templar
£10.99
0273662716
9780273662716

ALSO IN THE RULES SERIES

The Rules series is an international success and has sold over half a million copies worldwide.

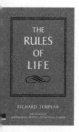

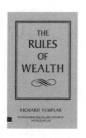

The Rules is a limited edition boxed set that brings together the bestselling *The Rules of Life* and *The Rules of Work*.

027370625X
9780273706250

0273710192
9780273710196

1405846534
9781405846530

THE

RULES

OF WEALTH

Books that make you better

Books that make you better. That make you *be* better, *do* better, *feel* better. Whether you want to upgrade your personal skills or change your job, whether you want to improve your managerial style, become a more powerful communicator, or be stimulated and inspired as you work.

Prentice Hall Business is leading the field with a new breed of skills, careers and development books. Books that are a cut above the mainstream – in topic, content and delivery – with an edge and verve that will make you better, with less effort.

Books that are as sharp and smart as you are.

Prentice Hall Business.
We work harder – so you don't have to.

For more details on products, and to contact us, visit
www.pearsoned.co.uk

THE

RULES

OF WEALTH

A personal code
for prosperity

RICHARD TEMPLAR

PEARSON
Prentice Hall
BUSINESS

Harlow, England • London • New York • Boston • San Francisco • Toronto
Sydney • Tokyo • Singapore • Hong Kong • Seoul • Taipei • New Delhi
Cape Town • Madrid • Mexico City • Amsterdam • Munich • Paris • Milan

PEARSON EDUCATION LIMITED

Edinburgh Gate
Harlow CM20 2JE
Tel: +44 (0)1279 623623
Fax: +44 (0)1279 431059
Website: www.pearsoned.co.uk

First published in Great Britain in 2007

© Richard Templar 2007

The right of Richard Templar to be identified as author
of this work has been asserted by him in accordance
with the Copyright, Designs and Patents Act 1988

ISBN-13: 978-0-273-71019-6

British Library Cataloguing-in-Publication Data
A catalogue record for this book is available from the British Library

Library of Congress Cataloging-in-Publication Data
Templar, Richard, 1950–2006.
    The rules of wealth : a personal code for prosperity / Richard Templar.
       p. cm.
    Contents: Thinking wealthy -- Getting wealthy -- Get even wealthier - part three --
Staying wealthy -- Share your wealth.
    ISBN-13: 978-0-273-71019-6 (alk. paper)
    ISBN-10: 0-273-71019-2 (alk. paper)
       1. Wealth--Psychological aspects. 2. Wealth--Social aspects. I. Title.

    HB251.T46 2006
    332.024'01--dc22

                                                                        2006050772

All rights reserved. No part of this publication may be reproduced, stored in a retrieval
system, or transmitted in any form or by any means, electronic, mechanical, photocopying,
recording or otherwise, without either the prior written permission of the publishers or a
licence permitting restricted copying in the United Kingdom issued by the Copyright Licensing
Agency Ltd, Saffron House, 6–10 Kirby Street, London EC1N 8TS. This book may not be lent,
resold, hired out or otherwise disposed of by way of trade in any form of binding or cover
other than that in which it is published, without the prior consent of the publishers.

10 9 8 7 6 5 4
10 09 08 07

Typeset in 11pt Berkeley by 30
Printed and bound in Great Britain by Clays Ltd, Bungay, Suffolk

The publisher's policy is to use paper manufactured from sustainable forests.

Contents

Acknowledgements

I would like to thank Dan Clayden, director of Clayden Associates – Independent Financial Advisers (www.claydenassociates.co.uk) who was so kind as to go through a draft of this book in the early stages and put me right on a few things and is one of the best financial advisers I have ever met professionally.

I would also like to dedicate this book to my delightful father-in-law who manages his money in a kind, generous, honest and moral way and still manages to make it work for him efficiently and expertly. He is an example to all of us. He is a Rules Player par excellence.

Introduction

Let's be honest. We all want to be well off, wealthy, rich, abundant. And we're fascinated by others who already are. How did they do it? How can we do it too?

The simple truth is that wealthy people tend to understand and do things the rest of us don't. From mindsets to actual actions, they follow behavioural rules when it comes to their wealth and these rules are what separate them from everybody else. This book codifies what those behaviours are so that you too can choose to be more wealthy. The basis of the Rules (as with the other Rules books) is that these are all things I have observed wealthy people do. This is, if you like, sympathetic magic. If we do like them, we'll become like them. This actually does work.

Quite simply, this book reveals:

● what people do to make money
● how they carry on making money
● how they hang on to it once they've got it
● how they spend it
● how they invest it
● how they enjoy it
● how they make use of it altruistically.

In all probability, we'd want to do as little as possible to get to be wealthy, rich, abundant. A staggering £50 billion is gambled in the UK each year. Gambling levels of £50 billion means there are a lot of people looking for an easy way to make some money. Gambling £50 billion also means a lot of them are going to be disappointed. Not all of them mind. Casinos work on percentages – just like any business. Roulette for instance, if the game is run properly, runs on about 28 per cent. That means if £100 crosses the table the house expects to pocket £28 of that. It returns £72 to the players – not necessarily the same ones who staked it. Some will lose. Some will win. And some will break even. But the house will always, always win – in the long term. That's a fact.

Now if so many people are gambling so much, it implies to me – and I did notice this a lot when I worked in a casino – that they:

- have too much spare cash and need to get rid of some of it[1]
- firmly believe in their own 'luckiness'
- like to lose so they can have a reason to feel wretched
- are desperate for easy money.

This book is not for people who are after any or all of the above. No, not even the easy money bit (sorry). However, it should make a significant improvement to your overall prosperity.

This book provides a set of principles, strategies and things to understand and to do that won't make you get rich quick, but they will increase the odds of your making money and growing your wealth while remaining a decent person. In effect we can become the house and always win. So, what do we have to do?

Well, there are a whole number of things we can do. No individual rule guarantees success. But each narrows the odds. They all increase our chances of making money. It's not as easy as a quick win on the blackjack table but it is more assured and long term and it doesn't make you an addict or have you chasing a losing streak.

No need for violins here but I was poor as a kid. I went without. I knew others had more, had lots. I also knew, really, really knew that I would work my way out of that poor upbringing. But it took a lot of false starts, a whole lot of nearly made-its before I

---

[1] Some of them are there to launder money – put spare cash across the tables and then not play but get it back in the form of a winner's cheque so they don't have to pay tax on it. Very naughty. Trouble is the house invariably takes its 28 per cent off them as well no matter how hard they try to get out without playing much.

got it right. And I only got it right when I took the time and trouble to observe what the really rich do. And that knowledge based on those observations I now happily pass on to you.

I'm going to assume you want to:

- get richer
- do it legally
- do something useful with it once you've got it
- put something back
- keep some of this stuff under your hat.

And that you are prepared to put in a bit of work.

To help you achieve this, I have divided this book up into five sections:

- thinking wealthy;
- getting wealthy;
- getting even wealthier;
- staying wealthy;
- sharing your wealth.

We start with thinking wealthy because that's the foundation on which all things wealth related rest. We all have money beliefs. Most of us believe that even if money doesn't make us happy (but secretly of course we believe it will) it will at least allow us to be miserable in some comfort. We almost all believe that money lets us buy better stuff and by buying better stuff we will be happier. It's not for me to discourage you in any of those beliefs, merely to give you means of finding out for yourself whether or not this is true.

Time to start. Shall we crack on? Whatever happens, here's to your greater prosperity.

Richard Templar

THINKING

WEALTHY

Money is a concept. You can't really see or touch it (unless you are holding a gold bar in your hand). You can only do that with some physical symbol of it like bank notes or a cheque. Bits of paper, yes, but bits of paper with enormous power.

The concept of money comes with a lot of baggage to most of us. We have an inherent belief that it is good or bad and that wanting it is good or bad. That loving it is good or bad. That spending it is good or bad.

What I am going to suggest in the first few Rules is that maybe, just maybe, how we think about wealth might be holding us back from having wealth. If, in our heart, we believe (even subconsciously) that money is a bad thing and having lots and lots of it is a really bad thing, then chances are we might be undermining our own efforts, unwittingly, to get lots of it.

I am also going to get you to look at how much effort you are prepared to put into making money. It's a bit like a sport – the more you practise the better you become. Likewise you can't make money while being lazy. You've got to put in some work here you know.

You've also got to know pretty intimately what you want, why you want it, how you think you are going to get it, what you are going to do with it after you've got it – stuff like that. No one said this was going to be easy...

Anybody can make money – it isn't selective or discriminatory

The lovely thing about money is that it really doesn't discriminate. It doesn't care what colour or race you are, what class you are, what your parents did, or even who you *think* you are. Each and every day starts with a clean slate so that no matter what you did yesterday, today begins anew and you have the same rights and opportunities as everyone else to take as much as you want. The only thing that can hold you back is yourself and your own money myths (*see Rule 5*).

> YOU HAVE THE SAME
> RIGHTS AND
> OPPORTUNITIES AS
> EVERYONE ELSE TO TAKE
> AS MUCH AS YOU WANT

Of the wealth of the world each has as much as they take. What else could make sense? There is no way money can know who is handling it, what their qualifications are, what ambitions they have or what class they belong to. Money has no ears or eyes or senses. It is inert, inanimate, impassive. It hasn't a clue. It is there to be used and spent, saved and invested, fought over, seduced with and worked for. It has no discriminatory apparatus so it can't judge whether you are 'worthy' or not.

I have watched a lot of extremely wealthy people and the one thing they all have in common is that they have nothing in common – apart from all being Rules Players of course. The wealthy are a diverse band of people – the least likely can be loaded. They vary from the genteel to the uncouth, the savvy to the plain stupid, the deserving to the undeserving. But each and every one of them has stepped up and said, 'Yes please, I want some of that'. And the poor are the ones saying, 'No thank you, not for me, I am not worthy. I am not deserving enough. I couldn't. I mustn't. I shouldn't.'

That's what this book is about, challenging your perceptions of money and the wealthy. We all assume the poor are poor because of circumstances, their background, their upbringing, their nurture. But if you have the means to buy a book such as this and live in comparative security and comfort in the world then you too have the power to be wealthy. It may be hard. It may be tough but it is doable. And that is Rule 1 – anyone can be wealthy, you just have to apply yourself. All the other Rules are about that application.

Decide on your definition of wealth

So, what, to *you*, is wealth? This is one you have to sit down and work out in advance if you are going to get wealthy. My observation is that wealthy people invariably have worked this one out. They know exactly what, to them, wealth means.

I have a wealthy and extremely generous friend who says that he knew long ago when he was starting out in business that he would consider he had made enough when he wasn't living off the money he had amassed (which we will call his capital). Nor would he be living off the interest on his capital. No, he would consider himself wealthy when he was living on the interest on the interest on his capital. Sounds good to me.

Now, this friend knows how much his interest on the interest is making him, pretty much by the hour. Thus if we all go out for a meal in the evening he knows (a) how much the meal has cost and (b) how much he has made while eating the meal. He says that as long as (b) is more than (a), then he is happy.

This is setting the definition of wealth pretty high you might think. Maybe you wouldn't want to set it this high. And that's fine of course. Then again, maybe you'd want to put some kind of figure on it. In the old days everyone wanted to be a millionaire. That was an easy one to judge if you'd got there or not. Today there are a lot of people who have houses worth more than that and they wouldn't consider themselves wealthy at all and yet haven't quite got around to upping the ante to wishing themselves billionaires.[2]

---

[2] Sorry, but to me a billion is a million million and I won't be persuaded otherwise.

My own definition, for comparison, is having enough so that I don't have to worry about having enough. How much is that? I never know. There always seems to be more to worry about – and less coming in. But seriously, I feel that I have been 'comfortable' since I started counting in thousands rather than in pounds. I know to the nearest thousand how much I've got, how much I need and how much I can spend.

For some people, not worrying might mean having enough to pay for any emergency that might arise in your family or home. So how will you define it? By the number of cars you own? Servants? Cash in the bank? Value of your house? Portfolio of investments? There are, of course, no right or wrong answers, but I do feel that until you've worked this one out you shouldn't read on. If we don't have a target we can't take aim. If we don't have a destination we can't leave home or we'll be driving around in circles for hours. If we don't have a definition how can we monitor or judge success? If we don't do this how will you know if this book has been helpful to you?

> IF WE DON'T HAVE A DEFINITION HOW CAN WE MONITOR OR JUDGE SUCCESS? IF WE DON'T DO THIS HOW WILL YOU KNOW IF THIS BOOK HAS BEEN HELPFUL TO YOU?

Set your objectives

By defining what you mean by wealth, you now have a destination. Setting your objectives is establishing a timetable to reach that destination. It's quite simple. If you know you are going to drive to a certain place it makes sense to know:

- what time you are leaving home
- what time you expect to arrive
- what route you are going to take
- what you will be doing when you get there.

Getting rich is exactly the same. You will want to know in advance what rich means to you, how you intend getting there, how long you expect it to take and what you are going to be able to do or want to do with your money when you get it.

> YOU WILL WANT TO KNOW IN ADVANCE WHAT RICH MEANS TO YOU, HOW YOU INTEND GETTING THERE, HOW LONG YOU EXPECT IT TO TAKE

So, having defined what wealth means to you, can you now see the importance of setting your objective? Think about how you intend getting rich and how long it is going to take you and then set your objective. It might be simple: 'I am going to be a millionaire by my fortieth birthday and I shall make my money by running my own property development company.'

That was easy. Well it was for me because I'm only making up an example for you. For you I wager it's going to be pretty hard. This is because you won't have thought about this before. Oh, I daresay you might have had a casual dream – I want to be very, very rich and/or famous and/or successful. But few people – only the rich, famous and successful ones in my observation – actually decide what and when and how. You have to if you too want to be wealthy. And I assume you do or you wouldn't be reading this far. Good for you.

Now set your objective. I can wait.

Back already? How did you get on? Your objective has to be realistic, honest and achievable. By realistic I mean that setting an objective of being the richest person in the world might happen but it isn't going to, it isn't realistic.

Honest means you have to be true to yourself and set an objective that you can live with and work with. Lying to yourself means it will fail. Lying to others means it will fail.

Achievable? Yes that too. If you know nothing about property and aren't interested in learning, have no capital and can't get a mortgage, then setting an objective to be a property developer isn't realistic, honest or achievable.

Happy with what you've got? Good. If not have another bash at it and let's get a move on, we want to get you up and running as soon as possible.

Keep it under your hat

Now you have embarked on a new journey, a new direction, it might be worth keeping it under your hat. There may come a time when you will need to discuss what you are doing with money mentors (*see Rule 64*) but for the moment don't broadcast what you are doing. There are several reasons for this:

- Other people's opinions can often be negative and this can put you off.
- If everyone is doing it, there may be less room for you.
- There's no need to give away all your best ideas.
- Having other people discussing your business amongst themselves is never good for you.
- You don't want to be seen as preaching or trying to convert people to your way of thinking.
- No one else really wants to know what you're up to – if they ask how you are, reply with a simple 'Fine' rather than a lengthy explanation of what you are doing.
- It's nice having a secret – gives you a warm, smug, glowing feeling.

If you go round broadcasting what you're doing, there will be people around you who will get jealous and will do pretty well anything to put you off. After all, you are saying goodbye to them in a way. You are proclaiming that the old you, the old lifestyle, isn't good enough any more and you are off to pastures new. Of course they are going to be unhappy about that. So keep it under your hat. That doesn't cost anything or require you to do anything.

> ## NOW YOU HAVE EMBARKED ON A NEW JOURNEY, A NEW DIRECTION, IT MIGHT BE WORTH KEEPING IT UNDER YOUR HAT

Let this be our little secret. Carry on learning and practising the Rules but just don't go telling all and sundry – no matter how much you think they might benefit from reading this book. Leave a copy around by all means of course.

The interesting bit is that even if you did go telling everyone, they're unlikely to do anything about it. Most people would rather watch television than drag themselves out of their pit of poverty. I am only thinking of you when I say keep it under your hat. Anyone who gets religion of any sort needs to keep a tight lip on it. People really hate being preached at, lectured at, encouraged to think about their lifestyle or told that what they are doing isn't good enough. Gaining prosperity is one of those things you do privately, clandestinely, surreptitiously. Not that there is anything wrong, just that it's best done alone.

Most people are too lazy to be wealthy

You have to get up early, work hard all day and go to bed still working on your objective. Yes, money *does* sometimes grow on trees – or so it seems. Yes, people *do* win the lottery, the jackpot, the big prize. People *do* get sudden inheritances from long lost relatives. Yes people *do* suddenly find fame and fortune where they sought for none. But it isn't going to happen to you. Well, the odds are that it won't. If you set your objective as: *Win the lottery and live in the lap of luxury for evermore* then read no further. Put this book down and go and buy lottery tickets. If your objective is a little more realistic then read on.

Most people are too lazy to be rich. They may say they want to be, but they don't. They may buy a lottery ticket as a sort of half-hearted gesture of wanting to be rich, but they aren't prepared to put in the work. They aren't prepared to make sacrifices, study, learn, work their socks off, put in the effort and make it a deter-mined and concentrated focus of their life.

> MOST PEOPLE ARE TOO
> LAZY TO BE RICH. THEY
> MAY SAY THEY WANT TO
> BE, BUT THEY DON'T

And for a lot of them – not you – it is because they believe that if you do so you are somehow tainted with evil (*see Rule 6*). But is it OK to work hard to make money? Is it a worthwhile thing to want? It depends on why and what you are going to do with it I guess (*see Rule 8*).

Most people don't want to do the work. Yes, they want the money but only if it comes to them by accident, by luck, by chance. Then it's OK. Then it's not tainted with sweat and work and passion and focus.

I think if you look at anyone rich enough to be a role model – Bill Gates, Richard Branson, Alan Sugar, Warren Buffett, Gordon Ramsey, James Dyson, Petr Kellner[3] – you'll notice only one thing in common . . . they work their socks off. They might make their money from computers, sales, cookery, business, the film industry, vacuum cleaners, pop music, radio stations, whatever. But the one thing they all share is the ability to do more in a day than most of us do in a month.

And that's the wonderful thing about wealth – it's lying around waiting to be claimed (*remember Rule 1*). And those who claim it are the ones who get up early, work hard and put in the hours.

And you are going to have to as well. I don't have loungers, weight shifters or decorative spongers on my team. I want hard-working, dedicated, focused, ambitious, driven money makers. With a sense of fun of course.

---

[3] I did have a bet with myself that you wouldn't have heard of him – the Czech Republic's first billionaire.

Understand your money beliefs and where they come from

We all grow up with money myths. We get a lot of them from our parents and the way they bring us up. I can still hear my mother saying, 'A penny saved is a penny found', and to this day I still have no idea what it means. Maybe I'm lucky. My money myths are based on a lot of nonsense like that. But most of us have the following ingrained beliefs:

- Money is the root of all evil.[4]
- Money is dirty.
- I don't deserve to be rich.
- Money is only made by the greedy and dishonest.
- Money corrupts.
- You mustn't brag about money – never say how much you earn, are worth or paid for something (unless it is a bargain).
- You can't have money and be 'spiritually pure'.[5]
- You lose your friends if you get rich.
- You have to work too hard to get rich.[6]
- Happiness and money make poor bedfellows.
- The more you have, the more you'll want.
- It is somehow better to be poor.
- I wasn't meant to be rich – if I was I would have been by now.
- I'm not the right type to be rich.

---

[4] It is actually the *love* of money that is supposed to be the root of all evil but is it a belief of yours?
[5] Whatever that means.
[6] See Rule 5.

Have a quick look through. Check which ones you believe. Check which ones strike a chord with you. Now you have to do a bit of that old-fashioned hard work. Write down ones that mean something to you. Add ones I've missed – there will be a few. Now work out why you hold these beliefs. Is it something you have actively thought about, reasoned out, dedicated some research to? Or are they inherited, left over, picked up along the way?

Get rid of any that you can question and accept are nonsense. Discard any that simply aren't true. And chuck out any that stand in the way, hold you back, stop you making some money.

> ## GET RID OF ANY BELIEFS THAT YOU CAN QUESTION AND ACCEPT ARE NONSENSE

What you should be left with is none at all, nothing, a blank sheet. Now you can write new beliefs such as:

- Money is OK.
- Wanting money is OK.
- I am going to be wealthy.
- I am prepared to put in the work.

Wealthy people have none of the troublesome money myths we poorer people have. They have purged them or never had them. If we too purge them, we stand a better chance of getting there.

Understand that wealth is a consequence, not a reward[7]

If you work hard at making money, you stand a better chance of becoming rich. You have to accept that money is a payment given to you for clever thinking and hard work. The harder and smarter you work, the more you will earn. You don't get given the money by a committee who examine whether you deserve it or not, whether you have been good enough or not. It is a direct consequence.

> ## YOU DON'T GET GIVEN THE MONEY BY A COMMITTEE WHO EXAMINE WHETHER YOU DESERVE IT OR NOT

We often look at someone who has money and make all sorts of value judgements about whether they deserve it or not. We all do it. I was reading about Calvin Ayre – the Internet bookie – who has grown very rich indeed running online gambling. He has something like 16 million customers in the US. The US

---

[7] I use the word 'reward' in the sense of a prize or bonus, not as a payment or renumeration.

Department of Justice isn't very happy about this and want to shut him down. Ayre isn't a US citizen and doesn't reside there. You can read all about him on the www.Forbes.com website (home of the really wealthy folk). If it isn't your home page it jolly well ought to be. You are in this to be wealthy, which means understanding where wealth comes from.

Back to Ayres. He has grown rich exploiting an alleged US law loophole whereby what he does is alleged to be illegal but he isn't in the country to commit any crime. Do we judge him? I don't. I study this information to see if I could make use of it. What might be wrong is the gambling. But I am aware that his consequence of hard work has been lots of money.

I was watching a TV programme the other day about a chap who cleans and polishes cars for rich celebs and such like. He charges £5000 for car washing. Mind you, this does include polishing. Now is his money a reward or a consequence? I don't think he would see it as a reward. It's the price he sets, and customers pay him because he is the best car cleaner in the world. The consequence of his business idea, skill and effort is to be very well paid.

RULE 8

See wealth as a friend, not the enemy

Writing this book has made me question my own attitudes to money in a big way. And it was a very interesting process to go through.

We all have to handle money. We all have bank accounts and credit cards and loans and overdrafts and mortgages. We all deal with all the paraphernalia of money every single day of our lives. We all need/want more. So what's the problem?

It's all about what goes on in our heads. Like you, I handle money, spend money, save money. And I want to do so more efficiently, more happily.

So before I could write this for you I had to undergo a rigorous investigation of my own motives, myths, inherent stuff. And I came to accept that money is neither good nor bad, neither friend nor foe. It is not the evil we have come to believe. Without it life disintegrates. Money is the oil that smoothes life for all of us. What we do with it – *see next Rule* – is the good or bad, the right or wrong, the friend or foe.

> ## MONEY IS THE OIL THAT SMOOTHES LIFE FOR ALL OF US

Repeat after me: *Money is fine. Money is great. Money is necessary. Money is OK. Money is my friend not my enemy.* Repeat this under your breath of course or your family and friends will think you've gone all wibbly on them. Learn not to fight money, or be embarrassed about having it, when you do.

Finally, having money, working towards getting wealthy, doesn't mean you have to change your politics at all. You can be left-wing, radical even, if you want. One of the richest men in Britain is a Labour minister (Lord Sainsbury). Having money won't detract from that at all. Having money won't lessen your spiritual virtues, your karmic harmonics or affect your future incarnations. I promise. What you do with it might, but money is inherently your friend, not foe.

Decide what you want money for

This is part of your defining, setting an objective process. There are no right or wrong answers. For example, making a fortune and spending it all on cocaine seems, to me, like a foolish thing to do. But that's personal. You might find a problem with me spending mine on a decent Châteauneuf du Pape. We all spend on what we think will satisfy us, make us happy. We all choose our own pleasures and it's not for me to sit in judgement on anyone else.

So what do you want the money for? Why do you want to be wealthy? The answers you give will tell you a whole lot about your hidden money myths and how you really see money.

> WE ALL SPEND ON WHAT
> WE THINK WILL SATISFY
> US, MAKE US HAPPY

Sometimes it's very simple: we have a dream and need the money to fulfil it. The dream comes first. Gerald Durrell had wanted a zoo since he was a small boy and wrote 36 bestselling books which helped to fund his zoo (on the island of Jersey). What's your dream?

It might not be that simple, however. I asked a close acquaintance why she wanted to be wealthier the other day and the results were quite revealing. She said she wanted to be 'better off' so that she could give her children more. And in giving them more, they would stay at home longer. And if they stayed at home longer, she wouldn't have to face a possible old age alone. So basically she wants to be wealthy to stave off loneliness.

Another acquaintance said he wanted to get wealthy so he could have adventures. When pressed further it seemed his adventures were the 'running away' sort where he could be young, free and single again.

Is money really the answer for either of these people? Is it for you?

When you know what you want greater wealth for, think also about alternative ways to meet your needs: I said earlier I wanted to be wealthy so I could pay for medical care for any close family member that might need it. I could invest in some simple medical insurance to cover that instead.

Consider also what you *don't* need more money for. I like my toys – cars and boats – but have found that my investments in such things hasn't increased as my income has gone up. I still like old cheap sports cars and old boats that need plenty of maintenance. My motivation isn't to be able to spend loads on new things. I don't need more money to buy new cars and boats. Do you really need as much as you think? If so, fine, you just need to be sure and be clear about it.

So what's your excuse? What do you want money for? Set your own agenda, my friend, and keep it to yourself. And whatever you write down – and I do recommend you write it down, it makes it so much more real – keep it secret, keep it safe. It is a useful exercise to look back on one day and see if your dream and achievements match.

Understand that money begets money

There is no greater truth than this – money makes money. It likes clustering together. It breeds quietly and quickly like rabbits. It prefers to hang out in big groups. Money makes money. The rich get richer; the poor get poorer. That's life. Yes, it is sad. But it does seem to be a fact. Now we can work hard ourselves and do something about it or we can sit around moaning and become part of the problem. The choice, as always, is entirely yours.

> ## MONEY MAKES MONEY. THE RICH GET RICHER

If you do want to do something about it, then it seems to make sense to me to make a tidy sum and use your money wisely to help the less fortunate than you. Or do whatever with it you so choose.

Once you have some money you'll be astonished at how quickly it can grow. I recommend you understand and learn the concept of *compound interest* as quickly as possible. And no, I am not going to tell you anything about it except it's vitally important that you know about it and make it a cornerstone in your building of wealth. The reason I'm not going to tell you anything about it is, firstly, this isn't that sort of a book[8] and, secondly, I'm

---

[8] Go and read *The Financial Times Guide to Investing* by Glen Arnold.

not going to do all the work for you. That would be too easy and you'd learn nothing. My observation is that wealthy people get the idea of compound interest and the rest of us don't.

If you spend all you get, then this Rule will never work for you; it'll never get your money working for you. You have to set aside money for breeding purposes. If you ran a rabbit farm and killed and ate all your rabbits, you wouldn't have any left to keep going. Forget the rabbit farm – you're going to start a money farm. Your money will breed. You can then reinvest some and spend some – but you can't spend it all or you'll have no more rabbits. Look, this stuff isn't rocket science but it is amazing how many people simply don't get it. But you do now. You have been given the best tip I can give you.

- Put some money aside for breeding purposes.
- Cream a little off for spending.
- Reinvest the bulk to build up a good and healthy stock.
- Keep it to yourself.

If you see money as the solution you'll find it becomes the problem

Having money doesn't make all your relationships flow smoothly – not by a long shot. It doesn't protect you from disease – it may buy you better medical care after the event but it doesn't protect you. It might buy a better diet but the rich half of the world has a pretty poor health record despite having all the money to feed itself extremely well so that doesn't necessarily go hand in hand.

> IT MAY BUY YOU BETTER MEDICAL CARE AFTER THE EVENT BUT IT DOESN'T PROTECT YOU

The more you see money as a solution, the greater the chance that you are missing the point entirely. Money doesn't do anything.

I know, I know. You'll be thinking, 'If only I had X amount, I could fix this problem in my life.' I think you'll find money would throw up a lot more problems in its wake. Money will not make you happier, thinner or more popular with decent people. Money does not deliver lasting, meaningful peace of mind. There are plenty of rich, fat, unhappy people with no real friends. I think we need to find the cure to our problems first and then find a way of funding that cure. Money isn't, and never will be, the cure. It is the oil that smoothes the wheels. It isn't the engine.

RULE 12

You can make lots of money, you can enjoy your job, and you can sleep nights

A lot of people hold one or other – or all – of these notions:

- Making money goes hand in hand with being a ruthless, manipulative, amoral, greedy lizard.
- To make a bit of cash you have to sell your soul, grandmother and principles.
- Being wealthy means you end up with a heart problem, insomnia and other stress-related disorders.
- To make money you have to turn into a slimeball who sacrifices their family, morals and happiness and all on the altar of wealth.

Well, it can be like that, but it doesn't have to be. In fact, it shouldn't be. That's the beauty of it. If it *is* like that, then you're doing it wrong. You see, money is so freely available – and to anyone (as we looked at in Rule 1) – that you really don't need to try that hard, or change that much. An awful lot of pretty ordinary, nice people make money – and lots of it. The staid old cliché of the cigar-chewing, high-pressure executive barking orders down a phone while signing dodgy deals probably went overboard off the *Lady Ghislane*.[9]

You *can* make money, enjoy your job and sleep at night. You just have to decide that is what you're going to do – no matter what. And then stick to it.

---

[9] Come on, come on, keep up – you know whose boat that was . . . don't you?

Remember, if you are starting to lose sleep or have stopped enjoying what you do, then you need to have a serious talk with yourself. Go back to the beginning of the book and remember what it is that wealth is all about to you.

> **IF YOU ARE STARTING TO LOSE SLEEP OR HAVE STOPPED ENJOYING IT, THEN YOU NEED TO HAVE A TALK WITH YOURSELF**

I remember a cartoon of a boardroom with fat-cat executives. A small girl pokes her head round the door and says, 'Money can't buy a kind smile'. The businessmen all look, momentarily, shamed. Then the chairman growls, 'Get outta here, kid, who the hell wants a kind smile?' and the others all look relieved and go back to their meeting.

Well, I for one would like the kind smile even if it does mean I lose a little money. I want to sleep nights and to enjoy my job and to make money. But I won't compromise my principles, spend too little time with my family or children, neglect to sit in the sunshine occasionally, take a day off. I won't worry about work or money once I've gone to bed, be driven so much by money that I lose my sense of humour or need to have fun. These I swear by. And it is possible – believe me, I've known and observed enough wealthy people to know this is true – to make money and have a life, to be ethical and rich, to earn a lot and be a thoroughly nice person. It is possible. It just sometimes *seems* it isn't. All part of debunking our money myths.

Don't make money by being bad

I like Google's mission statement – *Don't be evil*. It's probably an anagram of something but I still like it. If you have to lie, cheat, steal, defraud, lose sleep, hide, dodge the law in any way, break the rules or generally behave badly to make your money, then don't do it, it isn't worth it.

If earning money or being wealthy stops being fun – and by being bad it really will stop being fun – then there's no point doing it. If you don't enjoy the challenge of earning money in a decent way, then best go and do something different.

I knew a major criminal once. He told me it was no fun being 'bent' as, in fact, he had to be a lot more law-abiding than the rest of us. He couldn't risk getting pulled over by the police for speeding or any minor motoring offence; no late night parties in case the police got called out; no flash car to draw attention to himself; no lavish lifestyle in case it put him in the spotlight.

> IF YOU DON'T ENJOY THE CHALLENGE OF EARNING MONEY LEGIT THEN BEST GO AND DO SOMETHING DIFFERENT

But there is more to living a clean life than being able to speed or have parties. Living a life where you make your money from being good lets you sleep nights. You get to look your kids in the eye – and yourself in the mirror – with the added bonus of a feel-good factor. No amount of money that can buy that.

If you have to resort to being wicked, it means you've failed; you've lost the plot. It means you haven't been able to do it properly. It means you're scraping the barrel. It means you haven't been able to think of a proper idea. It means you've been lazy, desperate, non-creative, boring.

I can come up with lots of examples of famous wealthy people who've made their money out of being bad. Yep, they're wealthy it's true, but look in their eyes and what do you see there? Do you want to have that stay-awake-at-night-worrying look? Do you want that flinch-when-the-doorbell-rings kind of life? You want 'nobody trusts you' sort of relationships? Or would you rather relax and know that you did it legit, honest, fairly? It's a no-brainer really, isn't it?

As long as you can earn your wealth without ripping people off, being cruel or unjust, breaking the law or bending the rules, you'll be doing fine. All it requires is a quick check, staying conscious of what you – and your money – are doing.

Money and happiness – understand their relationship

There are lots of things that will make us miserable – losing a partner, being made redundant, getting sick. And loads more. There are quite a few related to money and gaining or spending thereof.

Remember:

- too little money can make you miserable
- too much money can make you miserable
- too much stuff can make you miserable
- not having enough can make you miserable.

I think what we have to grasp pretty well from Day 1 is that money and happiness are not necessarily the same thing. **Money doesn't buy happiness.** This is a common mistake people make. It isn't going to be one you make. You can be poor and happy. You can be rich and happy. You can also be either poor or rich and miserable.

If you are looking to wealth to make you happy, you'll be disappointed. If you are looking to money to make you powerful/younger/sexier/more vital/more interesting/better looking/whatever, you're going to be disappointed. Sorry but money doesn't do any of that. In your head it might. In other people's heads it might. But it doesn't in reality. You can be all those things with money it is true. It isn't money that does it. The switch is thrown in your head first. Money is a placebo, not a cure.

RULE 14

We've all seen the lottery winners who buy the big house and feel miserable because they've left all their friends behind. Or the tycoons who lose the lot and top themselves because they felt their life was over just because they were skint.

> # MONEY IS A PLACEBO,
> # NOT A CURE

But we won't make any of these mistakes because we shall practise this Rule diligently and understand the relationship between money and happiness. Ah, but I hear you ask, what exactly is this Rule? What do I have to do? Answer: nothing except not expect too much from money and don't buy stuff in the hope it will make you happy – it won't. When they build that brand new Beemer or whatever it is you covet, they don't build in any happiness. So when you first sit in it or buy it and you feel fantastic – and I'm not denying people do feel great buying stuff – that feeling isn't in the thing you buy. That feeling was inside you anyway. All this said, what money can do is buy away a lot of <u>un</u>happiness. It just can't go any further than that.

Know the difference between price and value

I once asked my delightful father-in-law to explain that thing about wine to me. You know, can a bottle that costs £100 in a top restaurant *really* be twenty times as good as a bottle that you can get for a fiver at the local shop?

His answer was interesting. He said that you aren't paying for the wine alone. What you are paying for is the ambience, the service, the location (we're talking Le Gavroche here), the wine waiter's expertise, the good company, the fine tablecloths, the privacy and discretion, the style and class, the tradition, the food and the trust, the humidity and storage, the tone and the surroundings, the fellow dining guests and the great conversation.

The wine is almost an irrelevance and that's the point. We think we know the price of something. But the value can spread out far beyond all of that.

> WE THINK WE KNOW THE PRICE OF SOMETHING. BUT THE VALUE CAN SPREAD OUT FAR BEYOND ALL OF THAT

I have an old Mercedes car (I like Mercs but am far too mean to buy a new one and lose all that depreciation). I didn't pay much for it. You never do, as people are scared of them in case they go wrong, and fair enough they do cost a fortune to put right *but* you need to remember that because they are better made, they rarely do go wrong. I was visited by a friend who was driving a brand new car he'd just bought. A modern Eurobox, a small hatchback thing that looked like a mini spaceship. He looked at my old, battered, mud-streaked Merc and exclaimed, 'Blimey, you must be doing well!' I tried to explain that wasn't the case and that he'd probably paid at least five times for his what I'd paid for mine but he wouldn't have it. He saw the Merc and had decided its value was a lot more than the price – i.e. what was actually paid for it. I learnt that day about price not necessarily equating to perceived value.

Remember too that something is only worth what others are willing to pay for it. A catalogue may say the value of a painting is £500 but that's only true if somebody is willing to pay that amount for it. An important lesson to learn. The price of something can be far less than its actual value, either to you or to somebody else. Or a lot more.

If you are going to be wealthy – and I sincerely hope you are, if you put into play the Rules in this book and work diligently at it – then it's worth studying the difference between price and value.

Know how the wealthy think

There is a simple test to determine whether someone will end up wealthy – or if they already are. All you have to do is watch someone read their favourite newspaper, especially if it's one of the big Sundays:

- Notice which paper they choose.
- Notice which sections they choose to read.
- Notice which sections they discard.
- Notice in which order they read their chosen sections.

This is a test for you too. Have a look at the above and make a mental note of what *you* do. The wealthy – those who have deliberately chosen to be wealthy rather than those who have won the lottery or inherited (God's lottery as I think of it) or married into it – invariably:

- choose the more serious of the papers
- choose the more serious sections
- discard the 'frivolous' sections
- read the money/business sections first.

If you are serious about being wealthy, you will have to learn how the wealthy think. This means studying the 'opposition' – although very shortly you will be a part of them. You need to know the lingo and the language, where they eat and live, how they work and relax, how they invest and save. In short, you need to study money if you are to increase your prosperity. Try to get to talk to wealthy people. Ask questions. Develop a thirst for understanding and knowledge. Read about wealthy people – interviews and autobiographies can be full of insight.

You may also benefit from a few well-chosen business and finance books. I'm not going to recommend any to you as I don't know your reading style – find ones that suit you. Also, why not log on to the FT site or the finance pages of other online papers to keep up with the latest developments in the money market. Get informed.

But what if this all feels a bit too heavy? If, like me, you like the gossip columns as well as financial pages then you, like me, will probably never be extremely, mind-bogglingly over-the-top wealthy. We can still be wealthy – and we might have more fun too. Prosperous and fun – sounds good to me. I think we have to be really passionate about money if we want lots. We have to live and breathe and sleep (yes, bearing in mind Rule 12) money. We have to study hard at the University of Wealth if we want to graduate.

> ## YOU MAY HAVE TO CHOOSE – MONEY OR FRIVOLITY?

Don't envy what others have

We all set our own objectives. We all have individual ambitions. We all work out how much work we are prepared to put into this business of becoming wealthy. We all set our own limits and know what we are prepared to do or not do. So what is the point of envying what anyone else has? Not unless you know what their agenda was and is. Not unless you know how much work they were prepared to put in. Not unless you know what they were prepared to sacrifice.

Of course you can cast an envious glance at the easy three – lottery, inherited, married (or divorced!) into – we all do. But money earned is entirely the business of the person earning it. They did the work. They had the idea or entrepreneurial spirit. They got up earlier than us. They were driven or fired up by what they wanted to achieve. Envying them is pointless; learning from them is invaluable.

> ENVYING THEM IS POINTLESS; LEARNING FROM THEM IS INVALUABLE

And learning from them is the greatest gift they can give us. Ideally you need a money mentor. Someone you look up to who has made a lot of money and in the right way – legally, enjoyably and nicely – who will give you the odd tip, tuck you under their wing, set you on the right path. And refuse to lend you any money of course. Not that you'd ask.

If I come across someone extremely rich, I immediately try to work out how they did it and if that route would suit me. What bits of information could I glean to help me get to that position, bearing in mind I only want to do it right – legally and enjoyably?

I think 90 per cent of getting these Rules right is to approach getting wealthy as sympathetic magic – do as they do and you'll end up as them.

I have my money mentor and I hang on to his every word when it comes to money as he's living on the interest on the interest on his money – and that's the place I'm heading for.

Use other people as a source of inspiration. Besides, envy is not a characteristic of a Rules Player – that's you now, by the way.

It's harder to manage yourself than it is to manage your money

So how well do you know yourself? Pretty well? Not at all? Vaguely? We think we know ourselves until we come to give up smoking, lose weight, get fit, get rich. And then we realise we are lazier, have less willpower, less determination, make less effort, get too easily dissuaded, fall by the wayside too readily.

If I wanted to tuck you under my wing and make you wealthy, the first thing I would need to know is: 'Do you have what it takes to be wealthy? Are you determined enough? Will you work hard enough? Will you stick at it? Do you have backbone? Stamina? Guts? Relentless focus?' You see, if you don't, the chances are you won't succeed. I'm not trying to put you off. I am trying to make you see, that making money is a skill that can be taught – as long as the person is ready and willing to learn and apply themselves diligently.

> THE FIRST THING I WOULD NEED TO KNOW IS: 'DO YOU HAVE WHAT IT TAKES TO BE WEALTHY?'

If you decided you wanted to win Wimbledon you would have needed to start playing tennis when you were about five and have been winning junior championships by the time you were fourteen. It's the same with money. You can't expect an overweight, middle-aged person to suddenly be in the final.

When I was a young struggling student I once sold a valuable book so I could eat. I made a direct choice between owning something that was going to increase in value, and thus potentially make me wealthy, and having a slap-up meal for one. You see what I mean? I, in essence, chose – at that time anyway – to be poor rather than wealthy. I saw the same book recently in a bookshop and, believe me, I made a bad call that day.

And what I have noticed is that the wealthy – when they are starting out anyway – have enormous drive and are prepared to make enormous sacrifices. They manage themselves and forego instant rewards for bigger payback in the longer term. Self-control and delayed gratification are useful arts to learn.

GETTING

WEALTHY

We've entered the dark uncharted waters of Part Two. This is where we get serious. This is where we start the real practical stuff. This is where you have to start taking a good hard look at your situation, doing some planning and taking some action.

Getting wealthy means being very honest with yourself and being willing to invest your time and efforts into the quest for greater prosperity. Many of the Rules are behavioural and changing your behaviour is never easy. Some Rules will seem stunningly simple, but for every Rule you have to ask yourself: 'I may already know this – but do I do it?' The willingness to put in the graft and do something, make things happen, is vital.

You've got to know where you are before you start

Before we can go forward we have to know where we are now. Or rather *you* have to. When Robinson Crusoe swam ashore from his shipwrecked boat, the first thing he did was check out what stores and guns and ammunition he had. Once he knew that, he could assess the situation and move forward.

> WELL, BEFORE WE CAN GO
> FORWARD WE HAVE TO
> KNOW WHERE WE
> ARE NOW

So you are going to swim ashore and begin your new life. The first thing you have to do is to take stock. Find out what you've already got, what can be used, what can be discarded or discounted, what you owe, what you are owed, what basically is your net worth.

We're going to do a full financial audit on you and your life. If you don't know where you are before you start, you can't really work efficiently towards becoming wealthy. It's a wise man who lays out his tools before he begins the job.

All you've got to do is collect all the information – what you owe at the bank (or have in there in your current account, deposit account, savings account), and what you owe on credit cards. Also start working out what you spend on a monthly and annual basis (and where you spend it).

Here's your check list. It may need adapting to suit your individual circumstances.

Start with the big figures to get a picture of where you are right now overall:

Starting balance	+	Item	-	Net worth
		House/mortgage		
		Credit/store cards		
		Bank		
		Savings		
		Pension		
		Loans/overdraft		
		Assets/cars etc.		
		Personal items – jewellery etc.		
		Investments		
		Debts		

Now you have an overall figure, you need to look at your typical inflow and outflow of cash on a monthly or annual basis – you can choose which you assess, but all figures have to be made either monthly or annual.

	Item	–	Balance
(Put your salary here)	Fixed regular expenditure (e.g. insurance, bills, food, memberships)		
	Variable regular expenditure (e.g. shopping, holidays)		
	Totals		

This may not be ideal for your circumstances but I'm sure you get the idea. Don't be tempted to skip this exercise. Even if your financial situation is none too rosy, it's good to face up to reality so you can take positive action to address the situation.

You've got to have a plan

Why are a fool and his money so easily parted? Because the fool doesn't have a plan. If you don't have a plan you'll be tempted to fritter your cash away, spend it instead of investing, or forget the new business idea or career move. If you have a plan you know exactly what does and what doesn't fit into it.

The last Rule helped you work out where you are now, and you already know where you're going (your objective). The plan gives you the important bit – how you are going to get there. Back to the Robinson Crusoe analogy. Once he had been shipwrecked and taken stock he made a plan. 'I'll need a shelter to keep warm, some food, and something to do.' And he set about building a thatched shelter on the beach, which of course got blown over in the first gale and he had to retreat inland to a cave. You see, even the best plans have to be open to adjustment.

> ## THE PLAN GIVES YOU THE IMPORTANT BIT – HOW YOU ARE GOING TO GET THERE

First things first. If you have a job you love and are happy then you'll probably want to stick at it. If it doesn't make you enough money, you need a plan to generate income another way. If your job is making you miserable and what's worse keeping you in a poverty trap then you must prioritise getting out of it in your plan.

Your plan should involve taking financial control of your life. If you have debts, it will definitely include tackling these as a priority, ditto spending excesses. The plan might involve a career change, investigating a business idea, investing money or generating some capital so you can enter the buy-to-let market. It may well include selling things. A lot of money is generated through selling things – whether it's a product, a service or your time and skill. That's why I like writing books – even while I sleep there is a bookshop somewhere that is selling books for me. In fact one of the fundamental truths about gettng rich is that wealth – *real* wealth – comes from doing deals, not from earning wages, salaries or fees.

As General Patton said, 'A good plan today is better than a perfect plan tomorrow'. Whatever the plan includes, just make sure you have one, and that you stick to it. Don't worry, the rest of this book will give you lots of ideas as to what your plan could contain. Just remember: never sit back and wait for somebody to give you money – ever.

Get your finances under control

There's been a huge fuss made recently in the UK about hosepipe bans. If you live elsewhere this may be a complete mystery. It's even a mystery to me to be honest. In the UK there are companies that are allowed to collect water in reservoirs and then sell it to householders. The reservoirs have been low recently due to a lack of rain – apparently. If you live in the UK you'll know that it never stops raining. A lot of the householders are saying that there is a shortage of water because the water utility companies don't repair their pipes and masses of water leaks away. The poor householders are being told they can't water their gardens because there isn't enough water. They say there is enough water and that they are being punished unfairly. See where I'm going with this?

You may well have enough money but it leaks away before you get to spend it. In a whole variety of ways – taxation, paying interest, lack of use (not invested properly), too much being spent on the wrong things. Before you can control your finances you have to stop the leaks.

> BEFORE YOU CAN
> CONTROL YOUR FINANCES
> YOU HAVE TO STOP
> THE LEAKS

RULE 21

If you carried out the exercise in Rule 19 (of course you did) you'll have a record of your credit card balances. Higher than you cared to admit? Probably. We are all encouraged to spend on plastic. We are all seduced into racking up debts monthly. If you want to stop the leaks, cut up all the cards and pay them off.[10]

Do a quick calculation and see what levels of interest you are paying. It's the same with your mortgage. Make sure you're not paying more than you have to through negligence. If your fixed rate deal has come to an end it could be time to check out the best deals that are now available.

Keep a record of everything you spend. *Everything*. Do this for a short while – even just a week – and see where the leakages are. If you are going to be wealthy, first you have to know where your money is going. Sorry if you thought this was going to be easy or this book was going to be full of get-rich-quick schemes. But stick with me, and you'll be glad you did.

When you carry out your financial stock-check, watch out for the hidden things which can easily be overlooked. For instance, direct debits and subscriptions that are too high, wrong or out of date. The rich are eagle-eyed and miss nothing.

[10] And spend what? I hear you ask. Spend what you can afford on what you have to and above that, spend nothing for a while. Make the choice: wealth or spending sprees. You've tried the spending sprees. We all have. Now take the prosperity route and see if it isn't better. You are only postponing spending, not cancelling it forever. You'll also be able to spend more later. Look forward to that as you tighten your belt. Think of the better belt you'll be able to buy.

Only by looking wealthy can you become wealthy

I once watched a man looking at a job vacancy board. He was dressed in scruffy trainers, wore a hood (up), was unshaven and slouched with his hands in his pockets. You just knew he was going to go for job interviews dressed just like that – and fail to get them. And then he'd claim it was unfair, nobody would give him a break, life sucks and so on.

I've held many job interviews and have always been seriously under-impressed with the way people turned up. The lack of effort is always staggering – as is the lack of research and interest. 'Why do you want to work for this company?' 'Dunno.' 'What do we do here?' 'Dunno.'

I'm trying not to be an old reactionary here. But I can't fail to notice that the lack of effort is directly related to the lack of results. The poor look poor. Not because they have to. They wear a uniform that marks them out. If they change that uniform they change their circumstances because people will react differently to them. We aren't too far removed from the great apes and they relate to each other based a lot on how they move and look. Those who look weak and needy are treated as such. The powerful will strut and look confident. What I am suggesting is that you need to look powerful and confident. We should all look powerful and confident.

> ## YOU NEED TO LOOK POWERFUL AND CONFIDENT

Ah, but how can we afford to dress as if we are more wealthy? Come on, come on. I expected better of you. Think laterally. The great apes do it with no clothes at all. It's about the way you walk rather than what you wear. It's about the overall image you project.

But this doesn't mean you can get away with dressing inappropriately or badly – anyone can dress smartly. Borrow a decent outfit or buy a good suit cheaply (no, no, don't buy full price and just put it on your credit card!). For the interview for my first casino job, I bought a fabulous jacket from a charity job – double breasted, wide satin lapels – and proper bow tie you had to tie yourself (none of those rubbish ones on elastic for me). I practised for hours until I got it right and turned up for the first night looking more James Bond than trainee. I made a dramatic impression. Obviously I had got it wrong and had to go and buy a simple black suit from the high street afterwards, but I was remembered as somehow standing out, stylish, not scruffy. And I got offered the plum trainee job despite not being in any way qualified for it. This stuff works you know. Dress wealthy and people will assume you are and treat you accordingly. Learn style, class, how the wealthy dress. Look poor and you'll get poor service. And whatever you do, no bling. Yes, rich rap stars can get away with it but you can't. Nor can I. Restrained elegance is what we shall aim for. Old money. Quality. Simple lines. Good haircut. Clean nails. You know the sort of stuff I mean.

Speculate to accumulate (no, this isn't gambling)

We all know the actor who achieves overnight fame after one starring role and everyone says how lucky they must have been. Luck? They starred in every school production. Studied at drama school for three years. Worked their socks off in some dreadful soap. Slaved on the stage for the whole run of *Mind Your Manners* by Agatha Christie. Played an extra in *Extras*. Did panto every Christmas – playing the pumpkin of course. And finally landed their plum job, their starring role, in some deservedly successful film. And everyone says, 'How lucky you are!'

Getting wealthy is a bit like that. You toil away for years and suddenly you are lucky. You scrimp and save and sacrifice and gosh, how wonderful to be touched by fate's fickle finger!

> ## YOU TOIL AWAY FOR YEARS AND SUDDENLY YOU ARE LUCKY

Well, the truth is that you have to speculate to accumulate. You have to be in it to win it. If you don't bet, you don't get. No, no, no. I am not suggesting gambling in any sense. If you invest on the Stock Exchange, after wisely taking advice and studying the companies and their performance, this is the safest form of gambling. If you stake it all on red, this is high risk gambling. If you work your socks off for 20 years and finally it pays off, this is not gambling.

Speculate has in fact four meanings – to discuss, to think deeply, to invest and to believe in something not entirely clear. I think that about sums up our pathway to prosperity.

- **Discuss** – talk to all and sundry about wealth and see what others think and do. Study them closely.
- **Think deeply** – understand your subject.
- **Invest** – speculate with your time and effort and life.
- **Believe in something not entirely certain** – there are no guarantees, but you should be able to shorten the odds considerably if you follow the rules others have forged for you.

I know you might have thought I mean you to speculate with your hard-earned cash. I don't. I mean you to speculate with your time and effort, forethought and planning, energy and dedication. The more you put in, the more you'll get out.

On the other hand you could go and blow it all on red. Only joking.

Decide your attitude to risk

Am I going to suggest that money can only be hard won by perilous investments and chancy ventures? No, I'm not. In that case, am I suggesting caution and that you should carefully hang on to every penny? No, I'm not advocating that either.

What I am suggesting is that it's entirely up to you what level of risk you feel happy with – it's no good me telling you what that level should be. You have to decide your own attitude to and appetite for risk. Personally I love the *idea* of sailing close to the wind financially. However, my attitude is definitely verging on the cautious side so I don't take the risk. I find the risky schemes where you could blow the lot or make a fortune hold some appeal but I don't indulge my whims. I have young children and they come first.

> IT'S ENTIRELY UP TO YOU
> WHAT LEVEL OF RISK YOU
> FEEL HAPPY WITH

Once you have decided your attitude to risk it makes your planning easier. It allows you to tailor how you intend becoming prosperous. Hare or tortoise I guess.

Obviously your attitude will vary depending on the project. Things to take into consideration are:

- **Your age** – we cope better with risk the younger we are.
- **Family commitments** – if, like me, you have young children it does make you more cautious. If they've all left home, you might be prepared to push it a bit further.
- **Income and/or assets** – you need to work out the percentage of your wealth you are prepared to risk. The more you've got, the smaller the risk might be – unless you are prepared to risk the lot of course.

If you are going to take risks, then do try to offset them. Take out insurance if you like:

- Don't put all your eggs in one basket (more about this later).
- Consider how much stress and excitement you can handle.
- Look at the timing – long term against quick returns.
- Think about how much you can afford to risk. Worst-case scenario stuff.
- How much information have you? Too little increases risk.

The other thing to ponder is how you respond to the risks of life. Life in itself is risky and nothing is certain. How do you cope when things go wrong? Are you positive, dynamic, enthusiastic and up? Or do you get all gloomy and depressed and feel the glass is half empty? Know yourself and know how you cope and how you respond to changes. And remember that risk doesn't mean bad. It means you don't know how it will all turn out.

RULE 25

If you don't trust someone, don't do business with them

It's such a simple rule: we don't do business with people we don't trust. What more is there to say? Apart from that this also includes companies, corporations, governments, you name it. And why don't we trust them? Because there is something adrift, something that rings that little warning bell inside us. There may be clear visible signs but as often as not there won't be. Mostly this rule is about using your intuition, listening to your inner voice.

If you feel something, anything, is wrong, then walk away. Listen to what is being said to you. There are unconscious clues your subconscious is picking up. If you ignore them you'll invariably regret it. I've done it. We've all done it. I nearly did it again the other day. I nearly bought a car from a dodgy dealer. I knew he was dodgy but I wanted the car. I knew the car would be dodgy. What is it that makes us overwrite all the warning signs? I did the only sensible thing – I phoned a friend. And he talked me out of it. Good man.

You can extend this rule to cover loads of situations such as 'If you don't trust your boss, don't work for them.' 'If you don't trust your childminder, don't leave your kids with them.' 'If you don't feel comfortable with your financial adviser, get another.'

Look, you can choose what you do and how you do it but if you want to be a Rules Player then you need to be assertive, stand up for what you know is right, don't accept second best – ever. Listen to your intuition, be the biggest, boldest and bravest. If the situation feels wrong, it probably is. If you don't get the right feelings about a person you are dealing with, find a way out.

If it waddles like a duck and quacks like a duck, chances are it's a duck. Avoid. Walk away. Hold on to your wallet and run.

> ## LISTEN TO YOUR INTUITION, BE THE BIGGEST, BOLDEST AND BRAVEST

It's never too late to start getting wealthy

It's very easy sometimes to believe that the hand we got dealt in life is all we have to play with. Or to say, 'Ah well, I should have started a pension in my early twenties – it's too late now.' But we can change anything we want – it's never too late to start being wealthy.

Look at Rule 1 again – anyone can make money. And it's not limited by your age or any other time factor. All it requires is that you shift your focus to becoming wealthy and already things will happen without you having to do anything more. Obviously if you want more than the basic that the universe is going to give you, you will have to do more. But by shifting your focus you will set wheels in motion and prosperity will come to you. And no, this isn't mumbo jumbo. It's a universal fact. The fact you do something – shift your focus – is enough.

No matter how long you have been going along a particular path – poverty, lack of success, whatever – it doesn't need much of a shift to alter course. And altering course can happen no matter how long you've left it. There is no such thing as too late. It's a bit like being an ocean-going liner. You may need a lot of space to stop but it doesn't take much to get you to change direction. A couple of degrees on the wheel and you'll be on a completely different course within a few miles.

In gaining prosperity, as in most things, there is a tipping point. Once you've added on those couple of degrees to port or starboard the resulting change in trajectory gets bigger and bigger in a sort of compound way.

late to start investing – in stocks, in shares, in
yle, in quality, in yourself, in life. By staying alert
resist that decline into inactivity and apathy which is
eing attitude. My father-in-law (always such an inspiration) rted another business when he was seventy-five, and not
just any old business either – it was in a new technology which
most fifty-year-olds were having trouble getting their head round.

> # IT IS ALSO NEVER TOO LATE TO START INVESTING – IN SHARES, IN A PENSION, IN STYLE, IN QUALITY, IN YOURSELF, IN LIFE

However, if you think it is too late, it probably is. The secret is
never to think that. If you think that you can give up easily then
you probably will. Don't think it. Look, we came into this book
together to make money – some for you and some for me. I'm
going to do my bit, my damnedest, to help you increase your
prosperity. If you think there are any barriers – age, sex, race,
ability – then you are already batting on a losing wicket. Dump
the preconceptions and trust me. It is never too late to begin.
Start now.

Start saving young (or teach your kids this one if it's too late for you)

OK, it might be too late for you to start saving young. We can't go back. But you can certainly teach your kids the importance of learning this trick. And I'm not suggesting we scrimp and save to be able to save. Saving should be something we naturally do. I guess it's a trick you learn quickly if you are self-employed – or not, if you go bust. Every time you earn money you put some aside for VAT and tax. Failure to do so means scrabbling around when the return is due and you have to find it. If you put aside more than you need, the leftovers become the savings. Obviously you only fail to do this once or twice before it

> IF YOU PUT ASIDE MORE
> THAN YOU NEED, THE
> LEFTOVERS BECOME
> THE SAVINGS

becomes a really easy thing to remember to do.

I find that it is easier to have a 'figure' so you don't have to think too much. My own figure is 50 per cent. Anything I earn, I put half straight into a savings account. I don't have to think about this. I know that some is for tax and some is for VAT and the rest is for savings. Every now and again I transfer the balance of what's left to a second savings account – a sort of super savings account. From the super savings account I can transfer money to a pension fund, ISA (Individual Savings Account) or whatever.

This, for me, is an easy way to save. I don't have to think too much about it. It is a method I pass on to my children – spend half your pocket money and save half. I hope they'll find this an easy method to pick up, a sort of savings muscle memory, so that they will have a quid or two when they need it at university or whatever.

I really wish I had (a) started saving young and (b) been taught to do so. Lots of really prosperous people have said that they had wealth management drummed into them from a very early age. It seems to be an essential part of prosperity gaining.

I am fascinated to watch my own children learning about money. There does seem to be a genetic predisposition for spending or saving. We treat all of them identically when it comes to money but one child finds it easy to save; another is a fanatic spender and couldn't save anything to save himself; and one is oblivious to money either way.

I'm a great believer in making changes to correct basic flaws in one's upbringing. It's no good sitting around blaming others, you have to change it. I have to take responsibility and train myself. Obviously this doesn't apply to being tidy.

Understand that your financial needs change at different stages of your life

Some cultures allow for a different focus, a different strategy, during different stages of your life. For instance, up to 20 might be for being young and foolish and getting an education. Age 20 to 35 could be for getting married and raising a family. Age 35 to 55 might be for running your business and making your fortune. Life after that is for spiritual contemplation and retirement from the commercial world.

> A DIFFERENT FOCUS, A DIFFERENT STRATEGY, DURING DIFFERENT STAGES OF YOUR LIFE

Essentially, your financial needs change over time, reflecting what is going on in your life at any stage, and the choices you make in your lifestyle at that time. You might need more money when raising a family, but maybe this is a time when you can usually cope better with a little adversity.

RULE 28

By the time your kids are at university you definitely need loads more cash or the poor darlings won't have enough to squander in the student union bar in the evenings, every evening. And once you hit retirement you can downsize again – unless you intend spending it all on expensive world cruises.

This rule is about checking where you are and what you need. And about knowing that the conditions which influence your needs do and will change. You have to make allowances for differing circumstances.

A bit of forward planning with this in mind will stand you in good stead. For example, if you're about to invest all your spare cash in a long-term investment scheme, remember that if you suddenly need a bit more money as you've taken maternity leave or you want to go on a world trip in a career break, your money will be tied up. Think it through and anticipate possible future needs and changes.

So, quick exercise. Where are you in your life? How much do you need? What is the next stage for you? How much are you going to need?

You have to work hard to get rich enough not to have to work hard

I cannot emphasise how strongly I feel about this one. I watch and learn from the seriously wealthy and have reached the conclusion that in nearly every single case they slogged their guts out to get where they are. They often started early. They worked late into the night. They sacrificed a lot. They didn't take long lunch breaks, they didn't waste time. They didn't watch television in the evenings. They worked their socks off. They know money doesn't grow on trees.

> ## THEY DIDN'T WATCH TELEVISION IN THE EVENINGS. THEY WORKED THEIR SOCKS OFF

If you too are serious about getting rich, then you too must do as they do. You are going to have to put in the hard work to get rich enough so that you don't have to work hard. But you must do the work first.

So how dedicated are you? How serious are you? This is the point where we sort the wheat from the chaff, the men from the boys, the girls from the women, the runners-up from the winners.

Still here? Good. You are obviously committed. If you are prepared to put in the long hours and you put them in on the right things, you should succeed. Maybe not immediately. Maybe not with your first idea. But by slogging away you will get there. How do I know this? Because I have done it. I'm not preaching from the wilderness (I hope I'm not preaching at all). I started out poor, and worked long and hard and chose where to put my efforts carefully. And now I'm rich. It really is that simple. On the surface it looks like luck. But that's because I make it look so. In *The Rules of Work* I wrote about looking cool, looking laid back, looking effortless. I practise that a lot. I often go back to work very late at night after everyone else has gone to bed – or get up very early in the morning. Don't tell anyone because I like the indolent image where everyone assumes I am a work-shy, lotus-eating, decadent loafer. But the reality is I graft. You have to.

I'll let you into the secret of the wealthy club – you need to work like you've never worked before. Work like there is no one watching. Work like you don't have a boss. Work like your life depended on it. The second secret is, you have to enjoy it. If it's a chore then you won't do it.

Let me make one very important point here. This Rule does NOT mean that if you work hard at *anything* you will become wealthy. An office cleaner on minimum wage will not become rich by working all hours as an office cleaner or by cleaning really hard and thoroughly. They might, however, become rich by starting their own cleaning company and working very hard at getting it off the ground and finding new clients and making sure their staff were great, happy and motivated.

What I'm saying here is that even if you've got a great business idea or have some money to invest in shares, you will only maximise your return if you work really hard at your idea or investing the money wisely and managing it carefully. You have to put the effort in before you can reap the dividends.

Learn the art of deal making

Deals are great. Deals make you money. Simple deal making skills will serve you time and time again. You need to learn to be bold, to ask for more, to trade what you have for what you want.

Here is an example of successful deal making in action. Kyle MacDonald from Montreal, Canada, traded his way from one single red paperclip to a house in the space of nine months. You can read more at http://oneredpaperclip.blogspot.com/, but essentially this is how he did it:

- He launched his website offering to swap his one red paper clip for anything.
- He swapped it for a green pen in the shape of a fish.
- He swapped this for a smiley face doorknob.
- He swapped this for a portable barbeque.
- He swapped this for a portable generator.
- He swapped this for an instant party pack and keg of beer.
- He swapped this for a snowmobile.
- He swapped this for a trip to British Columbia.
- He swapped this for a truck.
- He swapped this for a recording contract.
- And finally he swapped this for a house in Phoenix, Colorado – admittedly only a year's lease but hey . . .

Eleven steps. Eleven little deals. Not bad. He says he is going to keep going until he owns a house. That's deal making.

RULE 30

So, lessons to be learnt from Kyle:

- Never say you haven't got anything to start with.
- Always be open to opportunities.
- Be adaptable and flexible.
- Have a goal.
- Work diligently.
- Network like mad.
- Take advantage of free publicity.

In my business I prefer to talk about 'mutually profitable partnerships'. These deals, where both parties benefit, are the best deals of all. Everybody feels happy with the outcome.

> # WHAT DO YOU HAVE THAT
> # OTHERS MIGHT WANT?

What do you have that others might want? Think broadly here – not just possessions like Kyle, but also your skills and your knowledge. Your time and your ability and efforts. Who might want these and what might you be able to ask for in return?

Learn the art of negotiating

If you are going to deal and trade and swap, you have to learn the art of negotiating. Basically the art revolves around making the other person feel they are getting as much as you are.

I like to talk about partnerships. This is my way of making this happen. I'm genuinely not out to scupper anyone else's plans of getting rich. I don't need them to fail in order to make me succeed. I figure we can all go forward together and no one has to lose out. If I want someone to buy something from me I expect them to be able to make a profit on it and do well out of it. I don't want to sell and run. I want repeat business. I want a decent reputation. I want to feel good about what I do. I want a partnership.

> I DON'T WANT TO SELL AND RUN. I WANT REPEAT BUSINESS. I WANT A DECENT REPUTATION

The art of negotiating will stand you in good stead in so many different situations – from negotiating a simple pay rise to negotiating in your relationship with your partner to negotiating with your kids over pocket money. If you learn this art, everything slips along easily and smoothly and you get what you want – and they get what they want too. Win/win.

There are a number of rules about negotiating you need to bear in mind:

- Always know your bottom line – the point beyond which you will not go.
- Always know what it is you want – the goal, the end product, the target. There's no use negotiating if you don't know what you are negotiating for.
- Always aim for win/win.
- Always bear in mind that negotiating isn't just about stuff – it has powerful emotional ramifications as well.
- Know the importance of each point – some you can let go of, some you can't.
- Always be prepared to give up things to secure other things – be flexible and fluid.
- Always know as much as possible before you start – knowledge is power in these situations.
- Understand what they aren't saying as much as what they are – watch their body language and facial expressions.
- Stay cool and patient.
- Negotiate successfully for everything you want at the beginning – you can't negotiate afterwards, no one will go back over a contract you've signed when you realise you don't like it.
- Find out exactly what they want (what they'll trade or concede), and get all their shopping list before you start negotiating. Hide yours.
- Don't make concessions, trade them.
- Create more variables – discounts, delivery, payments, stages etc.
- Go for the best deal you can possibly justify. Coming down later is easy; going up later is almost impossible.

I am always stunned and horrified by how often people go into situations – anything from a job to a relationship – without first finding out what they are embarking on, what is expected of them, what they are going to get out of it, what they expect their partner (boss, business buddy, lover, offspring, whoever) to get out of it and where they expect to end up. You've got to discuss these things – and that really is the basic art, discussion. Bring things out into the open so there are no assumptions. Assumptions are bad.

Small economies won't make you wealthy but they will make you miserable

Is it penny wise, pound foolish? I don't think so. I think that trying to make small economies in order to become prosperous is doomed to failure. It won't make you rich but it will make you miserable. And being miserable isn't a good place to start out each day. You need a decent breakfast and a positive attitude. Cutting out your daily cappuccino might help you lose weight, and it might reduce your caffeine intake, but it isn't going to make you rich and it might well make you feel miserable.

> ## CUTTING OUT YOUR DAILY CAPPUCCINO ISN'T GOING TO MAKE YOU RICH

So what about all that penny-pinching stuff? It seems to have been invented by the puritans – if you enjoy it, it has to be wrong. Some people get satisfaction out of being frugal, but if that isn't you, then don't deny yourself small pleasures in the belief that that's the way to wealth.

RULE 32

Hang on though. Didn't I say in an earlier Rule that the rich are eagle-eyed and that you had to stop money leaks? Indeed. But that's different. While getting your finances in order is a good thing, going without isn't. Make sure you aren't giving money away by being careless (those are the leaks) but don't deny yourself the very small pleasures that enrich your life – just don't go mad. If you can't afford what you want, buy less, but buy quality. Save up by all means for those big purchases or ask if you really need them, but don't start thinking that giving up little luxuries, little treats, little life enhancers, will somehow increase your wealth. It won't. It will keep you trapped in the poverty cycle. Escaping from the poverty cycle and the penury mindset is your key to success, your path to prosperity.

Wealthy people don't scrimp and save. Sure some of them are quite tight fisted and you'd have to crowbar their wallets off them. But while they watch their money carefully, they don't cut the odd coffee or buy cheap jam in the hope it will make them more wealthy. It obviously won't.

Like being on a diet, if you deny yourself every small pleasure, you'll probably fail. Little indulgences are the way forward. Now who else is going to tell you that?

Understand that working for others won't necessarily make you rich – but it might

Most of us assume that we'll never make it to greater prosperity while we are working for someone else; that only by being entrepreneurial will we become wealthy. And for a lot of us this may well be true – there is a limit as to how much you can earn per hour in return for your labour. However, there are some who do make it good this way.

We shouldn't overlook the fact that being employed may be the best route for us and that we don't have to run our own business. There are whole categories of employees that are doing quite nicely thank you – for example, a friend of mine works in corporate insurance and he's extremely wealthy thanks to large commission payments. He says he wouldn't be any better off working for himself.

Many people working in the computer business opted to become contractors because they assumed they would earn a lot more. Some did, but at the cost of stability. When the contracts dried up some were worse off than when employed. But for some this was indeed the best way to go and they have made handsome sums by becoming self-employed.

I guess you have to keep an open mind about this one and not be driven by assumptions. You can make yourself pretty unhappy by forcing yourself into self-employment if this isn't the right way for you. Perhaps the stability of employment is a greater priority and you should stick with it and not feel compelled to start your own business.

> ## PERHAPS THE STABILITY OF EMPLOYMENT IS A GREATER PRIORITY AND YOU SHOULD STICK WITH IT

The converse is true as well: understand that working for yourself might make you rich, but it might not. Nearly two-thirds of business start-ups end in failure within three years. Look around you and you will see many examples of the small business owner struggling desperately. There's no certainty there. Working for yourself generally has higher earning potential, but not in every case. You have to look into it very closely – right business, right demand for your services, right time, enough effort and so on.

There isn't the space or time here to go into all the pros and cons of working for yourself. Except to say it's one hell of a lot easier and much more fun working hard for yourself than for someone else. But what we are aiming for isn't freedom from employment but prosperity. Hence we have to be open to whichever means will hasten our achievement of that goal. Employment or going it alone? It entirely depends on which one will get us rich easiest, fastest, slickest. And your day job doesn't have to be your route to wealth at all . . .

The secret is not to close your mind to any opportunity to get rich. And staying employed doesn't mean not having a little eBay business on the side or a buy-to-let property to create a new income stream.

Don't waste time procrastinating – make money decisions quickly

If you are out at sea and it cuts up rough, you make for a safe harbour. Any port in a storm. You don't spend time procrastinating over whether the harbour has shower facilities or a branch of your favourite restaurant chain or cheaper moorings. No, you just get the hell out of the storm, while there's still space in the harbour, and be grateful it provides the one thing you really need – safety.

Making money is a bit like that. Sometimes you just need to act. As long as you get some return on your action, it's better than doing nothing. This isn't complicated but you'd be amazed how many people overlook this and think 'I'll decide how to invest that little lump sum I've saved up later – I can't decide whether to buy shares or put it in a savings account.' So they do nothing and the money sits in a current account earning no interest or, worse still, gets frittered away by default and inflation.

You don't have to think too deeply about this stuff. You don't have to think too hard. You don't even have to really think at all.

The samurai lived by a simple creed – no hesitation, no doubt, no surprise, no fear. It is simply the most brilliant strategy for doing anything. It basically says that once you have decided on a course of action (or battle or combat) then be committed; know everything you need to know about it, don't be afraid and get on with it as quickly as possible. If you've ever seen a samurai sword fight you'll notice they circle each other and then there is a dramatic burst of activity, a flurry of intense violence and it's all over. One or other or frequently both opponents are dead. The circling is not preparation – that was done over years and years of training. The circling is sussing out your opponent – taking their mind. When they go into attack it is a direct, swift, no hesitation attack. And your financial plans must have the same razor-sharp incisiveness about them.

> ## THE SAMURAI LIVED BY A SIMPLE CREED – NO HESITATION, NO DOUBT, NO SURPRISE, NO FEAR

Doing something is invariably better than doing nothing. And sometimes acting fast can be a lot better than holding out on a possibility. Suppose you buy and sell antiques and collectables as a money-spinning hobby. If you buy a plate for £10 and think you can sell it for £30, but somebody offers you £20 within an hour, then you take the £20 and go and buy two more plates at £10 to sell on in the same way. In some industries it's called 'churn' – keep things moving. Quickly weigh up the odds, consider the pros and cons and then get on with it.

Work as if you didn't need the money

Most of us work because we *do* need the money. But some of us let it show and some of us don't. If somebody looks as though they don't need the money, it's for one of two reasons. Either (a) they put on a good act or (b) they genuinely enjoy their work and do it because they love it – they would do it even if they didn't need the money.

Clearly (b) is a fantastic place to be and one we should all strive to get to. But even if that's not the case for you yet, there's a very good reason to act as if you would work irrespective of the financial return. If people think (or indeed know) that you need the money, it gives them power over you and that puts you in a vulnerable position; it makes you insecure. If you work as if you don't need the money, they have no power and you have it instead.

> IF PEOPLE THINK THAT YOU NEED THE MONEY IT GIVES THEM POWER OVER YOU AND THAT MAKES YOU INSECURE

RULE 35

Many years ago I worked in a job I hated and I was unhappy. Later on I started a business that my heart wasn't really in and it failed. But I have always written. Am I a writer? Not really. I don't write highbrow fiction. I wish I could but I know my limitations and stick to writing about what I see other people doing. But writing is something I have always done – whether I get paid for it or not. Whether it gets published or not. And that's my secret; I do it because I passionately care about it. It is my heart and soul and belief and drive and ambition. It is so much a part of me that no one can touch it or have power over it or take it away. Do you know how happy that makes me? Do you know how rich that is making me?[11] Do you know how much power that gives me?

So what's your secret? What makes your heart turn cartwheels? Where does your dream lie? You've got to be driven. Being prosperous has no room for 'I don't know' or 'I'm not sure'. You've got to know, you've got to be sure. Why? Because that is what wealthy people do. They know where they are going and what they are going to do when they get there. They have passion and drive and ambition and determination. They work because they want to.

Ah, but I hear you say, the passion and determination is something they are born with; it's in their personality. Perhaps it is. But it's also something you can emulate, copy, mirror. Do like them to become like them. Work as if you didn't need the money. Aim for the point where you don't do anything unless your heart is in it.[12]

---

[11] And for once I don't mean financially happy, although that too is part of it in a big way.

[12] Obviously, even if you are following your dream, there will be moments, days, when you've had enough and you're sick of everything . . . We're talking about what you overall enjoy, on the whole find pleasurable, mostly glory in.

RULE 36

Spend less than you earn

I'm amazed how many people flout this simple but most golden of all golden rules. You have to live within your means. Control your spending. Allow yourself to create a little bit of savings, with which to generate more income. (Remember the rabbit farm? You can't breed more rabbits if you sell them all.)

This Rule doesn't contradict Rule 32 about small economies not making you rich, by the way. You should live within your means but live well enough to be happy. If you don't earn enough to have champagne every week, then have it only once a month. But do have it if it makes you happy.

This is about being informed and in control. You need to know what your income is and what your outgoings are. We'll talk later about how to curb spending and make savings and how to cut up your credit cards if they've let you down – they do that sometimes, evil little things.

You also need to know:

- any expenditure that is likely to come up
- any provision you've made for contingency plans
- any future income you may be entitled to in the way of interest or investments coming to fruition.

And that really is about it. Where people go wrong is *not* whether they earn enough or spend too much – both of those are fairly easy to overcome. No, the biggest mistake is not knowing what you are doing, where you are financially and what is up ahead.

> # THE BIGGEST MISTAKE IS NOT KNOWING WHAT YOU ARE DOING, WHERE YOU ARE FINANCIALLY AND WHAT IS UP AHEAD

I know it can be tough to live within your means but if you are constantly in debt, all the prosperity that is rightfully yours is going to some faceless bank. I bet they're enjoying spending it. I bet they're having champagne more than once a week. Why encourage them?

I want you to know to the very week, the very hour, what you earn. And I want you to monitor what you spend, what it costs you to live – where you waste money, where you save money and where you spend money wisely. As long as more is coming in than is going out, you're getting the basics right. If more is going out than coming in, you need to take swift and effective action to redress the situation.

Don't borrow money – unless you really, really have to

It's so important that I will repeat it: don't borrow money unless you really, really have to. And even then don't. Not unless you are borrowing off someone who is lending it interest free, no strings, not secured against your house, no potential for messing up friendships – and that sounds like cloud cuckoo land. Ha, there is no such thing as free money (or a free lunch).[13]

If someone lends it, they'll want it back – plus. And that plus is what kills most of us, stops us from becoming prosperous. It has to be nipped in the bud. And if it's too late for that, then it needs to be severely pruned. We have to get rid of that plus.

> ## IF SOMEONE LENDS IT,
> ## THEY'LL WANT IT BACK – PLUS

The plus is usually financial (i.e. interest on the loan) and this is what usually cripples people. However, the plus can be emotional also – if you borrow from friends and family it can cause all kinds of other complications – it's never ever simple.

Pay off your loans and debts before you do anything else. It's the only way to get rid of the plus. I know, I know, lots of people borrow money to start their own business and then go on to

---

[13] There is such a thing actually – check out http://myweb.tiscali.co.uk/freelunch/.

make millions and what am I talking about– we all have to borrow, don't we? Do we? I have a friend who started his own business with three friends. They all put in £500 and ran the business for 15 years. Then they sold it for £43 million. Yep, and not a penny borrowed. The upshot was they had to share with no one – and at times like this you don't want to share, no matter what your parents said about how we all should learn to share.

I have another friend who borrowed heavily to launch his business, which he successfully sold for £8 million. But nearly every penny of that went into loan repayments and interest. He was left with very little and, having not learnt his lesson, proceeded to start another business with capital raised by money loaned from the City. But he says he has learnt a lot because this time he's only borrowed £3 million. Ho ho.

When you are starting a business, advisers often say it's OK to borrow off people you know because they are willing to support you etc. But the novelist Jilly Cooper says she is wary of lending money to friends as it is terribly difficult to see someone at Christmas and give them a hug knowing they owe you £10,000. Personally I would find it hard to hug someone who owed me a lot less than that!

Try not to borrow from:

- your parents
- your children
- other people's children
- friends
- lovers
- passing strangers
- loan sharks
- the City
- the banks
- the credit card companies
- offshore investment bankers of any sort
- me.

Consider consolidating debts

Obviously the best advice is don't get into debt in the first place. If it's a bit late for that nugget of wisdom then you need to pay as little interest as you can while you are paying off your debts (which clearly you will be doing as quickly as possible). Consolidating debts is one way of doing this that might be right for you. What I am talking about here is stopping using three or four credit cards plus an overdraft plus a bank loan plus other borrowings. It is possible to consolidate all of them into one loan, tear up the cards (as if – you need industrial strength scissors, and here speaks a man who has cut up many a credit card) and pay off the overdraft. And yes I do understand the ease and usefulness of a credit card but don't forget that good old stand-by – cash.

A word of warning, however, if you do consolidate your debts make sure you aren't turning short-term debts into long-term debts. The idea is strictly to pay off debt quickly

> ## DON'T FORGET THAT GOOD
> ## OLD STAND-BY – CASH

If you do decide to consolidate your debts, here are some useful tips:

- I have a friend who wrote to all his creditors and offered them an immediate payment of 50 per cent if they would write the debt off – this included all his credit card people. Surprisingly every single one of them said yes and he took out a bank loan and paid them all off without having to declare himself bankrupt. He thus consolidated his debts and reduced them by half. Brilliant.

- Never ever respond to any adverts from companies offering to consolidate your debts for you – those ads are for people with more money than sense.

- Shop around for any pay-off loans – don't accept your bank's just because it is your bank, they may not be the cheapest by a long way.

- Don't secure anything against your home, ever, under any circumstances. If you do, you could lose your home if you don't keep up repayments. Is anything worth this risk? I don't think so.

- Check the small print regarding early settlements and make sure you aren't going to be penalised if you settle early.

- Only ever take out one loan to consolidate and only do this once – learn your lesson and move on.

- Pay off as quickly as you can afford – the longer the term, the more you'll have to pay in interest.

- If you must borrow, borrow against an asset you can resell (machine tool, delivery van) and try not to borrow more than the resale value.

- Buying on credit is a bit different. When Jack Cohen started Tesco he negotiated the rent for his shop to be paid 3 months in arrear, he paid for his stock 3 months in arrear, and started taking money over the counter on day 1. By day 90 he'd taken a lot more than he owed.

Cultivate a skill and it'll repay you over and over again

There's a saying that he who pays the piper calls the tune. And that's true. But the piper can decide how much he will charge for playing that tune if what he plays is:

- in demand
- rare
- particularly difficult (or in some way unique) to play.

Get yourself a decent instrument, a decent set of tunes, an unusual or quirky PR approach, a USP,[14] create a name for yourself and the world will beat a path to your door. And pay you handsomely.

Once you can do something no one else can do – or as few people as is possible – you can pretty well name your price. And believe me it doesn't have to be a particularly difficult skill, just one that somebody else wants and will pay for. Remember the guy who polishes the very best cars at a premium price? (*See Rule 7.*)

You could train to be a brain surgeon[15] but it takes over ten years and aptitude and dedication and steady hands. So putting that aside, think about what you've got to offer. What are your skills, your talents, your strengths and weaknesses? Who needs those skills? How could you put them to best use? How do you tell the people who need these skills that you have them? What skill might you be able to master in order to meet a need that's out there waiting to be met?

---

[14] Unique Selling Proposition.
[15] Neurosurgeon as they are properly titled.

> ## ONCE YOU CAN DO SOMETHING NO ONE ELSE CAN DO – OR AS FEW PEOPLE AS IS POSSIBLE – YOU CAN PRETTY WELL NAME YOUR PRICE

For this exercise you are not allowed to say:

- don't know
- not sure
- nothing really
- not a lot
- what do you mean? Talent? Skills? Me?

Come on, we all have something we can do or could do that is special to us, that we feel we could make a fortune from if only someone would give us a break[16]. We all have a dream we could follow, a plan we dare carry out. Perhaps all we need is a shove, a push in the right direction, a wake-up call to get up off our backside and actually do something. Well, this is it. WAKE UP. GET ON WITH IT.

---

[16] No one gives you a break – you create breaks, you go out there and wrestle breaks to the ground and beat them into submission, you lure them out of their caves with sweets on a stick, you track them down and hunt them with an opportunity gun, you stay in their face until they give in – but no one gives them away.

Pay off your loans and debts as a priority

Do you clear your credit card balance every month? If you do, and you don't have any other outstanding loans/debts then well done you. You're not wasting money paying interest and you're already in a strong position to go forward. Skip the rest of this Rule and carry on.

If you *do* have a credit card balance (or five), an overdraft and/or other loans or debts[17], then you certainly aren't alone. It's so easy to get credit these days, and we live in a 'have it now, pay later' society. Trouble is, debt bogs us down and holds us back. We're simply throwing money away paying off the interest (you borrow, say, £20,000 and can end up paying several thousand pounds extra back in interest – the actual amount you end up paying depends on how long you borrow for, as well as the interest rate you're being charged). Debt is a millstone round the neck – it makes you feel bad, it's always there nagging away at the back of your mind and it can easily become a major problem that affects your health as well as your wealth.

> ## DEBT BOGS US DOWN AND HOLDS US BACK

---

[17] We don't include mortgages in this category by the way – although strictly speaking it is a loan, it's an investment (we hope) and therefore is a special case.

There's no doubt about it. The very first thing you need to do on your wealth quest is to get loans/debts paid off as soon as possible and do nothing else until that's done. There's no point at all starting to put money into a savings account, earning say 5 per cent interest, if you are at the same time paying 10 per cent interest on money you owe to the bank or somebody else. It doesn't make any sense. The simple truth is that those who borrow almost always pay a higher rate of interest than the rate received by those who save.

I acknowledge that you may in fact have found a special situation where you can borrow money at a very low rate of interest and believe you can invest that money for a bigger return, but I say be very, very, very careful indeed. You are playing with fire here and unless the investment is absolutely risk free (which I doubt), pay the debt/loan off as fast as you possibly can.

I should stress here that there are a few possible special exemptions to this Rule; for example, if you've borrowed to invest in, say, a business and you really know what you're doing. We're really talking mainly about personal debt in this Rule.

I'm not playing down how difficult it is to become debt free, but it has to be done. Make a plan as to how you're going to get rid of your debt – start by paying off the highest interest debt first if you've more than one. Motivation is vital as this is short-term pain for long-term gain.

And of course once you finally make it to debt free, you're never going there again, are you? (*See Rule 36*.) Of course you aren't. You're a Rules Player now.

Don't be too busy earning a living to make some money

It's easily done. You needed a job because we all do, in order to live. Then you get into working for a living and it takes up such a huge amount of your time and energies that there's none left over to spend thinking about what you could be doing differently, extra or smarter in order to make more money. How many of us are guilty of letting our financial affairs slide because quite frankly we feel there are better things to do with our precious free time than get to grips with our finances or plan a long overdue life/career change?

Sometimes we're so busy doing our jobs, we forget the end goal – making some real money. Well, to become wealthy, you absolutely have to remember to lift your head above the parapet of your 9 to 5 (or 8 to 8 or whatever hours you work) and give yourself a chance to think about the bigger picture – and take action.

Lots and lots of people work to live – and without them the rich couldn't get richer. And this doesn't mean the workers are being exploited or used. Just that if people choose to be drudges and invest all their time and energy in working for wages, then there will always be other people who will be quick to see an opportunity and become prosperous, simply because they had their heads up and could see further.

If you do work for a living and don't confidently expect that job to make you rich, then you must be doing it for love, mustn't you? No, this isn't a trick question. It is about prioritising our ambitions. If we go to work solely for money it makes sense to earn as much as we can, as we want.

> # IF WE GO TO WORK SOLELY FOR MONEY IT MAKES SENSE TO EARN AS MUCH AS WE CAN

If you love what you do then if the money doesn't come with it, you need to create a strategy for wealth creation that doesn't rely on the 'day job' income. It's great that you love what you do, but if you also want wealth you need to make sure you aren't so busy doing it that you forget to work out how you're going to get wealthy doing it, or what other actions or strategies you need to create a second income or alternative revenue generator.

If you are unhappy with your pay and/or hate your job then you have to question why you're still doing it and what else you could do. The worst possible scenario is that you don't feel fulfilled or rewarded in your job but you are so busy doing it that you don't have time to create a plan that will bring you greater prosperity and happiness. While you've got your head down earning a living a million and one opportunities to become prosperous have just passed over your head and you didn't see them. Imagine waking up in ten years' time and realising that's what you'd done. If this is your situation then do something now. Change your perspective and seize the day.

Save in big chunks – or should you?

I always thought that if I could get my hands on a big chunk I would put loads of it away and that would be a brilliant way of saving. I have a friend who says that is a nonsense and that the drip-by-drip effect is the best way to save. Who is right and who is wrong? Obviously I must be right. It's my book, after all.

Let us consider it a bit more logically. Suppose I save a big chunk. Let's say I get £20,000 for some work I do or something I sell. I spend half and save half. And I do this when I am 50. How much do I have at retirement?

My friend saves a measly, miserly £10 a month – small potatoes I say. But he does start early – at 20 and never misses a month. Who is going to retire big time and who is going to be reusing tea bags? Come on, come on, you can work this stuff out in your head, can't you? No? OK there's the chart opposite (assuming a modest 5 per cent interest per annum).

See, I told you I was right … but not by much. Hope you have learnt a valuable lesson here. It's good to be prudent and save regularly but in the long run a big chunk saved later in life will bring home the bacon just as easily.

---

[18] I know, I know, he won't get 5 per cent on the whole lot because he won't have the full £120 until the end of year 1 but this is just an example.

[19] I'm assuming I invest at the beginning of the year.

RULE 42

Year	My friend aged 20 at £10 per month	Me, who doesn't save a thing until I'm 50 – ha!
1	£126[18]	
2	£258	
3	£397	
4	£543	
5	£696	
6	£857	
7	£1,025	
8	£1,202	
9	£1,398	
10	£1,594	
11	£1,800	
12	£2,016	
13	£2,243	
14	£2,421	
15	£2,668	
16	£2,927	
17	£3,199	
18	£3,485	
19	£4,163	
20	£4,497	
21	£4,847	
22	£5,215	
23	£5,601	
24	£6,007	
25	£6,433	
26	£6,880	
27	£7,350	
28	£7,843	
29	£8,361	
30	£8,905	This is the year I make my big savings killing with £10,000 + 5% = £10,500[19]
31	£9,476	£11,025
32	£10,075	£11,576
33	£10,704	£12,154
34	£11,365	£12,761
35	£12,059	£13,399
36	£12,787	£14,068
37	£13,552	£14,771
38	£14,355	£15,509
39	£15,198	£16,284
40	£16,083	£17,098
41	£17,013	£17,952
42	£17,989	£18,849
43	£19,014	£19,791
44	£20,090	£20,780
45	£21,220	£21,819
Totals	£21,220	£21,819

Don't rent, buy

We all need somewhere to live. We therefore have the choice as to whether to rent the roof over our heads, or buy it. Most of us can't afford to buy outright (I doubt you'd be reading this book if you were in this category), so in order to buy we need to borrow a lump sum of money to buy with. But hang on. Haven't we said that borrowing is bad, bad, bad and we shouldn't do it? Haven't we said that this way madness lies because you pay so much interest on what you borrow and so on? Indeed we have.

So how can you own and not borrow, buy and not have a mortgage?

The answer is that a mortgage can actually be viewed as an investment rather than a borrowing. If you buy a property with a mortgage, you make a monthly investment. The fact you pay that to a mortgage company we can gloss over. You see, in the longer term (and if you're lucky, the shorter term too) you can reasonably expect that the interest you pay on your mortgage

> SO HOW CAN YOU OWN
> AND NOT BORROW, BUY
> AND NOT HAVE A
> MORTGAGE?

will be less than the increase in the value of your property. What you are banking on is that the value of your home will, in the longer term, go up and therefore you have invested whatever deposit you put down, and your mortgage money.

Renting on the other hand is not an investment. You will never see that money again. Of that there is no doubt.

With a mortgage, you stand a good chance in the long term of seeing your mortgage payments lead to an increase in the value of your house. When you sell, you get that increase in value.

There are those who believe that buying your home instead of renting brings with it huge stresses, and means you have less fun. It's actually not the ownership that causes stress, it's how much you borrow to do it and what that means for your overall financial picture. The lesson is to think carefully about how much your mortgage repayments will be and that you are able and willing to pay them.

Of course if you buy, there are no guarantees your home will increase in value – there will be house price slumps – but over time chances are that they recover and go on to increase again. Ideally buy cheap and sell for a lot more. You then have a choice: invest the profits in the next property without borrowing any more and in doing so you decrease the mortgage each time. Eventually you own outright and without mortgage payments you have some-where to live and don't have to pay for it at all any more.

Alternatively you can do what most people do and buy a bigger, better more expensive house. This isn't a wealth creation strategy but it can be what you wanted your wealth for, which makes it fine by me.

Understand what investing really means

Many investments have a twofold purpose. They generate income and they increase in value. In other words, if you invest a lump sum (this is known as capital) you get regular small payments of some kind *and* the actual value of the capital itself increases, i.e. the lump sum gets bigger.

Let's suppose you invest in property. In an ideal world you should be able to rent it out, thus providing the regular small payments in the form of rental income, and the value of the property should go up also, so your capital increases in value over time.

Likewise shares should pay out dividends (generate income) and should be worth more than you bought them for when you come to sell some time later (increase in value). You get the idea. And notice I say 'should' rather than 'will' – nothing is certain in this game.

You can of course invest in pretty well anything you want:

- company shares
- your brother's harebrained buy-an-old-boat-and-do-it-up-and-sell-it-for-a-fortune scheme
- fine wines, paintings, krugerrands, classic cars, rare books, Georgian glass
- pension funds and such like including savings and deposit accounts
- inventions and new product development
- ideas and people
- theatre shows, films, TV programme development.

And it doesn't have to be just plain old investment. There is also:

- sponsorship such as race cars, football teams etc. to raise brand awareness (hopefully yours and not just the race car or football team)
- angelic capital – you invest in people and ideas in an altruistic way rather than purely as a money-making venture (as opposed to venture capital, where you invest in people and ideas purely as a money-making venture).

Remember that investments of any sort are a form of gambling no matter which way you look at it. And that you can lose. Ask Lloyds if you don't believe me.

> # REMEMBER THAT INVESTMENTS OF ANY SORT ARE A FORM OF GAMBLING NO MATTER WHICH WAY YOU LOOK AT IT

On the other hand, investing in a broad range of low risk investments can still net returns worth having.

Build a bit of capital then invest it wisely

Lots of people dont't get prosperous because, as we saw earlier, they are too lazy. But a lot fail because they don't know what to do once they start to earn some money. It's easy to think, once you've got your hands on a bit, that you have earned it, you deserve it, you're gong to spend it. You *have* earned it – assuming you haven't robbed anyone to get it – and yes you probably *do* derserve it. But no, don't spend it all now, no matter how much you want that new car, holiday, cottage by the sea, whatever.

I've done it. I guess we all have. I once got a massive tax rebate. I don't remember why I was being taxed so highly but I was for several years and when they repaid me it was quite a handsome sum. And of course I blew it, on a spendid holiday. But that's the difference between the rich and the now so well-off. The rich see a sudden windfall like that as an opportunity to make some more money out of it. The not so well-off remain not so well-off as they see it as an opportunity to have some fun. Nothing wrong with that if that's what you want in life – instant pleasure. But if you want greater wealth and pleasure (albeit delayed) then you must learn as I did that once you get your hands on a lump sum, or build some up, you must immediately put it to good use. And frankly the only good use is as a starter kit for prosperity.

And it isn't lost, merely put to one side to work for you. Once it has grown and attracted lots more lovely money, you can have all the holidays you want. But you have to wait and you have to use that starter kit well and wisely. See it as a 'loader'. this is a term guides who receive tips use for starting the tip collection off. You have to put a loader in the plate or no one else will tip.

Buskers do the same thing, put a coin or two into the hat to get the crowd going. No one will put anything into an empty hat. What you are going to so is load your prosperity hat.

> # NO ONE WILL PUT ANYTHING INTO AN EMPTY HAT

Ah, but I hear you say, i'm never going to get my hands on a lump sum. Not true. You get your hands on a lump sum every week of your life in the form of wages – I'm assuming you do have a job here. You choose what you spend that money on – mortgage, food, car, entertainment etc. But if you want a way out of that particular lifestyle and into another, you have to be proactive about it. And the way you start it to put something aside each week to build up tht lump sum. Once you have something built up, think about where that money is going to generate you more money, and get it invested. Ideally you need to turn that money into an asset that will generate more revenue for you – be it share, a property you can rent out, or something else. Wealth happens slowly over a period of time when you turn surplus can into something that will work for you.

Understand that property, in the long run, will not outpace shares

So, you've built up a bit of money to invest – where to put it? Property and shares are two popular choices, but which to choose?

In the aftermath of the 'dot com' crash of 2000 when share prices started to plummet, many people in the UK turned from investing in shares to investing in property. It's not surprising really – many people who invested heavily in shares in the late 1990s saw the value of many of those shares drop so much it really hurt – and some companies folded completely meaning investors lost all their money.

With people turning in huge numbers from shares to property, the buy-to-let market boomed and with greater demand from investor buyers, house prices rose. Eventually we reached a point where in some areas there was a glut of property available to rent and income from rental properties failed to match expectations (supply outstripping demand). However, those early into the buy-to-let boom who bought in the right areas did well. In the years since 2000, however, share prices have recovered and those who could hold on to their shares on the whole have seen their value climb again.

So what's the right thing to do? Property or shares? Well, shorter-term blips notwithstanding, in the longer run, shares will outperform property.

Don't get me wrong – there's always a place for property – it's about getting yourself a good spread of investments – a portfolio as the professionals like to call it. Any decent investment portfolio is going to include property as a matter of course.

> ANY DECENT INVESTMENT
> PORTFOLIO IS GOING TO
> INCLUDE PROPERTY AS A
> MATTER OF COURSE

One big advantage of investing in property is that you can live in it (as we said in Rule 43 you have to live somewhere and you can't live in cocoa futures). Alternatively, if you're buying to let, you will get income from the rental of the property (though you have to be extremely careful that the rent is as much as you hope it will be, that you are sure there is enough demand for rental properties in that area, and so on).

With shares, you hope to get regular income in the form of dividends paid to shareholders, but the greatest return usually comes from a long-term increase in share prices. And quite simply, as companies have greater potential for growth than property, the longer-term picture should see shares giving you a greater return. I stress potential here as it doesn't always get realised – the value of your shares, or your property, can go down as well as up. There's always risk. The other reason to prefer shares to property alone is that shares – especially a nice well-balanced portfolio – will give you a decent risk spread. The more variety the less the risk. Did you know that in a slump baked bean sales go up?

RULE 47

Master the art of selling

Just as deal making is a vital skill, so is selling – and they aren't always the same thing. You sell stuff outside of deals. Indeed one of the most important things you have to be able to sell in life to increase your prosperity is yourself.

Selling is the bedrock upon which every fortune is built. Whatever you do to make yourself prosperous will involve selling: selling your skills, selling things, selling ideas. You can't make money without selling. Selling is where it's at. Every rich person knows this simple fact. Every poor person doesn't.

In an ideal world you should aim to sell:

- yourself and your abilities, skills and attributes (every minute of every day)
- something while you're asleep
- in countries you've not only never been to but have never heard of
- via other people, so someone else is selling for you
- things that are incredibly cheap to produce and give you a really healthy return
- things other people make and finance for you
- things that have a 99 per cent penetration into every household
- things that store, transport and stack easily.

The list is probably endless. But where people go wrong is when they try to sell things that no one really wants. Unless of course you are Damien Hirst and you make pickled sharks. Now there's a market I never thought of.

And don't go thinking selling is for sales reps in shiny suits with a nice line in patter. Every time Richard Branson appears on television busy with a hot air balloon he is selling; selling his entire brand. Clever man. Clever selling.

I like the young chap Alex Tew who started at university recently. He wanted to become a millionaire and realised that if he had a million things he could sell them all for £1 (or $1) and achieve his goal. And he realised a web page has 1 million pixels. He then set about selling each one for £1 to advertisers. You need a block of around 400 (thus costing you £400) to be seen, but he sold half by Christmas and the rest within his first year at uni. Head down? I don't think so. You can see the result at http://www.milliondollarhomepage.com/ – and yes, I supported his venture and paid him $400 for advertising my business as I figured such an enterprising young man needed a monetary round of applause for ingenuity, cleverness and innovation.

RULE 48

Don't believe you can always win

There is a whole list of things and people you can't beat, so it might be best to be cautious around them. They include the bookies (and anyone else trying to take money off you for gambling – casino owners, card sharps, race courses, online gambling websites etc.), the tax authorities, speed cameras, the government, your mother, planning authorities, the police, your kids and death.

Dan Brown, author of *The Da Vinci Code,* was sued by the authors of another book, *Holy Blood, Holy Grail,* as they believed he had plagiarised their work. They lost. They lost big time. They lost somewhere, in the region of £1.75 million including costs.

They probably believed quite sincerely in the merits of their case, but did anybody tell them they were unlikely to win? It'd be fascinating to know whether anybody advised them not to proceed as they would probably lose …

The reason to be very cautious in your dealings with bookies, barristers, accountants and such like is that they have knowledge you don't. They are holders of secrets that can enable them (if they so choose) to make money out of you purely because of your ignorance.

And don't go getting all moralistic on me and trying to change the system. These are facts of life. Live with them. Work them. You won't get rid of them. You can't beat the bookies – or the odds – so don't go trying or attempting to get rid of them on the grounds that they are making money out of the poor, innocent and gullible public. Trouble is, the poor, innocent, gullible public walk in there with their wallets open crying, 'Help yourself.' And then complain they are broke, no one gives them a chance, life isn't fair, no one likes me, it's not my fault, there ought to be a law against it, etc. Remember that there are sharks out there. So don't bleed.

> REMEMBER THAT THERE
> ARE SHARKS OUT THERE.
> SO DON'T BLEED

Understand how the stock market *really* works

It's simple. People buy, sell and trade investments – called stocks – that they have made in companies. So, how does it all work? And, more importantly, *what* works?

The easy answer to the last question is 'Buy low; sell high,' but don't you just know that there's more to it than that. The question of deciding what to buy, how much to pay for it and when to buy (and then sell) it has been the subject of entire libraries of books, most of them bigger than this one, and so I'll limit my contribution to a few choice rules, and the first of these is to understand the real forces at play: *value* and *speculation*.

Now personally, I think economists were put on this earth to make astrologers look good, but I'm not averse to quoting them, and one of the most quotable – John Maynard Keynes – once said that the stock market is just like a beauty contest.

Now when he said that, he didn't mean that stockbrokers should abandon their suits for swimwear and profess a desire for working with children or world peace. He was referring to a type of British beauty contest that used to be run by London newspapers, in which readers could win a prize by picking the beauty whose photograph was deemed to be the most beautiful by the greatest number of other readers. This meant that winning was not about picking the prettiest, nor even about predicting which the average reader would think the prettiest, but instead winning became a game of anticipating what the average reader would expect the average choice to be. And this, believed Keynes, was how the stock market works. Investors try to make money by buying stocks that they think other investors will want to buy in the future, and the price that they're prepared to pay for a stock depends less on the fundamental value of the company than on their expectations of what everybody else will be willing to pay for it. That's the essence of speculation in the stock market, and that's why the fundamental value of a stock and its price on any given day can be so different.

Speculating on stock market movements is great fun if you want to observe mass psychology in action, but in an uncertain world it's not the road to wealth. If you really want to accumulate wealth in the stock market, then here's my rule. Get rich slowly, but surely, with value. Ignore all the noise, the clamour about what this piece of news or that piece of gossip means for a price; stay away from the 'proven' techniques for predicting what prices will do tomorrow based on what they did yesterday (technical analysis! don't be fooled by the rational-sounding label, it's irrational) and resist, please resist, the temptation to dive in and out of stocks chasing a quick buck. If you're going to invest in shares, look for value. Look for companies whose share-price doesn't reflect their worth; look for companies that make or do something that people will find more valuable in the future, and look for companies whose value is appreciated by the investment funds (we'll meet them in Rule 50).

Once you've found them, buy them, and unless the fundamentals change, buy them for the long run. Wait for their value to appreciate, and watch as your wealth accumulates.

So, to buy the right stocks, at the right price of course, don't follow the crowd, find the value. Easier said than done, you might say, and you'd be right. It can take a lot of research, but you can make it easier if you follow the next Rule.

RULE 50

Only buy shares (or anything) you can understand

Another Rule to engrave on your heart. Buying shares – or anything else to sell on in order to make money – is just another form of gambling. When I worked as a casino manager, it was well recognised that there was a hierarchy of casinos. At the bottom were the ones with the slot machines and noisy brash atmosphere. At the top were the gentlemen's clubs where it was all smoked glass and diffused lighting. Gamblers of course recognised the hierarchy and felt that the latter were somehow 'cleaner'. Similarly most people view the stock market as in some way more refined, sophisticated – and thus free of risk or odds or danger. But it is all gambling. Nothing is certain.

If you are going to gamble on shares (or anything else you want to buy and sell), then reduce the odds as much as possible and only invest in or buy things you know and understand. By doing this you eliminate a lot of the mystique which can lead you to stake more than you intend, take risks you wouldn't normally, or be bamboozled by slick marketing spiel.

> CUT THE ODDS DOWN AS
> LOW AS POSSIBLE AND
> ONLY INVEST IN OR BUY
> THINGS YOU UNDERSTAND

RULE 50

If you shop at Marks & Spencer, and you see that the new product ranges are good and that the stores are full and you hear people raving about how M&S has improved this year, then buy Marks & Spencer shares. If you keep studying the stores and listening to people shopping you will quickly notice if it continues to be a good investment.

Just be careful you are aware if you are buying with your head or heart. I have a friend who only invests in green companies. He swans about with an air of moral superiority. He believes he has bought a ticket to heaven by doing this. He is a gambler. He doesn't realise this. Is he buying with his head as well as his heart? If you find investments in something you love, be clear if you are buying as an investment on business principles, or simply because you want to. If your rational market analysis says that wind farms are the future, and will be a growing industry with big returns, then fantastic, you can invest with head and heart.

If you don't really understand a particular sector of business, and don't intend to put the work in to get to know it well, then you'll almost certainly be better off investing in something else. If you want to invest in shares, but don't want to do all the homework and make all the decisions yourself, then you can use an investment fund. And that brings us conveniently to our next Rule.

RULE 51

By all means, use the investment professionals (but don't be used by them)

As you've probably guessed from Rule 49, most of those who pick their own stocks like to think that they can see value where others can't. Of course, we don't like to look too often to see if our track record backs that up, and I'm sure many a Rules Player has made dumb investment decisions. If you don't trust yourself to make clever decisions every time, or perhaps simply want to save the occasional investment decision for yourself and let someone who knows more than you do take care of the rest, then it's OK to use the professionals.

When it comes to investment, the professionals cluster wherever you can find tall buildings and long lunches. Wall Street, Singapore, the City of London … they're all positively teeming with investment experts ready to put their big brains and even bigger computers to work on your behalf. All for just a teensy-weensy fee of course.

Well gold, as they say, may be bought too dear. I've often wondered just whose interests our chums in the square mile are serving. I certainly know a friend who's studied them and written about them, and who swears blind that there are crooks in the Stock Exchange, and that at least Dick Turpin 'had the decency to wear a mask and not a pin-striped suit'. Forgive me if you are a stockbroker – my friend may be just a touch paranoid – but personally I believe that if you're going to use the pin-stripes to manage some of your stock-market investments, make sure you use them wisely. That's a big if, and that's what this rule's all about. How to use them to *make* more money, not *take* your money.

> ## MOST OF THEM TRY HARD, THEY REALLY DO, BUT IN THE END MOST OF THEM FAIL TO GROW MONEY ANY FASTER THAN THE MARKET. SO, DON'T PAY THEM FOR TRYING

Now, pay attention to this bit – it's really, really important. First they will tell you that they can take your money, invest it actively and *beat* the market. That they *do* beat the market and that they *will* beat the market. They may even have some colourful charts to show you how they beat the market, *every* year. Apart from last year of course (and that was just a blip, a short-term correction you know, everybody took a bath on that one, but *next* year . . .). Just sign here, sit back and you'll soon be worth more than Warren Buffett on a hot streak. Sounds too good to be true? Yep, it's wishful thinking and flawed logic in equal measures.

To put it simply, for somebody to be doing better than average, somebody else must be doing worse, and since the big firms invest most of the money in the market, who are they beating? Themselves? Right, and here's the ugly little truth about the investment industry. In any given year, some will come out ahead and some will lose, but over the long term the market beats most of them, most of the time. Oh I'm sure many of them try hard, they really do, but in the end nearly all of them fail to grow money any faster than the market. So, don't pay them for trying.

A sure-fire scheme for predicting winners? Unlikely. A hot tip for technology stocks? Hot air. Ask yourself this. If, like most people, you read the brochure, listen to the adviser (who's on a commission) and buy into a fund aiming to beat the market, what's the *one* thing that you can be sure will be higher than average? The returns? Or the fees? You know the answer to that one, don't you?

If you want help to put your money in the markets, without putting much of it in someone else's pockets, keep it simple.

If you don't have the time or know-how to carefully research the best active fund then follow the rule that *less is more* (and usually comes cheaper). Put your trust in funds that don't charge you big fees for taking big risks with a succession of clever strategies to beat the house. Pick ones managed by people who know enough to know that, in the long run, they won't beat the house by chasing higher returns from one stock to the next. Pick ones managed by people who'll invest your money, with minimum fuss and minimum fees, in a good range of stocks that replicate the market and then go to lunch. Then you can sleep at night (or get back to reading this book) safe in the knowledge that your money is in the market, quietly working away on your behalf.

If you're wondering where to find these funds, they'll be called index funds or tracker funds. Of course, they pay less commission to middlemen and spend less money on advertising, and so their brochure may be the last one out of your financial adviser's briefcase, but when it comes to using investment professionals, start by putting your trust in time, not clever tactics. You can take a more active approach as your experience grows, but believe me, the fees will be smaller.

If you are going to get financial advice, pay for it

Boy are there a lot of people out there waiting and wanting to give you financial help, advice, information, tips and guidance. Great – learn early on to be very careful who you take advice from if you want to hang on to your wealth.

There are two groups of people to whom you may turn in the event of needing said advice, help, guidance, whatever. First, there are skilled professionals who carry indemnity insurance so you can sue them – and expect to get a payout – in the unlikely event the information they give you is erroneous, wrong, or dangerously bad. If they stand by their advice, you should make sure provision is there so that you get paid if it is wrong. That keeps 'em on their toes. These people you pay and their fee entitles them to talk to you about your money.

Second, there are very rich people. Listen to them unless they won their money on the lottery, inherited it, robbed a bank to get it or bought a load of drugs in Marrakech and sold them in the local nightclub (actually their entrepreneurial skills might be worth something even if their honesty or honour isn't).

Those are the only two categories open to you. The ones closed to you include: friends and family, well meaning acquaintances (even if they do have a quid or two of their own), TV programmes, the Internet and high street banks.

You must make sure any financial advice comes from someone who carries a recognisable qualification or membership of a suitable organisation – that includes the very, very rich club. Make sure you know that they know what they are doing. The textile millionaire Joe Hyman used to say that in order of honesty, the three types of bank were (1) high street banks (2) mountebanks and (3) merchant banks.

> # MAKE SURE ANY FINANCIAL ADVICE COMES FROM SOMEONE WHO CARRIES MEMBERSHIP OF A SUITABLE ORGANISATION – THAT INCLUDES THE VERY, VERY RICH CLUB

There are two types of advisers in my experience: (a) those who stop you making an ass of yourself and (b) those who tell you you've made an ass of yourself after you've done it. You want category (a). You'll get loads and loads in category (b).

When it comes to professional financial advisers, there are another two categories: (a) those who deal with your finances and (b) those who try to sell you products. Avoid (b) like the plague.

Any financial adviser you use should be independent – i.e. they should not be restricted to providing advice from a limited range of products offered by the company he works for – it's the difference between buying a suit off the peg – a best fit – or buying something tailor-made to fit your requirements precisely.

You should also insist on paying for the advice by means of an agreed fee – not by commission on the policies you take out or the products or investments they sell you. It's tempting to go down the commission route as it sounds like you get better value (the financial adviser gets paid by the companies whose policies or investments he sells you). It may sound like better value (great – somebody else pays the adviser for you!) but it may not be better advice. You want impartial advice that is exactly tailored to your circumstances and paying for the advice is the only way to be sure you get it, and you don't get sold a lot of policies or investments from companies that pay the best commission.

Don't fiddle

Once you've worked out a strategy, leave it alone. There is no point fiddling, you're unlikely to make it any better, and you might make it worse. Not only that but you could incur lots of extra charges or penalties if you start changing things after a short time. You have to know when to leave things alone. It's like the proverb 'look before you leap'. Look, look long and hard. Then make your plan and take your decisions. Then leave it alone – don't mess with it.

Looking is weighing up the odds, seeking advice, considering the pros and cons. Leaping is acting on all that information. But once you have decided to leap, get on with it. Once you have formulated your plan, your objective, your strategy, your goals and targets and ambitions and destinations, then be committed.

It is so easy to get scared or panicky. We all fear unemployment, poverty, financial traps, falling behind, falling below, falling in debt. I've been there: having made a plan I was paralysed by fear into staying in a job for years because I didn't believe I could survive outside it. Once I stepped outside, I survived just fine. We always do.

Plans and small fish require the same amount of cooking. Once they're in the pan, leave them alone or they'll fall apart. Don't keep stirring or they'll disintegrate. Don't keep fiddling, tinkering, changing your mind and changing it back again. If you do keep on fiddling you may end up achieving very little and worse still you will have frittered and wasted money on early redemption charges and the like. Many investments are long term and fiddling means paying more or not reaping the full benefits.

Sure you should keep your eye on things, and on the market generally, but stick with your strategy and, having done your homework, leave as well alone as possible. Don't panic and don't fiddle.

> **BUT ONCE YOU HAVE DECIDED TO LEAP, GET ON WITH IT**

RULE 54

Think long term

At the same time as not fiddling too much (*see Rule 53*), so too you shouldn't play the short game. You have to think long term, both in your planning, and in your expectations of a return. You also have to invest for the longer term.

If you expect a rapid and sudden catapult into prosperity then go play the lottery and good luck to you (you'll need it). Gaining wealth is a slow process and rightly so. If you get it all quickly you have no time to acquire experience and sense. Too quickly and it'll be all 'spend, spend, spend'.

Thinking long term is a bit like thinking in very fast motion while the rest of the world moves incredibly slowly around you. *Softly, softly catchee monkey as they say.* Ever tried to swat a fly? A fly's eyes are different from ours and they basically see in fast forward. By the time you raise your hand, they have already predicted the movement and flown away. You have to develop the same ability. You have to see what's happening before it happens and the only way to do that is to think long term.

Think of gaining prosperity as stalking a reluctant tiger. It'll be wary and cautious and you have to stalk it skilfully, quietly, almost lovingly. It's no use running up and shouting at it – it will either turn round and kill you or run off. Better to take your time and creep up slowly and quietly. Any sudden movements will startle the canny beast.

> # THINK OF GAINING PROSPERITY AS STALKING A RELUCTANT TIGER

In *The Rules of Work* I talked about having various plans in force – short-term, medium-term and long-term. The same is true for investments. You need short-term investments for money you might need access to in the near future; medium-term ones that you expect to deliver returns in five or ten years say; and then you need long-term investments that will reap greater rewards but that deliver in the more distant future.

I know in Rule 34 I said to be decisive and act quickly, and that is still true. But only after you have taken a long-term view; only after you have weighed and considered and pondered and evaluated. *The samurai only makes one cut but that cut was an entire lifetime in the making.*

Where are you going to be in five years' time, prosperity-wise? Ten? Fifteen? Twenty? Longer?

Have a set time of day to work on your wealth strategy

You have to have a life as well as gaining prosperity. It is my observation that happy, wealthy people's financial planning follows a similar set of four principles:

1 They set targets then get on with it.

2 They don't tinker too much.

3 They tend to work on their financial planning at the same time of day (I don't mean everyone works at say 9am but that each person tends to favour a particular time of day whether it's 10:30 in the morning or midnight).

4 They are able to take a break from their financial planning and have a life outside it – it keeps them refreshed and interesting.

The reason you need a set time of day is twofold. Firstly, it makes sure you actively manage your wealth rather than looking at it once a year and thinking 'Oh dear' and conversely it means you don't overdo it and spend all day tinkering (which as we've said is a bad idea). And secondly, it means you can take advantage of your natural biorhythms and put in the effort when you are at your brightest. If you are a morning person, you'll want to get your planning in early. If you are more of an owl, then an evening slot will take advantage of your sharpest mental acuity.

The other big advantage of having a set time of day is that you can plan for it, work it into your diary and make time for it. If you don't, it can get forgotten or the time used for other things. If, for example, you always spend half an hour on your plan first thing after breakfast, then it gets to be a regular function and one you feel oddly uncomfortable missing – yes, even on holiday.

Working on your prosperity plan at the same time of day – and for the same shortish length of time – means you can break things down into manageable chunks and not get overwhelmed. You can work for a bit and then take a break, put it behind you for the day and go back to it, at the same time of course, the next day. Bit by bit, things will improve. Believe me, I've been here before you.

Pay attention to detail

This is my biggest failing I'm afraid. My solution is easy. I employ someone to manage my life who takes care of the detail – someone who is very, very good at the detail. Yes, it's an expensive way to do it. Better to train yourself right from the word go to pay attention to the detail yourself and save the expense.

> ## TRAIN YOURSELF RIGHT FROM THE WORD GO TO PAY ATTENTION TO THE DETAIL YOURSELF

Detail is not keeping a note of every tiny purchase you make and looking at minute economies – we've already discovered (*see Rule 32*) going without that cappuccino isn't going to make you rich beyond your wildest dreams. Detail is:

- checking the small print
- checking the interest rates
- checking charges and fees
- checking you pay for things on time so you don't incur penalties
- checking when you will be paid and that you invest promptly to avoid your money lying idle

- not forgetting people
- not forgetting dates, times and appointments
- making lists and writing everything down
- remembering to ask for information
- remembering to ask questions in general
- remembering to keep good records of all transactions, and purchases and sales.

This is just muscle training. I take it you know all about muscle training? When you are in training for any sport, if you repeat an action often enough your muscles retain the memory of that action. The more you repeat the action the easier it gets and the less effort you need to put in.

It's a bit like driving a car, tough at first but it becomes automatic (excuse pun!) after a while. I am writing this in France and I have been getting used to (a) driving on the right and (b) driving a left-hand-drive car. I've had to concentrate hard and shout at the children because I can't think if they are beating seven bells out of each other in the back seat. It's been a bit like learning to drive all over again. Added to the fact that all the signs are in French and it's a steep learning curve. But it's getting easier and becoming routine. I don't have to think about it any more and can take in the passing scenery and enjoy the journey.

Create new income streams

When it comes to wealth-creation strategies, investing wisely and managing your money actively are important, but nothing beats having more coming in in the first place. Everybody benefits from some thought about where their income comes from and how they could create another source of revenue.

It's a bit like being a busker and having several pitches. If one is proving unprofitable, you can pack it in and go somewhere else. But instead of packing it in what you are going to do is duplicate yourself – a cloned you if you like – and not only carry on busking but also be busking in a new place at the same time. The more hats you have out, the more they are likely to return a profit.

Look, don't take my word for this. Check it out yourself. Look at any prosperous person you admire and see if diversity isn't their tool for unlocking greater prosperity. The rich usually have several money-making schemes going for them.

This is especially important for anybody who loves their work, but it doesn't pay well. What you need is another income stream.

There are a couple of ways of doing this. The first is to turn surplus cash into assets that will work for you and bring in income, even when you aren't there. Rent from a buy-to-let property would be one example, or annual dividends from shares you've bought.

The other way to create new income streams is to find ways of using your skills and expertise in more than one setting, so you aren't just swapping your labour for a pay check in your day job.

This doesn't mean packing in your day job necessarily. It might mean, for example, doing some freelance work either in the same area or a completely unrelated area where you also have skills and expertise (maybe you have a hobby which means you have other skills and expertise that could be used?). Is there anything you could teach or consult on, or that you could set up as a business?

When I say 'create' new income streams, what I mean is create them *for you*. They can be old ones in the marketplace. Just make sure that you are maximising all your skills to bring in income, and that you are actively investing in assets that will earn money for you without you having to be there (I do realise you can't physically clone yourself).

> THE RICH USUALLY HAVE
> SEVERAL MONEY-MAKING
> SCHEMES GOING
> FOR THEM

Learn to play 'What if?'

When deciding how to earn your money and how to invest your money, you need to ask yourself a lot of questions starting with 'What if . . .?'

I'll start you off here:

- 'What if there is another recession?'
- 'What if this bank goes bust and I can't get my money out?'
- 'What if these shares suddenly take a turn for the worse?'
- 'What if gold prices plummet?'
- 'What if all my customers went elsewhere for a cheaper service/products?'
- 'What if I was made redundant?'
- 'What if property prices bottom out?'
- 'What if the oil runs out?'

The 'What if' game is one we can all play. All together now… 'What if…?' I call it 'looking for loopholes', only it isn't loopholes, more a sort of gotcha clause. Every time I start making some serious money, I figure someone somewhere is playing a gotcha clause whereby the unexpected happens and that particular income stream dries up rapidly. Part of the fun of being prosperous is in spotting the gotcha clause long before it happens and getting your money out and into another investment. It's also vital to consider when you are thinking about where to find extra income from. That's where having lots of hats comes in.

A good example of the dangers of putting all your eggs in one basket are the footballers who have been forced to retire while in their twenties. One minute they are earning millions and seemingly at the peak of their career and then they shatter their ankle, and their financial dreams too. They haven't trained for anything else because it never occurred to them that they might need another string to their bow.

> ## DIVERSIFICATION IS THE NAME OF THE GAME

Diversification is the name of the game – by having more than one income stream, and a nice broad spread of investments, whatever happens in the 'What if' scenario you will be in a much more secure position than if all your proverbial eggs are in the one basket. By asking 'What if…?' you are minimising risks to your wealth and wealth creation.

RULE 59

Control spending impulses

The surest way to scupper your wealth creation is to go out and spend everything you earn or receive (and a bit more just for good measure). This particular addiction is very strong in me. I blame it all on giving up smoking. I have nothing to do now with my hands so fiddling with a credit card seems to satisfy some deeply buried addictive urge. But you have to resist if you are going to turn what little you have into a bigger something. Forget notions of new cars and holidays in the sun. You are going to turn into a bit of a Scrooge for a while, hanging on to what you've got in order to prepare for the future when you will have so much more. This means you have to control your urges.

Look, I'm going to let you into a secret. Prosperity is a race, a prize, a winning line. We all set out wanting to race towards it, claim it. Some can't be bothered to even make it to the starting line because they are so weighed down with unhelpful beliefs that floor them before they start. And a whole lot of people fall by the wayside from laziness early on. And many more fail to make the grade because they get daunted by the hard work needed. And still more at this point, where you're at now, stumble because they give into temptation and spend, spend, spend like there is no tomorrow.

Well, there is a tomorrow and it comes quickly enough. And that shiny new car now looks sad and rusty, the holiday is gone with only a few snaps of people and places you can't even remember and the new clothes are outgrown and unworn.

The simple truth is the rich know how to control their spending urges – that's why they're rich. When they need to tighten their belts they can do it.

> ## THE RICH KNOW HOW TO CONTROL THEIR SPENDING URGES – THAT'S WHY THEY'RE RICH

And you need to do it too, tighten your belt that is. In fact what you need to do is not loosen it in the first place. We've talked about delayed pleasures in earlier Rules and I hope you've absorbed that one by now. Curbing those spending urges is absolutely vital and the best way to do it is to never buy anything instantly. If you see something you just have to have, wait a week. Do you still really need/want it? Chances are the urge will pass if you give it a chance to. Make it harder for yourself by putting time and distance between you and temptation.

Don't answer ads that promise get-rich-quick schemes – it won't be you who gets rich quick

If you type in 'Opportunities to make money' into Google you get over 150,000,000 hits. That's not quite as many as 'sex'[20] but still a pretty good indicator of what we want. There are a lot of get-rich-quick schemes in there. Now, believe me, they do work. What? I hear you cry. Yes indeed they do work. But not for you, not for the poor mugs who sign up. They work for the instigators, the beginners, the ones who launch such schemes.[21]

In the 1980s there were a lot of water purifier selling schemes about. I was invited to a couple of their meetings and went along out of interest (strictly research I promise) and was amazed at how quick people were to join in, to sign something, anything, that promised them loads of money with minimum effort. After all, what did they have to do but sell a water filter to a few friends and relations? Easy pickings they all thought. Where are all the people now who signed up, invested their savings, were promised untold riches? Funny, I can't find any either.

Maybe a few did indeed sell some and alienated their loved ones in the process. Maybe there were a few at the beginning who did make quite a bit of money. But any pyramid scheme isn't sustainable and will collapse once it reaches a certain level because there just aren't enough people on the planet to sustain the promise.

I like what Woody Allen says about a fool and his money – how did they get together in the first place?[22]

RULE 60

> ## A FOOL AND HIS MONEY –
> ## HOW DID THEY GET
> ## TOGETHER IN THE
> ## FIRST PLACE?

When I was a kid I remember reading about a couple of scams that set me thinking about how gullible people are. The first was a pest killer. You sent off £5 (it may have been pounds or dollars or whatever) to buy a pest killer guaranteed to kill any household pest including fleas, cockroaches, mice, etc. What you got back were two small blocks of wood with the instruction to catch and place the pest on block A and then press down block B with great force. I kid you not. And the perpetrators made a lot of money before they got caught. Might be time to try that one again. The second scam was someone offering a yard of silk during a silk crisis for a similar small fee (notice how the amount is always small enough to tempt you in) and what you got back was a yard of silk thread – they had never specified the width.

Now you might be thinking you are too clever to be taken in by such obvious hoaxes. Yes? Well they aren't all as obvious and you might not believe the schemes that otherwise very smart people sign up to. There are no get-rich-quick schemes. Repeat after me: There are no ...

---

[20] 688,000,000 if you Google 'sex' but God is up there with 624,000,000 and 'work' is a staggering 5,670,000,000 so maybe there's hope for us yet.

[21] 427,000 if you Google 'get-rich-quick schemes'.

[22] It may not have been Woody Allen of course – he does get a lot of quotes attributed to him, especially cynical ones about money and God. Woody also said – and it was definitely him this time – that money was better than poverty if only for financial reasons.

There are no secrets

Just as there are no get-rich-quick schemes, so there are no secrets – so don't go buying any of them either. You will be offered loads. Once your attention is focused on becoming prosperous, all sorts of offers are going to come at you out of the woodwork. And they'll all offer to let you in on the secrets only the really rich know.

You'll get offered very expensive newsletters that will tell you the hidden secrets of Wall Street, how to play the Stock Exchange and win, how to invest and make a fortune, how to move your money around in offshore accounts to avoid paying taxes. And it'll cost you so little! All you've got to do is sign up for 12 monthly issues.

Guess what? The only secret being sold is the one that says there's a mug born every minute. And now you know that secret, you too can just say no. No one but you is going to make you wealthy. No one in the whole wide world. They don't know more than you. They don't have access to any more information than you do.

> # NO ONE BUT YOU IS GOING TO MAKE YOU WEALTHY. NO ONE IN THE WHOLE WIDE WORLD

The secret of making money is that there are no secrets. You buy something and if you sell it for more than you paid, you've done well. And that applies to anything and everything in the financial world – stocks and shares and investments and property portfolios and ISAs and budget funds and finance management and commodity futures and FTSE and gold reserves and conch shells.

One of the earliest rules we had to learn was that only industrious people can be prosperous. Can you see why now? You have to put in a bit of effort to learn how to do it by studying the wealthy. If you think there are shortcuts, like buying get-rich-quick schemes or buying secrets, not only are you going to be disappointed but you'll be worse off than if you hadn't invested in such nonsense. Lazy people not only don't get rich but they often end up poorer because they look for such shortcuts.

Don't just read this – do something

Time to shift some weight off that backside I'm afraid and actually do something. Reading this book is a start but it'll count for nothing unless you actually take action. You've probably thought to yourself while reading this book 'Oh I know that!' or 'That's so obvious …' OK, you know it, but have you actually done something about it? Sure, parts are obvious but does that mean you've got it sorted? For most of us there is a huge gap between what we know and what we do. There's no point just reading this, you have to act on whatever it spurs you to think would be a good idea.

Let's take it as slowly as you want. I do appreciate that changing direction is often hard; developing new character traits can be painful. Begin by changing what you watch and what you read. Begin by simply reading/watching a bit of business news. Begin by changing your awareness of what money is all about and how our money myths influence each and every interaction we have with it.

> **CHANGING DIRECTION IS OFTEN HARD; DEVELOPING NEW CHARACTER TRAITS CAN BE PAINFUL**

The way to change our mindset is to change the way we behave and the way we conduct ourselves.

- Watch how you talk, and think, about money. Do you praise its many virtues or denigrate it as something evil and negative? If you begin to talk it up you'll be surprised how quickly it materialises.

- Watch how you walk. Do you slouch and give off an air of resigned acceptance? Or are you upright and confident and looking as if you are hungry for change? (*See also Rule 22.*)

- Watch your overall image too. Plead poverty all the time and people will assume you are poor and act accordingly. The best thing to do is to 'act as if' you are already rich and people will adjust their perception of you and reaction to you accordingly.

Many people will fall by the wayside, despite claiming they want to be rich or richer, but they will do so not from a lack of desire. Instead it will be from a lack of motivation, a lack of doing something. Start now, right now, today, immediately.

GET EVEN
WEALTHIER

Once you've got a bit of money behind you, the whole thing gets a bit easier. Money begets money. You won't pick up a lot of bargains at an antiques auction for £50. But there's a hell of a lot more if you've got £5000. It's that first million that is difficult – ho ho. But seriously, once you have started to move towards prosperity it isn't a good idea to sit back and start counting your loot. It'll disappear faster that way than by any other means. Instead you've got to get slicker and quicker, stay on your toes, be even busier and more focused and definitely don't take your eye off the ball.

As you start to get richer, you might need to start gathering a few advisers around you, people you can trust and, most importantly, listen to. The reason? Because as your investments and capital start to grow, you will need advice and help to make things grow even more. Obviously you can listen, but you will need to make the final decisions about what you are going to do.

Not sitting back on your laurels means you have to be on the lookout for hidden opportunities to take your prosperity further. You've got to stay abreast of current developments, play your hunches, understand the market, know what you've got and what you can spend/invest/save.

Now is the time to start stepping up how opportunistic you can be – thinking laterally, not following the herd, being creative and innovative – that sort of thing. There's no point in doing what everyone else does if you want to make some serious money …

Carry out a finance health check regularly

It is essential if you are going to increase your prosperity that you maintain a healthy awareness of your bank balance. You should be carrying out a finance health check on a regular basis. I think, personally, it should be weekly. Of course, you are free to do it as often as you want and if that means monthly or even longer, then that is entirely up to you but I wouldn't recommend that you leave it too long.

My observation is that the tighter a grip you have on the pulse of your financial life:

- the quicker you can react to changes
- the more information you have to make decisions
- the less chance there is for things to go drastically wrong without you noticing
- the better a focus – and thus interest – you'll have in your finances.

Sorry, but you do have to be disciplined about this. You have to have a regular time when you sit down and:

- carry out a bank reconciliation
- list your creditors and debtors
- check credit card balances against receipts
- check outstanding cheques – the ones that you've written that haven't yet arrived in the bank
- check what future income you have and what major expenses you might have looming on the horizon

- check your standing orders
- check pensions contributions
- check investments
- check any loans
- check any overdrafts etc. (I know, I know, I have said not to have any but you are human).

If you don't do this stuff money will leak away. Forgetting a debt doesn't pay it.

FORGETTING A DEBT
DOESN'T PAY IT

You've got to be disciplined and have a routine – every Monday morning without fail. Yep, even when it's sunny outside, even on holiday, even when you're feeling a bit off-colour, even when there are more exciting things going on. Because if this doesn't excite you, then you're not going to make it I'm afraid.

Personally I think you should know what you are earning every day by the day. And you should know what big outgoings you might face in the next 12 months and that does include a most often forgotten one – the tax bill. Watch that little baby like a hawk and don't ever take your eyes off that ball because it will get you every time.

Get some money mentors

When not writing books, I do have a proper job. I have several in fact, which all involve running companies. I'm no fool when it comes to knowledge. I know there are things I should know that I don't know. And there must be millions of things I don't even know I don't know. My solution is to use other people's knowledge to supplement my own deficits. I have money mentors. In fact I have mentors for all sorts of situations but we'll stick to the money ones for the moment.

Now why should you use money mentors?

- They bring a wider range of experience to the table.
- They make you present your ideas in a clear and concise format – which makes you think long and hard about what you are doing.
- They will make you justify what you are doing – this makes it much harder for you to go off like a loose cannon.
- They are on tap to provide answers, advice, as a sounding platform, a reigning-in service and a 'Have you thought it through?' facility.
- They will individually keep their ear to the ground so you can benefit from their collective (a bit like a news-gathering service).
- They are independent and so will have no vested interest in what you do as competition.
- They are independent and thus will be loyal, supportive and on your team.

Many successful entrepreneurs use mentors when they start out in business. They find somebody who has been successful in starting and running their own businesses, and they ask if they would be prepared to offer guidance and advice (and sometimes contacts and more) to the new entrepreneur as they start out. The vast majority of experienced businesspeople approached will say yes – it's fun for them to pass on their expertise. They enjoy it.

Yes, but I have questions, I hear you say. Fire away.

- What sort of mentor do I need?
- Where do I find them?
- What's it going to cost me?
- Can I ignore them if I don't agree with their advice?

For a money mentor you need people who have proved their financial acumen by making a bit of money themselves – and not by inheritance or lottery winnings. You find them by looking around you. Anyone you admire who has been successful – approach them – they may well be flattered.

> MONEY MENTORS ARE PEOPLE WHO HAVE PROVED THEIR FINANCIAL ACUMEN BY MAKING A BIT OF MONEY THEMSELVES

It shouldn't cost you more than about four decent lunches a year. You take them out to lunch. In return they give you advice, information, suggestions, restraint, support and encouragement.

And can you ignore what they say if you don't like it? Yes, of course you can. I ignored mine once. Just the once. It cost me a lot to ignore them. I publicly apologised to them and wouldn't ever ignore them again.

Play your hunches

Have a hunch. Listen to your heart. Follow your intuition. Listen to your inner voice. Have gut feeling. Have an inkling. These are all saying the same thing. There are times when:

- you know something stinks
- you know when something is absolutely right
- you need to nod your head and believe in yourself.

Of course having a hunch, following a hunch and going off like a loose cannon are not all the same thing.

> OF COURSE HAVING A
> HUNCH, FOLLOWING A
> HUNCH AND GOING OFF
> LIKE A LOOSE CANNON
> ARE NOT ALL THE
> SAME THING

RULE 65

There is a format to this intuition lark and it is a little bit more sensible than you'd think.

- have the hunch
- do your research and see if your hunch is worth following – it usually is but best to just check first
- prepare a well-worked proposal to present to your money mentors
- present
- listen and act on their advice.

And there is no point whingeing, 'But I had this really brilliant hunch!' If you can't back up your hunch with facts and figures then it is just a stab in the dark. A hunch is a sudden flash of inspiration, a moment of sublime intuition, a clever and brilliant realisation. And these can all be justified with facts and figures. Just because the inspiration was a hunch doesn't mean you don't have to justify it and research it. You still need to prepare a some figures and develop a plan. Having a hunch doesn't let you off being sensible and practical and realistic.

Lots of wealthy people got there by having that one truly brilliant moment of inspiration. But they then turned that inspiration into perspiration (sorry) and worked their guts out to make their dream come true. And I bet loads of people said to them, 'But you're so lucky.' Bah. No such thing as luck. But there is a hunch followed by hard work.

Don't sit back

There's a saying that 'Nothing wilts faster than laurels that have been rested upon.' It's very true. There is a temptation once we have made a bit of money, when an investment has worked out, or it seems to be all paying off, to sit back and relax. Yes, we can. But we don't want to. Now is the time to speed up a gear or two, put more irons in the fire. Now is the time to look around and work out our next plan of attack. Now is the time to strike, capitalise, consolidate. Now is not the time to take your eye off the ball.

> ## NOW IS THE TIME TO STRIKE, CAPITALISE, CONSOLIDATE

We can all stir from the swamp and then settle back into the mud. But the really prosperous keep struggling until they are completely free of the slime forever. If you take a day off the slide begins and will, inexorably, continue. And the next effort will be even harder. I know, I've been there.

So redouble your efforts. Rekindle the enthusiasm. Relight the fires of desire and let's get back to work.

RULE 66

You mustn't sit back. The wealthy don't take days out, tea breaks, lunch breaks, holidays. They keep their nose to the grindstone, shoulder to the wheel, ear to the ground, back to the wall, finger on the pulse, iron in the fire, fire in their belly and hand on the tiller. Wow! Tall order. They work harder and enjoy greater rewards – and get told how lucky they are.

You've got to keep on doing whatever it was that made you make it. If it's a cash cow, ride that baby until it dies under you. If it was a one-off brainwave, have another. If it was sheer hard work, keep going. If you've found a successful formula, make some more. But whatever you do don't turn off the tap unless it's run dry. And even then keep it turned on just in case.

Remember, don't get clever. Don't think you know it all. Keep using those money mentors. Keep working harder than anyone around you. Keep it under your hat and keep at it.

But don't forget how you got to where you are – location, method, plan, mission. Remember the 'Don't fiddle' rule and don't change anything until you are sure it will only improve results and not make the boat sink.

Get someone to do the stuff you can't

I have money mentors because there is loads of stuff to do with business and making money that I know nothing about. There are also loads of things which have to be done which I don't know how to do. I could learn, but it isn't where my talents lie. So why go learning how to do things when there are eminently more suitable people out there who can do them? Do what you are good at and get others to do the things you can't. Simple. Pick really good people, and let them get on with the job of making you really prosperous.

> **PICK REALLY GOOD PEOPLE AND LET THEM GET ON WITH MAKING YOU REALLY PROSPEROUS**

Now there are ten rules to making sure you (a) get the right people and (b) keep the right people.

1 Know exactly what it is you want done and who you want to do it.

2 Be very clear about what you want them to do for you and how much you will pay and what guidelines you will give them.

3 Care about them – they are human and mustn't become a mere tool.

4 Keep them informed and motivated – inspire loyalty.

5 Tell them your long-term strategy – they too have a stake in your/their future.

6 If they muck up – and they will from time to time, we all do (even you Mr Templar? Well, maybe not me) – then correct it and move on. Forgiveness is a good thing.

7 Praise them constantly – nothing inspires more than praise (oh, yes, and money of course).

8 Set realistic targets but don't expect the impossible.

9 Set a good example – be someone they can respect and look up to (no one likes working for a jerk) – and set high standards and live up to them yourself.

10 Remember you're the boss, not their friend. Try to maintain dignity, distance and authority.

That should do it. There may be other things you will try, adapt, implement and use. All this stuff is adaptable and entirely up to you. Just make sure you treat your people well and have fun. Don't be an insensitive bossy boss – as if!

At the moment I have a wonderful accounts person. She sighs a lot as I'm always trying to find ways to ensure I'm not paying more tax than I need to – don't we all? But all I do is ask her questions. The rest I leave entirely up to her and the relationship works. Apart from the sighing that is.

RULE 68

Know yourself – solo, duo or team player

If you are going to change direction – in this case to prosperity from wherever it is you are now – then you need to know

(a) your strengths and weaknesses and

(b) what you are good at – and bad at obviously (and this isn't the same as strengths and weaknesses).

For example, I'm good at broad strokes, big picture stuff but I'm not the greatest when it comes to detail.

Get what I'm on about? You just have to know yourself pretty well and then you will be confident in the areas you are good at, can brush up in areas you are weak, can trade on your strengths and get someone else to do all the stuff you are bad at (or haven't yet learned or researched or studied).

And then you've got to know if you are at your best working as part of a partnership, a team or going it alone. Personally I always need the steadying hand of a partner to curb some of my business excesses – a overwhelming tendency to shoot from the hip, be a bit undiplomatic at times, to rush headlong into things, to spend money wastefully on advertising and not to attend to the detail. I am, however, really bad in a team of more than two. So if a business opportunity comes up that requires teamwork I know I can turn it down or tailor it in some way, because I know if I say yes, I will make a pig's ear of it. If, however, it requires a partnership, I'm much more likely to be interested.

> ## I ALWAYS NEED THE STEADYING HAND OF A PARTNER TO CURB SOME OF MY BUSINESS EXCESSES

I am also good working alone. I make decisions easily (not always the right ones but at least I don't prevaricate), I am happy in my own company for long periods and don't need to bounce ideas off anyone to make them seem real. I can travel well alone and can speak up for myself. See what I mean about knowing yourself?

You have to do this exercise if you are to forge ahead with the rest of the moneymakers. Questions to ask:

- Am I good on my own or do I need other people around me?
- Do I have a role to play in a team and feel happier in that role?
- Can I work well with just one trusted partner?
- Do I know where my strengths and weaknesses are and do I know the difference?
- Do I know what I am good and bad at?

My business partner says we work well together because we are the 'brains and brawn'. The only trouble is we both see ourselves as the brains and the other as the brawn. Oh well.

Look for the hidden asset/opportunity

You've got to be a vigilant, never-sleeping, never-taking-time-off machine. Always alert, always on the lookout for that opportunity. An old Senegalese proverb says that the opportunities that God sends do not wake up those who are asleep. Wake up! Sleep is for the lazy, the indolent, the poor. Wide awake, restless, prowling is for the hungry, the lean, the opportunity taker, the rich. All around us all of the time there are opportunities to make a fortune. All we have to do is be open to the possibilities, to the magic of such events.

There are only five things you need to take on board if you are going to be a treasure seeker:

1 **Timing is crucial**. React too slowly and the opportunity is gone. Too fast and you might startle it. Markets shift, fashions change and products fade.

2 **You have to be serious**. There is no point in being on the ball every other day or only in the mornings. Hidden opportunities only reveal themselves when they feel they want to. I always imagine them as small shy beasts coming down to the waterhole for a drink. If you want to catch one you have to creep up really quietly, really skilfully.

> ## THE OPPORTUNITIES GOD SENDS DO NOT WAKE UP THOSE WHO ARE ASLEEP

3 **You have to be quirky.** If there are only a few hidden opportunities then you need to stand out. Quirky, unique, special, creative, unusual – name it however you will, but you have to stand out from the herd (to complete the animal analogy).

4 **You've got to know what you're doing.** Wealth, like any other skill, needs to be learnt. To spot opportunities and to be able to take advantage of them you need to give yourself the best chance. You can't pick up a financial paper and say you are going to understand it from Day 1. It takes time, dedication and commitment. Know your stuff and you'll see the opportunities much more clearly. There's a management technique called 'SWOT anaylsis' – an acronym for 'strengths, weaknesses, opportunites and threats – keep looking at all four.

5 **Be attractive.** If you smell horrid that shy beast is going to bolt. You have to dress smartly, smell fresh, look good, be well turned out and radiate attractiveness.

All around us all of the time there are opportunities to make a fortune. All we have to do is be open to the possibilities, to the magic of such events.

Have you ever noticed that when you are thinking of changing cars to another make or model you immediately start noticing hundreds of that make on the roads. Were they there before? Of course. It's just that you never noticed them. But once your attention is focused like a narrow beam of intense light, it throws them into sharp focus.

Opportunities are a bit like that. Once we start noticing them they are all around us. We just need that kick-start, that beginning of the search. Just like changing cars, we change our focus.

It is essential that we wake up our opportunity detector. Once we do, they will appear as if by magic all around us.

Don't try to get rich too quickly

We've already said you need to think long term. Trying to get rich quick only leads to disappointment and over-anxious hustling. And you do need to build a good base or your financial castle can topple at the first gust of wind. The longer you take to make your money, the more diverse you'll be with investments and income streams.

The quicker you make your money, the more likely it'll be a single strand and thus easy to break.

> **THE LONGER YOU TAKE TO MAKE YOUR MONEY, THE MORE DIVERSE YOU'LL BE WITH INVESTMENTS AND INCOME STREAMS**

Getting rich over time usually means you'll:

- build long-term income streams
- be insured against recession or sudden and negative market downturns

RULE 70

- have time to have a life as well – that old work/home relationship is less likely to be fractured
- be better at making money honestly and decently
- have time to make the relevant adjustments and thus not so likely to rush out and spend inappropriately
- gain the experience necessary for long-term financial security as you go along.

If you make your money too quickly there is a tendency to:

- spend it inappropriately
- not have time to learn to handle it well
- risk losing it by having your income coming from one area only.

If you really do want to earn a lot quickly you might like to take a leaf out of 81-year-old Stella Liebeck's book. She sued McDonald's because she burnt herself with spilt hot coffee and was awarded initially $2.9 million – later knocked down to a mere $640,000.

This may not have been a deliberate game plan but it did pay off – and quickly. Personally I would rather make my money slowly and enjoyably and not have to sue anyone to get it – or win the lottery, or have a close relative die, or have to marry someone inappropriate merely because they had a quid or two. Make your money slowly and you'll enjoy it more. It will last longer and you'll sleep nights.

Always ask what's in it for them

I don't want you to be paranoid generally but it is OK to be paranoid when it comes to your money. There are a lot of sharks out there looking for easy pickings from the less awake amongst us. Watch out.

Jeremy Paxman, the UK broadcaster, always interviews politicians with a basic underlying assumption that they are hiding something and he has to find out what and why.

Obviously we don't want to go round believing everybody is out to get us, but there is a good technique here that we can adopt to question anyone:

- offering us a money-making proposition
- offering to 'look after' our money
- looking to invest in our future or schemes
- offering us any financial advice
- offering to work for us
- offering us a partnership
- offering us products or services.

You have to be suspicious of anyone and anything that could make inroads into your wealth. Be very wary of anybody who:

- promises to help you get rich quick, by short-cuts, using tax loopholes or dubiously legal schemes
- uses the word 'offshore'
- uses the letters MLM or pyramid selling

- claims to be incredibly wealthy and is offering to share their secrets with you – the secret is they make their money out of people like you (*see Rule 61*)
- offers to increase your wealth by using the Internet
- asks for money upfront to seed investment, pay for promotional material or carry out a survey.

And three things to always remember:

- if it waddles like a duck and quacks like a duck then it is a duck and don't let anyone tell you it isn't
- if it looks too good to be true it probably is
- not all that glitters is gold.

> # BE SUSPICIOUS OF ANYONE AND ANYTHING THAT COULD MAKE INROADS INTO YOUR WEALTH

Remember also to keep asking 'What's in it for this person?' Don't trust anyone. Don't give your money to anyone to look after for you. Check the small print of anything you sign. Be on your guard.

RULE 72

Make your money work for you

An awful lot of us are guilty of wasting money by not making the best use of it – whether it's a small amount or large, long term or short term. From not cashing cheques to leaving cash in low interest accounts because you've forgotten about it or can't find the time or be bothered to move it.

Here, are a few tips to get you thinking about whether you are making all your money work for you:

- Don't leave money inactive in bank accounts – move it around to high interest accounts, even if it's only for a few days. Electronic banking means money can be easily and simply switched from one account to another – even for very short periods.

- Never be satisfied with the interest rate you are getting – there's always a better one out there. Keep actively looking.

- Shop around for all services you pay for. There are always cheaper options. Don't just pay for a name, pay for what you are getting.

- Don't leave property empty – it may be increasing in value but you are missing valuable rental income.

- If you invest in anything that is appreciating in value, could it also be useful? Would a classic car you can drive be more useful to you as opposed to a painting you can only look at (although that could be regarded as useful in the sense it might be relaxing or therapeutic but let's not go there).

RULE 72

- Explore all options. Don't be content ever with what you are doing but always be on the lookout for ways to improve, enhance, perk up, progress and advance. This does not mean fiddling of course.

- Crack on. Don't put anything off for tomorrow. Do it today. Do it now. If you take 4 months to bank a cheque then that's 4 months interest you've lost.

- Always remember idle money is wasted money – use it or lose it.

> ## NEVER BE SATISFIED WITH THE INTEREST RATE YOU ARE GETTING

RULE 73

Know when to let go of investments

I have my own little calculation which I am happy to pass on to you. I learned it from an Internet site a while back and it has stood me in good stead. Basically for an investment to work for me means I am looking for a return that will double my money in five years.

The calculation I use is to divide the interest rate into 72 to find out how long it will take me to double my money. For example, if the interest rate on a particular investment is 6 per cent, then it will take me 12 years ($72 \div 6 = 12$) to double my money. Too long for me. So I would be looking for an interest rate (known as a 'return') of around 14.4 per cent (I know, I know, you'd be lucky at the moment but this is only an example). This works for any amount of money incidentally.

So, if you want to know what interest rate to look for divide 72 by the number of years you are prepared to wait. $72 \div 5 = 14.4\%$. Gosh, something useful for you there and I did all the work for you.

For me, therefore, any investment that looks like it won't double my money in 5 years I pass on or, if it makes financial sense to get out (i.e. no penalty for doing so), I will let go of. I have my criteria, you need yours.

Perhaps you need to let go when:

- You feel in your waters that something is not right.
- The market has taken a downturn.

RULE 73

- You read something that makes you curious or suspicious of a particular investment.
- You need the money for something better, hotter.
- The investment hasn't been doing well for a while and is sluggish.
- You've achieved your maximum profit and it's time to get out.
- You've lost interest in a particular investment and simply can't be bothered any more.
- You have changed emotionally or ideologically and need to move on – perhaps you only invested green and now want mainstream or vice versa.
- The investment isn't fashionable any more – old hat can be costly if the return isn't there.
- You need to spread your portfolio around to minimise losses in a recession or down market.
- You bought blind and now have more information – and can see our fingers getting burnt.
- Throwing good money after bad will just aggravate the situation – cut your losses and get out (*see Rule 74*).

> PERHAPS YOU ONLY
> INVESTED GREEN AND
> NOW WANT MAINSTREAM
> OR VICE VERSA

RULE 73

There's a Chinese proverb: 'The more you know, the more luck you have'. So it is that the more money you gain, the more knowledge of the markets you'll need. Take it slowly and build a portfolio based on experience, knowledge, decent advice, up-to-date research and helpful friends. And if an investment isn't working, know when to let it go.

I know a man who bought shares in his company when he worked there – a good investment at the time as he bought them at a discount as an employee perk. After he left the company, he found out from contacts that the company was beginning to get into trouble and read about industry changes that he knew would be bad for the company. Sadly he was too lazy to do any-thing about his shares and didn't sell when there was the first sniff that all wasn't well. The value of these shares is now a half of what it was. He knew when to let go – but he didn't do it.

Don't chase bad luck runs

We all have a tendency to buy on tips from other people, buy on a whim, buy glamorous, invest too much in any one thing, ride a winner to death and, most fatally of all, fail to quit a loser. This is the one we really must learn to let go of.

There are four types of investors and it is clearly important to check which one you are – and which foibles you present. Thanks to Merrill Lynch (www.ml.com) for letting me reproduce this:

- **The Competitive Investor**. Makes up around 17 per cent of all investors and that's a 60/40 split male/female. Their biggest pluses are that they usually start investing early, have a lot of energy and are knowledge about their investments. And the biggest minuses? They are greedy, over-confident and love chasing a losing streak.

- **The Measured Investor.** This is the biggest group making up some 32 per cent of all investors with a 55/45 split male/female. They are secure in their investments, confident and think long term. Their one real big downside is they really find it hard to let go – they too chase a losing streak.

- **The Reluctant Investor.** This makes up 26 per cent of all investors with a 47/53 split male/female. They are more likely to use an adviser, wait too long before investing and find it easier than any other group to let go. They also don't like 'wasting time' on their investments.

- **The Unprepared Investor.** Represents 11 per cent of investors and a 47/53 split male/female. The description says it all really. They wait too long to start, put in too little money and don't let go soon enough. They tend to concentrate on one investment too much and are easily swayed by 'hot' tips.

RULE 74

Hannah Grove, chief marketing officer of Merrill Lynch Investment Managers says: 'Money is an emotional instrument, but emotions can get in the way of making the right investment decisions... If we can fathom our individual emotional tendencies, then we can take steps to anticipate and correct them.'

> # IF WE CAN FATHOM OUR INDIVIDUAL EMOTIONAL TENDENCIES, THEN WE CAN TAKE STEPS TO ANTICIPATE AND CORRECT THEM

It is imperative that you know what type of investor you are – and when to quit riding a losing streak. Nothing clouds your judgement more than throwing good money after bad. You have to learn to cut your losses and walk away. And yes, I do know how hard that can be.

Know why you should be able to read a balance sheet – and how

If you are going to run a company or invest in companies, you need to be able to read a balance sheet. This is different to knowing what profit or loss a company has made (i.e. reading a profit and loss account). Why? Because a profit and loss account only shows you half the picture.

For instance, Company X might have a turnover of 1 million and expenses of 500,000, thus it has made a profit of 500,000 and must be doing really well, n'est-ce pas? No, actually. Because what you can't see from this simple profit and loss account is that it owes the bank 2 million, the 1 million in turnover is very dodgy and there is a 4 million tax bill hanging over its head from previous years' accounts, a franchise expiring, tax loop hole about to close and a powerful competitor about to start up. Invest in Company X? I don't think so. It's bankrupt and fraudulently trading and not worth a pig's ear. Stay away. So you need to see a balance sheet. Without fail. And because of what it is *not* telling you.

A balance sheet has to balance. That's why it's called a balance sheet.[23] The basic formula you need to know is Assets minus Liabilities = Equity or A – B = C. Into even simpler terms: what you own less what you owe equals what you are worth. This applies to yourself, companies you work for/own and companies you intend investing in.

---

[23] The actual balance is Equity + Liabilities = Assets, thus balancing. You get assets on one side and liabilities and equity on the other.

RULE 75

A BALANCE SHEET HAS TO BALANCE

Let's have a closer look.

- **A: What you own – your assets**. Made up of current assets including cash and anything that can be realised (i.e. turned into cash) within say a three-month period (this might include cast-iron debtors, money in transit etc.); stock (stuff ready to be sold and raw materials that have value and can be made into products); any property you or the company may own; equipment and goodwill.

- **B: What you owe – your liabilities**. This includes your creditors, long-term loans and bank loans. Basically what you would have to find in cash if everyone called in what you owed them.

- **C: What you are worth – your equity.** This is A minus B. It tells us what you or your company is really worth. There is a formula that says that you take your current assets and divide it by your liabilities and if the answer is bigger than 1.5 you're doing OK. Obviously you need to adjust this for different industries and businesses but it serves as a basic indicator. I also take the equity and divide it by the assets as a percentage. And if the answer is higher than 50, I feel confident. For instance equity 35 million ÷ by assets (capital employed) of 70 million as a percentage = 35,000,000 ÷ 70,000,000% = 50 which is fine. But assets of 120 million and equity of 35 million is not so hot – around 29.

So if you just hear about a company that has made a profit of 1 million and are offered the chance to invest, don't be impressed by that single figure. Ask to see the balance sheet. Read it thoroughly. In fact, don't just read the balance sheet, important as it is, there are other things you need to know, such as a company's financial statements in total. The more information you can get (and should get), the more solid your decision will be.

Be one step ahead of your tax collector

You must never ever try to evade paying your taxes. If you do you will go to prison – and quite rightly so. No, I am not on the side of the tax collector. There's a difference here between evade (criminal) and avoid (sensible). There is a line between making sure you aren't giving money unnecessarily to the tax collector – avoiding – and deliberately evading tax illegitimately. Cross that line at your peril. But there should be no need to do so. There are many good people out there who will give you all the advice you need.

> ## THERE ARE MANY GOOD PEOPLE OUT THERE WHO WILL GIVE YOU ALL THE ADVICE YOU NEED

The more money you have, the greater the need to avoid tax – I stress this is not the same thing at all as evading – and the more expensive it becomes to do so. Obviously there is a tipping point whereby you are obliged to hand over your tax affairs to experts – who naturally cost an arm and leg – so you can avoid paying the tax collectors the other arm and leg you have left.

As you move up the prosperity ladder the tax issues get more complex. And there are all sorts of options. But remember the tax collectors are closing loopholes, changing laws, cutting off avenues as fast as you and your expensive experts can devise ways of avoiding tax. It's like a chess game only much more exciting and expensive.

I am not going to give you any specific advice because it changes too quickly and I don't want to get sued but areas worth bearing in mind are:

- Consider establishing a Limited Company – it can attract less tax and give you all sorts of options not available to the 'self-employed'. I'm assuming you are making some money – if you aren't, there is obviously no tax to save as there is no tax to pay. Bear in mind also that anyone can get your company records from Companies House so if you are bigging yourself up you can get caught out.

- Always make sure you make full use of your allowances – use them or lose them.

- Always consider if something is tax deductible before you buy it.

- Become a resident in a tax haven – but be quick as they are being shut down fast.

- Invest heavily in your own pension fund – it's tax free – or as about tax free as you can get these days.

- Become a tax nomad and wander the world not paying tax anywhere – watch out as a UK tax liability will arise when either income or a capital gain is remitted into the UK and there are circumstances when you can be based abroad but still pay tax (it depends on residency, ordinarily residency and domicile).

And of course make sure you are well up on investments that you don't have to pay tax on – get good advice and be willing to pay for good advice.

| |

Learn how to make your assets work for you

First off, do you know what assets you have? I mean you to include both long-term assets (fixed assets) and short-term assets (current assets). The fixed assets are the ones it would take you a while to turn into cash and the current assets are the ones easily converted into readies. Have you listed them? If not, do so now. I'll wait.

Back already? Got your list? I hope it has some of the following on it:

- property
- land
- motor vehicles
- pension funds
- cash
- goodwill
- works of art, antiques etc.
- investments
- money owed
- furniture and other possessions
- patents
- stocks and bonds
- intellectual properties.

If you have a business it may also include things like:

- stock
- work in progress

- raw materials
- plant and machinery
- equipment
- trade marks
- mailing lists

Once you start writing it down as a list you begin to see endless possibilities for using assets to make more money. Basically the personal advice is:

- Don't let an asset sit idle – if you own property, rent it out. And I don't just mean buy-to-let. Some enterprising people have rented garages or small bits of land they don't use in areas where there isn't enough parking for commuters and so on. Think laterally and don't discount anything!
- No asset is beautiful unless it is working for you – it has to be accumulating, increasing in value, to be worth keeping.
- Never leave cash sitting around – it tends to get bored and wander off. Make it work.

> YOU BEGIN TO SEE
> ENDLESS POSSIBILITIES
> FOR USING ASSETS TO
> MAKE MORE MONEY

And on top of those the business advice is:

- Keep stock and raw materials to a minimum – more is less.

- Depreciation is a dirty word – keep its use to a minimum and then excuse yourself every time you use it. But if you don't depreciate equipment you are fooling yourself about net worth.

- If you own something, borrow against it to buy more and then borrow against that to expand further. All businesses are expanding or contracting, they are like plants, flourishing and growing or wilting and dying, you choose. (I know I said earlier don't borrow, but you can borrow against assets – don't borrow for revenue expenditure.)

- It is a false economy to extend the life of plant or equipment past its safe-to-use date; the legal ramifications are enormous.

- Don't give more credit than you need to – money owed is money wasted.

- Chase debtors.

Don't ever believe you're only worth what you are being paid

Those who believe they are only worth what an employer pays them are almost always selling themselves short. Big companies depend on people not questioning their worth. Don't let them get away with it.

There are several points here. Firstly, it's a fact that if you work for an employer, those who change their jobs fairly frequently tend to get pay rises each time and therefore end up earning more than those who stay with the same company (maybe for very good reasons, like being happy). If you are staying put you have to learn to ask for more and demonstrate how you are adding value to an organisation to justify being paid more.

Secondly, no company is ever going to pay more for anything than they really have to. You need to be proactive and ask for more, and show you are worth more. It requires you to take action, however. Don't wait to be recognised. If you are freelance the same applies – nobody will suddenly offer to pay you more for your work – you need to be proactive and show you are worth more.

Thirdly, if you think you are always worth more, it makes you restless, ambitious, keen to get on. If you accept what is offered and never question it, then it makes you complacent and you'll get taken for granted.

> # IF YOU THINK YOU ARE ALWAYS WORTH MORE IT MAKES YOU RESTLESS, AMBITIOUS, KEEN TO GET ON

Now this is not a book about how to get a pay rise[24] but here are a few tips:

- Don't accept you are only worth what they are paying you – that's always the starting point. Pick your moment and ask.

- Be very clear about what you think you are worth – and why. If you have worked harder, achieved more, produced more, got better results, then you are entitled to say so and ask for recompense.

- Don't bargain just for money – always take into account cars, pensions, holiday entitlements, responsibility, working environment and space, staffing, whatever it is you want.

- If you do get turned down, always find out why and what it is you could do to get what you ask for.

- Return after putting right whatever was wrong in the previous point.

- Remain calm at all times.

- Never compare yourself with anyone else – you are unique and there is no comparison.

---

[24] Check out *How to Get a Pay Rise, a Bonus, or Promotion, or Whatever It Is You Want* by Ros Jay (Prentice Hall 2001) if you want the definitive guide.

- Never threaten to leave. Leave if you don't get what you want but no histrionics or threats or bullying. They might just call your bluff and if they do give into your tantrums, you'll never respect them afterwards.

If they say you can't have what you want, find out what it is you have to do; do it and return. Then they can't say no, can they? Getting more money – or anything else – is a matter of negotiating. Those who are good negotiators get more. It's a simple as that. Brush up on your negotiating skills (*see Rule 31*). And don't moan if you don't get what you want. Work harder and go back again.

Don't follow the same route as everyone else

Obviously you can follow whatever route you want, but you might end up in the same place as a lot of other people. If that is a good place, you'll have to share a lot. And if it's a bad place, why be there at all?

Being creative is a brilliant way to make money. Look at all the best moneymakers and one of the things they share is the ability to be one step ahead, to think creatively (out of the box if you like), to come up with schemes and ideas that other people haven't thought of. This doesn't mean you have to be reckless or a gambler. It just means thinking differently from other people. But that's the problem most people have. Following the herd is terribly comforting. If it all goes wrong, being in a herd gives a collective feeling of shared grief and the opposite of shared blame. Be a loner and going wrong is a tough cookie to swallow.

And the converse is true. If it all goes well and you are in a herd you can celebrate together – shared joy. A bit like being at a football match. It's a good feeling.

> IF IT ALL GOES WELL AND YOU ARE IN A HERD YOU CAN CELEBRATE TOGETHER – SHARED JOY

It takes a person of real courage, confidence and maturity – not to mention creativity and drive – to stand up and go your own way. You've got to be pretty confident to turn your back on shared joy and shared grief. In the great stock market crash of October 1987 an awful lot of people lost an awful lot of money. Two who didn't, and got out of shares and into cash in August, were the billionaires Kery Packer and Jimmy Goldsmith. And remember that the closer you get to becoming a winner, the less risk you want. And the nearer to losing you get, the more you are inclined to gamble.

I saw a website the other day – an investment broker's one – which claimed to show the five most popular stocks and the reasons why you should sell them now no matter what your friends, neighbours or family say. These stocks have been so high for so long that they must crash soon. Sell now and get out ahead of the crowd. I was thinking that real moneymakers wouldn't have been there anyway but would have been out there investing in something none of us had even thought of.

Lots of people invested in ostrich farms. Where are they now? Lots of people invested in worm farms. You bought eggs and turned them into worms and the big worm farm would buy them back. Loved that one. Yeah, right. Of course they'll buy all your worms back off you.

One of my sons invested £10 to start his own giant snail business. He bought two giant snails to breed with (or should that be from?). He fed and looked after them for about six months when I had to break it to him they were snails out of someone's garden he'd bought. He wasn't alone. Loads of kids at his school were sold the same dream. And the same snails.

STAYING

WEALTHY

Now you've got it, you don't want to let it go, so the next section is how to hang on to it once you've got it. Assuming you now know to avoid the giant snail scams and the ostrich farms. How to preserve, protect, enjoy and maintain it. After all, when you've finally got it, you don't want to waste it, squander it, throw it away or give it to me. Actually the last one isn't true. You can if you really want to.

There are endless websites all offering to look after your money for you. Ignore them all. They usually say something like: *Start Your Own Wealth Freedom Journey Today – No Time To Lose*! All you have to do is sign up for a newsletter and buy a 'get rich quick' book right away. They promise to make you a millionaire within three to five years.

Perhaps you should ask for a refund on this one because I promise you nothing beyond hard work, dedication, focus, creativity, standing out from the crowd, forward planning and the honest sweat of your brow. Gosh. No promises there at all.

Shop for quality

My lovely wife taught me this one – credit where it is due. When we met I was a great one for finding a bargain – two chickens for the price of one at the supermarket, that sort of thing. She, on the other hand, bought less (I never did do anything with that other chicken) but bought quality. So I would cook a thin and sick-looking chicken and drink it with cheap white plonk and she would provide lobster and champagne. You can see why I fell for her.

> I WOULD COOK A THIN AND SICK-LOOKING CHICKEN WITH CHEAP WHITE PLONK AND SHE WOULD PROVIDE LOBSTER AND CHAMPAGNE

I bought five cheap T-shirts in a pack and she bought one immaculate of much better quality. Now her stuff:

- lasted longer
- washed better
- looked better with age

- kept its colour better
- kept its shape better
- said more about her in a positive way
- took less maintenance (I drove a cheap car that was always breaking down and I missed meetings etc. whereas she drove a better car and always arrived looking calm and immaculate).

She taught me that the money I was spending, although less, was being wasted because I had to replace stuff much more often. I was throwing money away and looking cheap at that.

Shopping for quality rather than price was a hard lesson to learn. I had to discard all those money myths from my childhood:

- Don't spend more than you need to.
- No one needs to look that expensive.
- It is somehow wrong to spend money on yourself.
- It is somehow better to get a bargain than to buy quality.

Shopping for quality says masses about the way you live, the way you conduct yourself and your business. It says quality to others who will adjust the way they treat you. It also saves you money in the long run – cheap can often be a false economy.

Check the small print

I could write you a contract promising you a cast-iron, no get-out clauses, guaranteed, money back without quibbles, cross my heart and hope to die in a cellarful of rats, sort of thing that would stand up in a court of law and withstand any scrutiny you cared to put it under. What am I selling? It doesn't matter. Small print can cost you dear. Check it carefully.

> ## SMALL PRINT CAN COST YOU DEAR. CHECK IT CAREFULLY

I love the sort of small print classics, such as taking shoes back that don't fit only to be told they can't be refunded if they have left the store. Or the small print on medications that say they can make you sick and you can't sue. Or the small print on computer software that says you are bound by the agreement if you break the seal on the packaging – and the software can't be tested until it has been run and you can't run it until you've installed it and you can't do that until you've broken open the packaging. Agh!

There's a wonderful story of someone who sold their soul to the devil. The devil wanted five years off their life and the person reckoned it was worth it. Oh no! He didn't check the small print. The devil took five years off his life all right – the *first* five years. Agh! Can you imagine what missing the first five years would do to you? And you thought credit card companies were bad?

What do I mean by 'checking the small print'? What do you actually have to do? Three basic things:

- Obviously check that it covers you for what you want.
- Check there are no hidden clauses that will twist the basic meaning of the contract.
- Check for penalty clauses – ones that penalise you for late or non-payment of anything.

It's a bit like checking the small print on food packaging. If you don't like what's in it, don't buy it. Move on up the aisle and buy organic, green, fresh, unpasteurised, whatever. If there is small print, the hairs on the back of your neck should be rising. There is only one reason for it to be there – to trip you up. Move on.

Don't spend it before you've got it

Gosh this is a hard one for me. I have to admit I find this one of the most difficult to take on board.

How am I to learn this one? Any tips? I know I should:

- Budget for today and only for today. If I don't have it, I don't spend it.
- Ignore what I think or know is coming in, in the future.
- Put loads aside for tax – no, even more than that.
- No loans, overdrafts, no borrowings of any sort so I won't be tempted to use future income to pay off debts run up today – or the reverse, run up debts today knowing that income from the future can be used to pay them off (very naughty).

The downside of spending future income is:

- The income may not materialise or be less than you thought. (Counting chickens that never hatch…)
- The bubble has to burst somewhere and if you are always spending in advance you will get caught out one day.
- It encourages sloppy financial planning.
- Whatever you bought will have long lost its appeal or wear out, get broken or even completely forgotten.
- You lose touch with reality – the future isn't real until it becomes today – and as such you can overspend only too easily.

I guess I need a four-point plan:

1 Question whether I need a particular thing today or could wait until later to buy it – a useful ploy as once the 'blood lust' has worn off the appeal often wears off too.

2 Question whether it is worth it. Obviously, if buying today against tomorrow's income, you will incur interest – so is it worth the extra?

> # BUYING TODAY AGAINST TOMORROW'S INCOME, YOU WILL INCUR INTEREST

3 Question the risk factor. If I commit myself today, what if my circumstances change and I need that future income for other purposes?

4 Question that if I spend today I might not have income for a really exciting spend that might come up – better to keep it just in case.

Follow this with me and it should reduce our credit card balances considerably.

RULE 83

Put something aside for your old age – no, more than that!

When you realise you are cracking along fast in the outside lane of the age motorway and can see less road ahead than there used to be, you should be keen to make sure that if you do stop earning you will still be able to afford the level of style, luxury and comfort you now enjoy or want to enjoy.

> IF YOU DO STOP EARNING YOU WILL STILL BE ABLE TO AFFORD THE LEVEL OF STYLE, LUXURY AND COMFORT YOU NOW ENJOY OR WANT TO ENJOY

There are some really good reasons why you should put aside money for your old age:

- You can't rely on the state any more.
- If you don't save for yourself, then you may have to rely on the kindness of strangers – or family, which might be worse.
- If you have no old age plan, you may lose control of your level of comfort, style and luxury.
- You will lose control of your financial freedom.

- You may lose control of bodily functions and will need money to take care of medical bills.

- As you age you do slow up, and working as hard as you are now will be impossible.

- You also don't want to *have to* always work hard (though you may choose to) – for most of us there is a time for sitting in the sunshine and if it isn't when you're old, then when is it?

So why haven't we put something aside already? Well, when we are young it's hard to envisage a time when we won't be. So we don't need to prepare for it. Also we are too busy having a good time to think about such things. Also we are too busy looking after other members of our family to have much time to think about ourselves. Also we are mortgaged up to the hilt and work is hard enough. Also we haven't entered our earning boom period of our fifties so don't have lump sums to salt away. Also, also, also.

So, if we are going to put something aside, perhaps we need a few guidelines:

- It's never too late to start, but the earlier you do it, the less it will hurt. Prioritise spending – list what you are going to spend on and see if 'the future' is there. If it isn't, put it there and make it top of the list ahead of that new boat or trip to Paris.

- If you haven't saved much by your fifties put in a lump sum to seed your retirement plan.[25]

- Get your finances in order and curb waste – spend it instead on your plan.

- If you don't have a pension, make sure you have something that will fund your retirement/later years (property to sell? shares to cash in?) and that they will be sufficient.

- Always think high interest and move money around to get the best out of it.

Trade down property as you get older and your needs get smaller – once the kids have all left home you don't need so much space so invest the profits and downsize.

---

[25] God, don't ever 'retire', you'll drop down dead immediately you do that.

RULE 84

Put something aside for emergencies/rainy days – the contingency fund

As well as saving for your old age you'll always need to have a contingency fund. I can't give you a definitive list of emergencies but here's a few to get you thinking. Don't have nightmares now:

- accidents – motoring, industrial, work-related
- illnesses
- sudden legal problems – like being sued or arrested wrongly
- land disputes – very expensive indeed
- problems with children – don't start me off, there are too many to list here including drugs, unwanted pregnancies, trouble with police, motoring, illnesses, travel problems (it's expensive to get them back from Thailand when they run out of money and/or enthusiasm)
- acts of God – floods, earthquakes, tsunami, droughts, subsidence, forest fire, pestilence (whatever that is)
- sudden unemployment
- sudden liquidation of your company
- recession.

So how much to put aside and where do we put it? Well, the wise move is to put aside enough to keep you going in the same style as you live now for three to six months without having to even think about money for that period. Roughly half your annual income if you like. Obviously if you get completely wiped out in a tsunami or forest fire you'll be insured so can collect, but you will need something to tide you over. Medical bills can also be covered by insurance.

So where to keep it? Most people keep it as a savings account – high interest of course, but instant access. Personally I've noticed the shrewd rich ones keep a safety deposit box with cash for emergencies as well. Always handy in desperate times.

You only have to look at humanitarian disasters to realise how quickly money runs out and how conventional sources become desperately difficult to access. Surviving the storms of Louisiana was bad enough for most people but it was a great leveller because no one could access the banks because they too were under 10 feet of water. And money quickly becomes a useless currency – food and water become the priorities then (and guns I believe, but I don't want to go there).

You might choose to take out sizeable insurance policies to help alleviate the problems sudden emergencies can cause … Alternatively you might prefer to squirrel away an emergency fund in a highly liquid account (easy quick access), such as a saving account or money market account (which pays higher interest rates). But, as usual, take detailed advice from a proper financial expert – not me.

> **PERSONALLY I'VE NOTICED THE SHREWD RICH ONES KEEP A SAFETY DEPOSIT BOX WITH CASH FOR EMERGENCIES AS WELL**

You paid what for it?
How to shop around

I know I said shop for quality, and I do really believe that, but I don't believe in throwing your money away on expensive stuff that could be bought just as cheaply from another source. For instance, a dear friend was recently buying a very expensive car, a wonderful car. I was most jealous. I was so jealous I broke all my own rules and asked him what he was paying for it. I couldn't believe my ears. 'You're paying what for it?!'

He said he could afford it – as indeed he most certainly can. But it was the principle of the thing. 'You can get it a lot cheaper here, here or here,' I suggested. 'Yes,' he replied, 'but then I would have to get up off my arse and do something instead of just reaching for the phone.'

I offered to buy it for him at the cheaper location and then sell it on to him and split the difference. But he was having none of it. He explained he had earned his money so he could stay on the sofa and lift a phone and have the world brought to him, delivered with the minimum of effort. That was what he thought great wealth was all about.

Now, unlike my friend, the sensible rich don't just throw money away because they can. Instead they:

- always get at least three quotes for work being done and don't just accept the first quote they get
- shop around to make sure they aren't wasting their money
- are cautious about spending if they have had to work hard for their money. They aren't miserly, just cautious and selective and discriminating.

RULE 85

There is an old Russian saying that spending is quick but earning long. That's true. We can offload the work of years in a few moments. We have to be prudent when it comes to spending. Not to deny ourselves anything – God forbid I should recommend that. But instead just be a bit cautious and don't go throwing money away needlessly.

> ## JUST BE A BIT CAUTIOUS AND DON'T GO THROWING MONEY AWAY NEEDLESSLY

I think wise spending is something we should be teaching our kids from a very early age. They are all too often persuaded by advertising that if something is brightly coloured, noisy, messy or in some way repugnant to parents, it must be a good thing. And they rush home and strip off all those wrappings and disappointment sets in so very quickly. Teach 'em young.

As for you, time to discover for yourself the joy of getting value for money in everything you buy (if you haven't already). The Internet makes it all terribly easy to compare prices and shop around and make sure you aren't paying more than you have to for anything. Use it.

RULE 86

Never borrow money from friends or family (but you can allow them to invest)

I think we might need to have a quick recap of what friends and family are there for – and what you are there for, for them as well. Friends are for:

- caring
- loving
- supporting
- nurturing
- helping
- advising – and getting advice from
- comforting
- having fun with
- sharing.

Nowhere in that lot does it mention:

- borrowing from
- stealing from
- conning.

Put simply, it is very bad manners to borrow from friends and family. It sets up too many issues and agendas. It causes resentments and recriminations and suspicions. It jeopardises relationships that are important. Don't do it.

> ## IT IS VERY BAD MANNERS TO BORROW FROM FRIENDS AND FAMILY

Besides which, friends and family aren't proper sources of loans because they aren't licensed for it. I'm not talking here of the odd fiver to get a round of drinks in but significantly large amounts – how much that is will depend on your circumstances ... You do need to be licensed to be a credit broker (no seriously) and if you borrow from friends (or conversely lend to the same) you have no, legal recourse if it all goes wrong – and it will, as sure as eggs is eggs.

I know technically you could get proper agreements drawn up and all that but even then, and even if they are charging you the proper interest rates, it's dangerous. If you fail to pay them back – due to circumstances beyond your control of course – you risk losing their friendship, which of course would mean much more to you than the loan would in the first place.

The only exception to this is if family and friends want to invest in say a business you are starting, and they fully understand that, like any investment, they may not see a return and all the usual risks apply. (*See Rule 90* for more on this.) What you can't afford is for it to cause a rift if things don't work out. Family and friends are too important for that.

Don't surrender equity

This is a Rule for anybody who runs a company, or who is a free-lance and is thinking of setting themselves up as a sole trader business. Essentially the point is not to give away bits of you or your company.

The aim of the exercise is to preserve wealth so don't surrender equity (shares or a stake in your company) or you'll be paying someone a share of your hard work, time and energy. Better to give them money, even if it is with interest, rather than a share of you.

In a later Rule on spending your money I'll tell you to ask for equity, but that's different – that's you as a lender of money. The shoe is on the other bank account then, so different rules apply.

There is a misconception that having total control of one's business is a bad thing and many business advisers will advocate giving away equity as a good thing. But I have noticed that the really successful wealthy don't do this. They hang on to every bit they've got. They may borrow and take out loans and run up overdrafts but they don't give away equity.

Advisers will suggest steering clear of a bank loan because the bank can close down your business so quickly. A business angel will lend money instead, but they will demand equity.

If you do have to surrender equity then make sure you swap it for:

- business skills and acumen
- hands-on directorships
- a freedom-from-hassle agreement so you can run the business the way you want

- a realistic percentage so you don't give away too much
- a buy-back clause so you can buy back the equity for cash at a later stage when you are cash rich.

I run a company and have some shareholders but the shares they hold don't give them voting rights. So, although they do get some equity, they don't get control, and in fact the shares were given as a reward for advice rather than money I borrowed.

> ## NEVER GIVE VOTING
> ## SHARES AWAY TO ANYONE

Only take money into your business from people who have experience of your business and understand its ebbs and flows and industry-related problems and remember, never give voting shares away to anyone.

Know when to stop

What? I can hear a gasp of surprise. Know when to stop?! Didn't you say earlier that you shouldn't rest on your laurels or they will wilt? Yes I did, but that was when you were starting to get results, not when you'd done really well and were wealthier than you thought you ever would be. Look, there has to come a time when enough is enough. There has to come a time when you want to:

- spend more time with your family
- enjoy your life
- have fun
- go travelling
- get the work/life balance tipped a bit in favour of the life
- use your time to pass on what you have learned to others.

> ## LOOK, THERE HAS TO COME A TIME WHEN ENOUGH IS ENOUGH

Of course you might be able to do all of these without giving up the gaining wealth ideal. But it is the focus that stops perhaps. Being driven to gain prosperity is a good thing. But once gained, you should return to the fold so to speak. I am always impressed by people like Bill Gates, who decided to retire from his work to run his charitable foundation. In his case he probably didn't need and couldn't spend or count any more money than he already had/has and it's probably accumulating faster each day than he can count. He's probably living on the interest on the interest on the interest on the interest ...

And I see his close second in the wealth stakes Warren Buffet is doing the same – and actually contributing to Bill's foundation.[26] I know these boys are playing around with sums well into the billions but their hearts are in the right place. These sorts of people are where this rule comes from. Others doing the same include Thomas Monaghan, the Domino Pizza founder, who is reputed to have given away over a billion dollars and founded Ave Maria University.

You're thinking that you aren't anywhere in the same league. No, but you can still have an end game strategy whereby you build an 'enough is enough' clause into your plan. Otherwise where do you stop? How much is enough? Where do you draw the line? There is an Arab saying: '*If you have much, give of your wealth; if you have little, give of your heart.*' So when you get a lot, give some of it away – we'll speak more of this in a moment.

I'm not going to browbeat you about giving to charity but I am suggesting that knowing when you've got enough money is important. I know there is an expression that you can't have too much of a good thing but focusing on prosperity is only one part of a rich and varied life and you can be too dedicated.

---

[26] Sorry, it is actually called the Bill and Melinda Gates Foundation – BMGF – sounds like something from a story by Roald Dahl.

SHARING YOUR WEALTH

Once you've worked hard to earn it, it does seem a bit unfair to share it. But if you don't you run the risk of your hardworking outstretched hand turning into an arthritic grasping claw. Money can be earned, grown, guarded, fought over, used well, used badly, won, lost, buried, invested, given away, bought back, exchanged and divided up. But the nicest thing to do with it is surely to share it.

I'm not talking do-gooding here. I'm talking sharing because sharing is a kind thing to do. It won't buy you a ticket into heaven but it will help others. I know you've worked hard, grafted, and burnt the midnight oil to get to where you are today and why should you give it away to those who are lazy or less focused or indulgent or plain liberty-takers? Yep, good point. But I'm talking here about the less well off, the unfortunate, the weak, the needy and the deserving.

Wealth is a bit like a beautiful painting. Sure you can hang it in your study and only you get to look at it. But you can also share it and let others look as well. Ah, but you'll say wealth decreases if we share it. Does it? Does it really? I doubt it somehow. I think for every penny you give away – or share with someone less able to gain prosperity – you double its value. Maybe not in hard cash but in other ways.

As I say, I don't want to browbeat you. It's just I've noticed that the really successful, happy rich people do feel at ease sharing their wealth and that is a lesson for all of us.

Use your wealth wisely

I read of a nice couple the other day – both rock musicians – who had bought a big house in the countryside in Oxfordshire (or some other Home County) with nine acres and were settling down to raise kids and I thought what a good investment as it provides:

- a stable place to bring up kids
- a sound investment as long as the current boom in house prices continues
- a nice place to live in the sense of peace and quiet with no city pollution
- a friendly place for the children to grow up with neighbours looking out for them
- a sound investment in history and heritage.

On the other hand, I read in the same paper of a fashion model who was in the news a lot because of her drug habit. An expensive habit I have no doubt. I guess you can see where my interests lie from these two snippets gleamed from the newspapers. One is a sound and wise investment and the other is just self-indulgent trouble that lends nothing to the wisdom of wealth.

I'm not a party pooper but I have noticed that those who handle their wealth sensibly and share it and are generous with their time and money get back a whole lot more than those who squander, misuse, indulge and generally behave as if their wealth gives them a licence to show off. Enough moralising and preaching. I did promise not to. But these are genuine observations and I'm sure you've made similar observations yourself. Those who abuse their wealth don't tend to stay wealthy for long. Here are a few questions regarding our wealth and how wisely we might handle it:

- Why did we get wealthy in the first place?
- What is the best use of wealth?
- What are our long-term goals and expectations for our wealth?
- What do we think our wealth will bring us?
- What could we do with our wealth that would be beneficial to others?
- What sort of world do we want?
- How do we and our wealth wish to be seen?
- What will they say about us after we've gone?
- What legacy will we leave behind?

> ## THOSE WHO ABUSE THEIR WEALTH DON'T TEND TO STAY WEALTHY FOR LONG

I personally think the best use of wealth is to teach children how to earn it, invest it, save it and spend it wisely. As we all get more and more affluent, there is a real need to introduce some element of monetary discussion into the curriculum. Children need to learn about tax, insurance and spending and all the stuff we never got taught and have had to learn the hard way as we went along. Mind you, I would also make sure every child could read and write before they left school and could drive a car.

Never lend money to friends or family unless you are prepared to write it off

Can you share your wealth with family and friends? Yes, but if you want to retain your sanity I would strongly suggest you don't lend anyone any money unless, mentally, you are prepared to write it off. That way when they don't repay you – and I bet they won't – you'll feel just fine about it. If you expect them to repay you and they don't, imagine how hurt and let down you are going to feel.

I know. I have sons. But my money is for them as much as it is for me, so we play this game of them asking for a loan and me giving it to them. Sometimes they pay it back and I am pleasantly surprised but sometimes they don't and I write it off and that's fine too. (I really hope they don't read this or I'll be cornered like a rat in my own home.)

> I REALLY HOPE THEY DON'T READ THIS OR I'LL BE CORNERED LIKE A RAT IN MY OWN HOME

I value them and their relationship with me and I wouldn't want to fall out with them over something as squalid as money when there are so many better things to fall out with them over anyway.

If you do lend money to friends and don't get it back, you lose more than just the money – you lose the friendship as well. They feel embarrassed because they aren't repaying you and thus don't come round to see you. You feel grieved and don't invite them because of it. Result: end of friendship.

Write it off though and you'll still be happy to see them and they'll quickly forget the embarrassment and regard you as one of a kind.

Of course you don't have to do either. You can just say no (*see Rule 93*). Or you could just give them money (*see Rule 94*).

I've been reading an advice blog on the web about a young man who lent his room-mate at college $350 – not a huge amount – but the repayment never materialised. He had asked various friends first if they had ever lent his room-mate money and they said he had paid them back. Now he has of course fallen out big time with his room-mate – despite offering him the option of repayment terms at $50 a month. Worse still, he has fallen out with all his other friends because they 'approved' the loan in his eyes.

The advice was to take the friend to court but I figure he won't see the money anyway and will cop a lot of legal expense into the bargain. Better to chalk it up to experience and walk away whistling. I know, for him, it is a lot of money but any decent education doesn't come cheap. The discussion did go on into his rights to 'seize' his room-mate's possessions etc. I still say walk away whistling and don't ever do it again.

Don't lend, take equities

If you are asked for a loan by somebody for a specific project such as starting a company or expanding one, there are a variety of answers including:

- no
- yes
- yes but
- yes on the condition that
- yes with equity
- yes with a convertible loan.

Obviously 'no' can cause offence (*see Rule 93*). 'Yes' is a no-no, if you see what I mean. Lending friends and family money isn't on unless you are prepared to write it off (*see Rule 90*) and generally people who want big loans aren't that close or they'd know you better.

This leaves us with the last three – conditions, equity or convertible? There may be others of course.

Conditions: A mug's game if you ask me. On the condition you repay me when you've made your fortune. Hmm. On the condition you don't do anything silly with this. Hmm. On the condition you only use this for the good of mankind. Hmm. Conditions is such a tricky one but there are many who'll ask for conditions – 'If you would just be so good as to lend me this I promise to … blah blah'. Yeah, right.

Equity: Better. You don't lend, you offer to buy a share in whatever project it is. If it is successful you recoup with interest. If it fails, you shouldn't have been lending – or buying into it – in the first place. More fool you. The trouble with equity is that it's often black and white, hit or miss. You get your money back if the project is successful – and perhaps that should be *when* the project is successful.

Convertible: Much better. You lend as a proper loan with repayment details all worked out legally so it is a binding loan. But if the project is successful – it should be or you shouldn't be lending in the first place – you convert the loan into equity. This way you get your money back plus a big share of the profits. It sort of makes lending seem worthwhile.

> # ASKING FOR A CONVERTIBLE LOAN WILL SORT THE WHEAT FROM THE CHAFF

If approached for a loan, asking for a convertible loan will sort the wheat from the chaff, the serious from the not so serious. It makes the serious stand up and be counted. If the project then fails you get your money back – in theory at least. Obviously if the project fails there may not be any money but you will have secured it against their property of course (I know I said never to do that, but that was advice for you as a borrower; as a lender always make sure you do). I even do this with my children if tempted to lend them any money for big items like cars and houses. Yes you can have the money but I want to own a share, so you can't sell it if you get bored or restless or whatever without my permission. Amazing how often they back off when they know I'll be their partner. And I also then know that they did buy the item rather than something they'd rather not tell me about.

You really, really can't take it with you

I know there's a saying – whoever has the most toys at the end wins. But you really can't take it with you and you can't buy anything with it when you go – no tickets into heaven, no indulgences, no get-out-of-hell free cards. When you go, you go alone and with nothing, just as you came in. So all that effort, in a way, is wasted. Unless of course you did something useful with it when you had it and had the ability to do it. Left drooling in some old folks' home isn't the time or place to start being philanthropic is it?

Not getting rid of it is known as *wealth bondage* – being tied so tightly to your money that you really do try to take it with you – and that really is kinky. Sure you can leave it to your kids but you should have given most of it away long before you pop your clogs or you'll be leaving a massive tax liability for someone down the line.

> NOT GETTING RID OF IT IS
> KNOWN AS WEALTH
> BONDAGE

Whatever you decide to do, do take the proper advice – nothing grates so much as a poorly thought-out will and lots of tax after you've gone.

You can of course insure against tax liabilities after you've gone. You have to calculate what you think your tax liability is likely to be and then set up a whole-of-life insurance policy to cover it. But the policy has to be written into a trust to ensure the proceeds from the policy aren't included with your estate – but for heaven's sake be careful on placing anything in trust because if you use the wrong one you can make things even worse – also legislation can change, for example the latest budget and changes to taxation of interest in possession trusts.

Gosh, I'm not a financial adviser (except on a behavioural level – you need somebody else for the nitty-gritty-which-investment-is-best-for-me detail) but it seems to make sense to have all this tied up before you go. And of course you can leave the lot to your spouse and then they don't have to pay death duties[27] but by golly their tax bill is going to be high when they go, so you are only delaying rather than off-setting. You can establish a trust to ensure that both husband and wife's nil rate bands are fully utilised – but again be very careful using a trust.

I was reading about the Dalai Lama's wealth the other day. He gets paid the equivalent of around 38p a day expenses, owns two robes – one on and one in the wash – and his only indulgence is a new watchstrap every now and again (I did wonder if he bought leather ones). And yet he is the head of an entire country – albeit one in exile. Now that is cool in my book.

---

[27] Spouse's exemption – it must be your spouse or civil partner and if they are domiciled outside the UK the exemption is restricted to £55,000.

RULE 93

Know when/how to say no – and yes

Now you've made some money there will be those who see you as:

- a target – easy pickings
- owing them something – after all, they have known you for years …
- worth taking a chance on – you never know
- a genuine source of low-interest loan or free gifts – and so much easier than preparing a proper business plan and going to the bank.

I'm not saying you will always get the outstretched hand. In fact some requests will be cloaked in the most attractive brochures of potential investments. So how do you know when to say yes and when to say no? And how to say either?

Saying no to friends and family is easy, in a sense. Right from day one you make it a policy – and a very easily identifiable one – not to lend to friends and family (*see Rule 90*). You never do, so they learn not to ask.

Saying no to business acquaintances is also easy. Just ask them to refer everything to your accountant or business adviser. Say you never make a decision without their input and you can't proceed until they have studied everything in close detail. That puts off the ones who are just arm-round-the-shoulder trying it on. The others might be worth considering if they have genuine plans. In which case it might be worth having a look.

RULE 93

Now *when* to say yes or no. Say no if:

- your gut instinct says to say no
- they haven't done any work on their presentation – if they are lazy at ground zero it strikes me they'll be lazy right through
- you have no connection with them – always say no to strangers basically.

To say yes is fine. To say no is fine. It's your money and you can do with it what you want. You have to:

- Let go of any guilt – this is business.
- Make sure you understand exactly what is being asked for – that's why calling in advisers is always a good idea.
- Keep a closed-door policy to stop yourself being overwhelmed by requests – make it hard for them to get to you.
- Avoid saying yes because you think it will make people happy – they are emotionally blackmailing you and thus get themselves crossed off the list automatically and without guilt.
- Always be very clear when you are saying 'no'. No 'maybes' or 'we'll see' or 'I'll have to sleep on that one'. Say no and put everyone out of their misery – including you.
- Don't allow yourself to be badgered. Be assertive.
- Stop them in their tracks – a simple 'I'd rather you didn't ask me' before they've even got started.

Find ways to give people money without them feeling they are in your debt

I love this one. It is such a challenge to give money to people who:

- haven't asked for it
- need it
- deserve it
- will use it wisely/well.

And the challenge is to get them to accept it without feeling indebted to you, beholden, grudging, guilty, whatever. This is one of those rules we all ought to practise no mater how much money we have. I reckon you get to start as soon as you become a parent and give your kids big money for cars and things. They are always saying: 'I'll pay you back', and you know they won't. But if you can give them money without all that stuff being attached to it, you are doing well.

> IF YOU CAN GIVE THEM MONEY WITHOUT ALL THAT STUFF BEING ATTACHED TO IT, YOU ARE DOING WELL

There are a variety of tips to help you give your money away without them feeling guilty or you embarrassed:

- The 'You might win the lottery one day' approach. This is a good one as it implies that there, but for a bit of luck, you go. All they've got to do is be as lucky as you and they'll pay you back.

- The 'Fortunes change and they go down as well as up' approach. Basically what you are saying is that you are flush at the moment but that might not always be the case and when your fortunes go down, they can help you out.

- The 'I like my friends to be happy' approach. How can I be happy when I see my friends in misery/trouble/debt/whatever? If you aren't happy then I can't be, so I'll help myself to become happy by helping you to become happy. How can anyone refuse?

- This is the 'Why shouldn't I help my friends?' approach – a subset of the one above but still valuable and useful. Look, it's what friends are for. You've helped me out in the past/are helping me by…/have always offered help anyway so why can't I do the same for you?

- The 'Help me out here, I've got a tax problem' approach. Look, if I can offload some of this cash I can alleviate my tax burden, so can you help me by taking some? I would be ever so grateful.

- The 'Taxman will only get it after I'm dead approach' so can I give it to you now and see the pleasure it'll bring you rather than you be grieving and moping after I've gone?

- Help them with a housing upgrade by taking equity in the new house. They pay nothing until they snuff it, at which point your investment will probably show better appreciation than the interest rate it would have earned on deposit. And if it doesn't so what? Profit was never the point anyway, but they can feel happy about it.

I'm sure if you put your mind to it there will be many more you can come up with. Hey, this one is fun. You get to help others, give loads away, share your wealth and be creative all at the same time.

Don't over-protect your children from the valuable experience of poverty

Look, if you're about to ask your parents for a really big loan (gift?) then you'd better buy up every copy of this book you can and burn the lot of them because you're not going to like what I have to say next.

Parents, if you are reading this then don't give them that loan (gift). It is OK not to mollycoddle them, to make them learn the value of money, to make them treat money with respect right from the word go. And just because you have lots doesn't mean they are entitled to stand there with their hand out right from the day they get out of nappies.

> ## A MONTHLY ALLOWANCE IS ALWAYS A GOOD IDEA

I'm the world's worst at this one but I am learning. There are various ways you can go from being utterly mean and not giving them a bean to being overly generous and giving them every-thing. Now, I was going to talk about setting budgets for children and setting up trust funds for them.

RULE 95

A monthly allowance is always a good idea as they then have to live within their means. It teaches them to budget and to scrimp and save at the end of the month – or halfway through it in most cases. When they first go off to uni is probably the best time to do this as they are also learning a whole new batch of things about being grown up – sex, drugs, staying out late, wrong sort of friends, binge drinking. Learning to balance their own books at the same time is good for them.

You can set aside lump sums for them as well so they can buy a house, business, decent car. If you administer it, then they can't blow it on a plasma TV or a £600 designer handbag but only a sensible thing that they have to explain to you in some detail. And of course a trust fund for when you have shuffled off. Or of course let them have such a fund when they are of an age sensible enough to enjoy it without it diverting them from their education. Personally I would give it to them after it would make any real difference to them; in effect after they have started to earn their own money in worthwhile amounts.

And for goodness' sake don't ever tell them they are getting a lump sum aged 25 or whatever you decide. Nothing demotivates a child more than thinking they're coming into money. They'll think they don't have to make any effort. Let them think they'll always be poor and watch them go.

And how do you set a good allowance figure? Only you can work it out for your child and it obviously varies depending on age but once they reach their teens it's as well to thrash it out with them – a process sometimes of painful discussion (who said rows?). But make them argue every penny and justify it. It'll make them value it when they get to spend it.

Know how to choose charities/good causes

Once you have some money you get inundated with requests to give to charities. I'm not talking about the emotional blackmail ones we all get through the letterbox – these three pennies could pay for food for an entire family forever and a rainforest and sight for all the blind people in the world and all you have to do is send them back with whatever you can afford. Oh the guilt when you spend those three pennies – not!

I'm talking about big charitable donations, supporting a particular cause, supporting a particular person. I've always had my doubts – and this is entirely subjective, entirely personal – about supporting a penguin or endangered fish or threatened albatross. How do you know which is yours? In the zoo you can at least go and have a look at your own saved pet but in the wild it is so much more difficult.

> I'VE ALWAYS HAD MY
> DOUBTS – AND THIS IS
> ENTIRELY SUBJECTIVE,
> ENTIRELY PERSONAL –
> ABOUT SUPPORTING
> A PENGUIN

Anyway here are a few tips for choosing a good charity – a good one for you:

- Decide what is important to you – the planet, saving whales, small children, the poor, cancer research.
- Work out what you want to do – just give money, get involved, be an adviser, raise funds (I've always wanted to drive one of those inflatables for Greenpeace; I just think those boats are so cool).
- Check out charities you might think suitable on the Internet and see if your ideals fit in with theirs.
- Check out the charities themselves – financial statements, accounts, brochures, campaign information, membership, mission statements.
- Trust your gut feelings.

Personally I reject any charities that directly approach me. Not because it makes me cross but as a way of weeding out the ones I don't want to support. I have my own mission statements when it comes to charity giving and not being approached is part of that. I also like charities that set out to help directly instead of merely churning out aid – teaching villagers to fish and all that. I also only support small charities as I figure they need it more.

And I will only support small charities that are doing things that seem attainable. I figure feeding the poor of the world requires a bottomless pit. Not that it isn't a decent objective but one I find too remote. But one that seeks to provide fresh water for a particular village I can relate to; or providing a breakfast for an inner-city schoolkid.[28]

---

[28] www.magicbreakfast.co.uk is something I *can* get my head round.

Spend your own money because no one will spend it as wisely as you

What! Surely we all spend our own money? No, we don't. As we get richer, the need to have others spend it for us grows stronger. Believe me, it becomes a real risk to hand things over and lose value and wealth because of it. It is so easy to figure that because we are busy and someone offers, it is a good thing to hand over.

I have noticed that the successful rich don't hand over anything; they carry on paying attention to detail all the time. Obviously there might come a time to hand over as we grow too old to administer our own affairs but until then, give up nothing.

> I HAVE NOTICED THAT THE SUCCESSFUL RICH DON'T HAND OVER ANYTHING

Examples? Of course. I have a friend who has considerable wealth and who is happy to hand over his spending to anyone around him who offers to do it for him. His gardener buys all his equipment, including mowers and chain saws and the like. Top of the range? I should say. This gardener is driving around on mowers that are the gardening equivalent of a Rolls Royce. My friend just signs the cheques and the gardener is laughing all the way to the tool shed. My friend also pays caterers to come in and organise meals every time he wants to entertain. Again he signs the cheque and the caterers supply him with a complete dinner party.

Ah, but I hear you say, 'So what? He can afford it.' Yes, indeed he can but he is also:

- being ripped off repeatedly
- not getting good value for money
- slowly losing control over his own financial affairs
- losing the respect of his employees and hired service companies who see him as a bit of a joke – too much money and not enough sense (it would be all right if he was aristocracy as you expect it of them but he is a self-made rich person).

He's the same when it comes to buying a new car. He just rings up the showroom and they deliver what he wants. Trouble is they frequently deliver what they've had sitting in their showrooms for too long and can't shift. Ask him about the pink Bentley he bought that no one else was going to touch in a million years. I tease him and ask him if the showroom had a big glass office where they could sit and see him coming.

You've got to retain control of your own spending if you want to retain control over your finances – and dignity. No pink Bentleys for you. Don't hand out credit cards. Don't give anyone authority to sign personal cheques. Don't use a personal shopper. Set people proper budgets. Get them to submit proper proposals for spending. Check the small print. Check everything. Question everything. Stay on top. Stay in control. And if you want my advice – no joint accounts ever. There's no need for it in this day and age.

Take responsibility before you take advice

This is a follow-on from the previous Rule. If you are going to take advice you need to know in advance:

- what you expect to get
- why you are asking
- your exact position – if you don't know, how can they advise you of anything?
- what you want to happen next
- what role they will play in that
- what action you can take if their advice is wrong/out of date/harmful
- what further advice you might need.

And before you can do any of these you need to take responsibility.

We all start out – or at least I did, and so did most people I've ever talked to about it – somehow expecting that we would end up rich. It was/is an assumed process, sort of by osmosis. As you get older and add years to your life, so in theory you add riches. Then you wake up one day and it isn't/is just like that. For me it wasn't, so I went into hyperdrive to change the situation and am now fabulously wealthy.[29] But it took hard work and tremendous effort. Now you've made it, it is time to review. Time to take responsibility. Time to take stock. You need to know:

- where you are
- how you got there

---

[29] If you are the tax collector I was only joking and/or I've already paid my tax bill.

RULE 98

- what you are worth – both financially and spiritually
- where you want to go next
- how you expect to get there.

When you have answered these questions you are ready to take advice about your plans. And it doesn't have to be advice of the paid kind, the expert kind, the man-in-a-suit kind, the all serious and heavy kind. Sometimes advice can come from unlikely sources and unlikely people. Learn to listen. Learn to take in what is *not* being said. Learn to be happy (gosh that's a big one for all of us).

> ## AND IT DOESN'T HAVE TO BE ADVICE OF THE PAID KIND, THE EXPERT KIND, THE MAN-IN-A-SUIT KIND

The wealthier we become, the easier it appears to be to hand over our affairs (financial ones) to people we think have our best interests at heart or who we assume know what they are doing or are on top of the latest developments and laws. My observation is that (a) they're not and (b) the shrewd wealthy ones don't hand over anything unless they are really, really sure of their advisers. And that's my advice.

Once you've got it, don't flaunt it

Wealth is lovely. Having money is great. Getting rich is a worthwhile and enjoyable activity. Buying the pink Bentley is just plain gross. As is a lot of other things that shout nouveau riche, over-the-top, flaunting, bling. So tacky. Take lessons in how to handle wealth by all means but do handle it well.

I read a nice story the other day of a young lad who got to stay in a millionaire's mansion – a relative I assume – and when he went to bed he left the light on. The millionaire popped his head round the door and told him it was wasting money and he should turn it off. He even threatened him with a $1 fine. But instead he tossed him a $1 coin and turned the light out himself. The kid never forgot the incident and is still turning lights off when he goes to bed or leaves a room to this day. And he still doesn't know why the reverse psychology worked. As he says, he went from a possible $1 fine to a big windfall (it was 1953 when a dollar was a lot).

Be frugal. Be careful with your money. Don't flaunt it. And as you now belong to an exclusive club, could you please observe a few rules:

- no flash cars
- no castles, ranches or ranch, style house – this isn't Dallas you know
- no bling
- no glitz or showing off
- no impulse spending
- no wild animals as pets

- no buying islands
- no private jets
- no flying all your relatives to a foreign county for a party
- no flying your relatives to a foreign country for your latest trophy wedding
- no huge diamonds – or big jewellery of any sort, it'll only attract the robbers and thieves.

Be a discreet, tasteful, refined, cultured, less-is-more, more-is-tacky, quiet sort of rich person. Someone we can all look up to. Someone who will inspire and not cultivate ridicule – they do laugh at those leopard skin trousers I'm afraid (not that you've got any). Someone who will set a good example to the young, the impressionable, the not so well-off.

We've all seen those who come into money too suddenly and flaunt the fact that they have loads and we all think 'God, how tacky'. I know we shouldn't sit in judgement on others but I do find my toes curl at … no, I can't say in case you've got one.

Flaunting it creates envy, jealousy (different from envy), criticism, snobbery, condemnation, censure – and all quite rightly. Discretion, on the other hand, encourages respect, admiration and emulation. Don't ever mention how much you've got, what you are worth or how much you earn. Ever. If you tell people, half will despise you for not having more and the other half resent you for having so much. Only reveal such information to your bank manager and even then they should have to drag the info from you.

> DON'T EVER MENTION HOW MUCH YOU'VE GOT, WHAT YOU ARE WORTH OR HOW MUCH YOU EARN

What's next? Pacts with the devil?

It's the last Rule and I guess we can have some fun. Creating wealth is as varied and different an adventure for each of us as anything else. We can work for it, win the lottery or a poker game (mind you it would have to be a pretty big one), inherit it, steal it, be awarded it as a prize (Nobel Peace Prize for literature – you do get around $1.3 million[30]. Gulp. Put my name forward at once please, somebody. Or what about the Templeton Prize, which gets you $1.4 million),[31] or find it in the street (lots of examples on the Internet of people finding huge wads of cash), marry into it, you name it. And of course if you are really desperate there is the old pact with the devil – but beware of gotcha clauses.

> ## THERE IS THE OLD PACT WITH THE DEVIL – BUT BEWARE OF GOTCHA CLAUSES

---

[30] 10 million Swedish krona – the actual value changes with fluctuating currency conversion rates.

[31] The Templeton Prize is awarded annually by an international, multifaith panel of judges to a living person of any religious tradition who has made a unique contribution to progress in research or discoveries about spiritual realities.

RULE 100

The Chinese believe, via feng shui, that if you leave your loo seat up, your money will get flushed away. I wonder if this is a modern invention because I have no evidence of flushing loos in China when feng shui was being established in the Taoist eras.

Then there are affirmations – you write down the wealth you want and pin it up so you can see it everyday and chant it out hundreds of times. Might work. Then there's writing it down and putting it under your pillow so you'll dream of where your wealth is buried.

Then there's the cosmic ordering service – you tell the great cosmic bank how much it owes you and it repays you immediately – there has got to be a catch there somewhere knowing banks; they're all the same I reckon.

Then there are money maps and money boards – you cut up pictures of expensive stuff you can buy and would want and make a sort of scrapbook but as a board, and look at it a lot I guess. Might work.

Then there's crystals – you wear one/sleep with it/carry it around. Certain crystals resonate with the cosmic bank (them again) and it's a sort of rock cheque I guess.[32]

Dowsing? You follow hazel rods (or bits of bent coat hangers and empty Biros depending on which books you read) which twitch when you are above buried treasure or a seam of gold or one of those ring-pull things off the top of a beer can. Bit like a metal detector but doesn't need batteries.

---

[32] Citrine, ruby and tiger eye are supposed to work but I figure if you can buy rubies you don't need the wealth or you're giving it all to the crystal seller, so I suppose it works for them.

I suppose you could buy a racehorse but it seems so very risky to me. How about painting a masterpiece and hanging on in there until (a) it gets valuable or (b) you get dead? Laying down fine wines? Could work but I couldn't resist the temptation I think.

I am not scoffing at any of these methods. However you intend gaining prosperity, you should get on with it, believe in it, follow it, give 100 per cent to it and not listen to others. Including me. Especially me. Good luck.

Richard Templar

The Rules of Parenting

By Richard Templar

It seems pretty clear to me how you can spot a good parent. You just have to look at their children. Some kids go through bad patches for a while for all sorts of reasons, many of which you really can't pin on the parents, but I've found that once they leave home, you can see what kind of a job their parents did. And I figure the parents whose kids are able to look after themselves, to enjoy life and to make those around them happy, to be caring and kind, and to stand up for what they believe in – those parents are the ones who are getting it right. And over the years I've seen what kind of parenting produces those kinds of adults 18 years on.

So what are they doing right? That's what intrigued me when I first became a parent, and over the years I've distilled what they do into certain Rules of parenting...

Don't try to be perfect

Have you ever thought what it would be like to have perfect parents? Well, think about it now. Imagine your parents had been faultless when you were growing up (I'm betting they weren't[2]). How would that have felt? Suppose they were textbook parents now – that your mother was *always right*. Sound like fun? Of course it doesn't.

Look, kids need something to kick against when they're growing up. They need someone to blame, and I'm afraid that's your job. So you might as well give them something to blame you for.

So what's it going to be? You don't want to be cruel or abusive – you need to pick something that's not unreasonable and shows a bit of human frailty. Maybe a short fuse? Putting a bit too much pressure on them? Being slightly neurotic about keeping everything tidy and ordered? Or tell you what, better still, why bother to choose? Just go with your own natural imperfections, and then you don't have to make an effort.

Of course this doesn't mean that you're off the hook, that you shouldn't try to improve your parenting skills. Apart from anything else, that would make the rest of this book redundant. It just means that you shouldn't give yourself too hard a time when you fall a bit short of the standards you set yourself. After all, what kind of an example would it be to your kids if you were unable ever to fail, even a little bit? I wouldn't fancy having to live up to parents like that, and I don't suppose your children would either.

Your children are going to blame you for something, because that's how it works. If you were perfect, they'd have every reason to

---

[2] Please don't write in to accuse me of insulting your mother. I'm just making a point.

blame you for that. You can't win. You can only hope that eventually, especially if they become parents themselves, they'll come to see that actually they should be grateful to you for not being perfect.

> ## YOUR CHILDREN ARE GOING TO BLAME YOU FOR SOMETHING, BECAUSE THAT'S HOW IT WORKS

Different children need different rules

Broadly speaking I don't consider this book controversial. That's not my aim – I'm just trying to flag up some common-sense Rules that are easier to follow once they've been put into words, and which maybe you hadn't consciously thought about before. But I suspect that if anyone wants to argue with me, this is the Rule they'd pick to dispute. It appears to contradict Rules 24, 33, 54 and probably several others we haven't got to yet. But it only *appears* to.

Your children are not the same as each other and it therefore stands to reason that a one size fits all approach to rules simply can't be right. Of course your children won't appreciate this when they think they're on the wrong end of things, so some rules must apply to everyone. Call them house rules if you like. It's only fair that everyone has to go to bed when they're asked to, or clear up after meals. But other rules will have to be adapted to your child's personality.

I'll be honest with you. When I first started out as a parent I thought it was unfair to bend rules for one child and not another. It seemed obvious to me that you had to have the same rules for everyone. And then my children started to grow. And I realised that certain rules were asking far more of one child than another.

Here's an example. I have one son who is pathologically untidy. He is messy on an industrial scale.[3] He has no idea that he is, because he has a strange condition that renders him unable to see the chaos he leaves around him. Asking him to tidy up after himself is simply not the same as asking his siblings to tidy up. We'd be

---

[3] Yep, there goes Rule 35 again. But I'm not saying which son.

demanding 20 times as much of him because a) he can't see the mess, b) he doesn't understand why it's a problem anyway (it's not bothering *him*), and c) it would take him several hours a day. So actually, applying the same rule to all of them would be hugely unfair on him.

Of course, we don't let him off the hook. But we do settle for less than the others. He has to do some tidying, and we help so long as he's genuinely working at it too. As he gets older, so the onus gradually passes to him.

This son, I should say, has a very good attention span, and is expected to sit down and work at his homework for a good half hour at a stretch, which he does with no problem. One of his (tidy) siblings, however, finds it really hard to work in more than ten minute bursts, so he's allowed to spread his homework over a whole weekend in shorter sessions.

In other words, sometimes the same rules for everyone is the only fair approach, but there are times when it can be unfair, and you have to look out for these. The important thing is how much you're asking of each child.

THE IMPORTANT THING IS HOW MUCH YOU'RE ASKING OF EACH CHILD

Remember Newton's Third Law

The thing is, you love your kids desperately. So it's incredibly hard to watch them making mistakes that you think will come back to bite them later on. Over the years you've got used to letting them make small mistakes – helping themselves to too much pudding, or riding their bike too fast downhill. As time goes on, the mistakes get bigger.

So now you have to watch them drink too much at their mate's party, or wear clothes that are far too low-cut (or high-cut). Maybe you even have to stand back when they decide to leave school at 16, when you'd hoped they go to university, or jack in a brilliant Saturday job because it's too much effort getting up in the morning. It's a much bigger deal than letting your two year old take too much pudding. The stakes are getting higher.

And worst of all, you may even have to watch them repeating your mistakes. Dropping science just because they hate the teacher when they could have a brilliant career ahead of them. Or saving all their money for a gap year when the time comes, and then blowing it in a moment of madness on a car that doesn't even go properly. You could have told them. You probably did tell them. Quite possibly loudly and forcibly... But then, did you listen to your parents when they told you all those years ago?

Unless your child is putting themselves in serious danger, you really do have to put up with it. Sometimes even if it is dangerous you have no choice. The more you try to tell them, the more you push them in the opposite direction. They're looking for something to kick at, to rebel against, because they're programmed to. The more force you use, the more they'll use. Remember Newton's third law of motion? For every action there is an equal and opposite reaction. He could equally well have called it the first law of teenagers.

So what can you do when you see them going wrong? You can tell them what you think, but don't tell them what to do. And tell them in the way you'd tell a grown-up and an equal. Not, "I'll tell you what I think! I think you're a fool!" More along the lines of, "It's your decision, but have you thought how you'll fund your gap year if you spend your money on this?" Talk to them like an adult and maybe they'll respond like an adult. And if not this time, maybe next time. They'll certainly be quicker to ask your advice if they know it will be given as an equal.

> ## DID YOU LISTEN TO YOUR PARENTS ALL THOSE YEARS AGO?

ISBN: 978-0-273-71147-6

Price: £9.99

THE
RULES
OF PARENTING

is available from all good bookstores

or buy online at

www.pearson-books.com

Available from January 2008